Proceedings of the 2015 Business Research Consortium of Western New York

Proceedings of the 2015 Business Research Consortium of Western New York

CAMBRIA PRESS

Amherst, New York

TABLE OF CONTENTS

List of Figures.. ix

About the BRC... xi

Divorcing Your Job French Style: An Argument to End At Will
    Employment in the United States
    Vincent Agnello.. 1

Sustainable Revenue Generation System for Nonprofit Institutions
    of Higher Education
    Graig P. Arcuri.. 13

Testing the Excess Return Hypothesis: The Canadian Case
    Trevor W. Chamberlain and Abdul-Rahman Khokhar.......... 43

Taxation Changes and the Cross-Border Pricing of REITs
    Trevor W. Chamberlain and Hesam Shahriari................... 59

Cost Accounting Variance: Blended Learning
    R. Mithu Dey.. 75

Latent Employee Turnover and Prevention—When Job Creation
    Catches Up with Economic Recovery: An Employee
    Retention Model and Case Study
    Barry A. Friedman* and Lisa M. Schnorr....................... 89

Recommendations for Implementing Sustainability in New
    Product Development for Supply Chain Management
    Lynn Fish.. 119

Using TQM to Implement Sustainability in Supply Chain
    Management
    Lynn A. Fish.. 151

A Literature Review and Directions for Future Research on
    International Student Perceptions of Online versus Face-
    to-Face Education: Student-centered Characteristics
    Lynn A. Fish and Coral R. Snodgrass........................... 177

A Literature Review and Directions for Future Research on
    International Student Perceptions of Online versus Face-
    to-Face Education: Program-centered Characteristics
    Lynn A. Fish and Coral R. Snodgrass........................... 199

Using Text Analysis to Assess Qualitative Student Works, Deal
    with Inter-rater Reliability, and Simultaneously Comply
    with AACSB Standard 8 and Middle States Standard V
    Guy H. Gessner* and Karen M. Kutt-Doner.................... 229

A Suggested New Approach to Management Science Topic
    Coverage
    William Leslie Langdon... 251

How to Build It So They Come: Using the Interrelationship
    Quality Function Deployment Matrix to Design a
    Professional Business Student Club
    *Nate Luciano, Mary Bolo-Blum, Tyler Lokietek, and Lisa M.
    Walters*.. 263

The Financial Statements Articulation Fence: An Expanded and
    Refined Visual Model of Financial Statement Articulation
    John Olsavsky... 285

Application of Marketing to an Evolutionary Business Framework
    Mark Parker and Paul Richardson.............................. 297

Resources and Speed: Entrepreneurial Strategies of US Biomedical
    Firms
    Ronald M. Riva... 307

Cross-discipline Collaboration in Business Research: Filling a Gap
    in Business Education
    Mary Tone Rodgers and Lisa Dethridge........................ 317

Table of Contents

The End Before The Means: A Critique of Muhammad Yunus'
Concept of Social Business
Zachary Rodriguez and Jim Mahar............................ 329

Client-Firm Relationship Dynamics: A Model for High Risk
Clients
Susan L. Wright and Hema Rao................................. 341

LIST OF FIGURES

Figure 1: Employee Retention Model 107

Figure 2: Effective Human Resource Practices that Promote
Employee Retention 108

Figure 3: Case Study: Constellation Brands, Inc. Employee
Retention Resource Practices 109

ABOUT THE BRC

The Business Research Consortium of WNY promotes academic scholarship related to business, economics, and the scholarship of teaching. The first annual conference was held at Canisius College (Buffalo, NY) in Spring, 2006. The 2007 conference was held at St. Bonaventure (St. Bonaventure, NY). The 2008 conference was held at Niagara University (Niagara University, NY). The 2009 conference was held at St. John Fisher College (Rochester, NY). The 2010 conference was held at SUNY Geneseo (Geneseo, NY). The 2011 conference was held at SUNY Brockport (Brockport,NY). The 2012 conference was held at SUNY Oswego (Oswego, NY). The 2013 conference was held at Canisius College (Buffalo, NY). The 2014 conference was held at Nazareth College (Rochester, NY). The 2015 conference was held at St. Bonaventure University (St Bonaventure, NY). Program archives and additional information are availalble at http://www.businessresearchconsortium.org

Proceedings of the 2015 Business Research Consortium of Western New York

Divorcing Your Job French Style: An Argument to End At Will Employment in the United States

Vincent Agnello

Vincent Agnello
Professor of Law
College of Business Administration
Niagara University
Niagara University, NY 14109
Email: agnello@niagara.edu

Abstract

The United States and France are at opposite ends of the spectrum in protecting employees from employment termination. France has developed an elaborate regulatory and judicial scheme to protect workers, while the U.S. still allows workers to be in an at will relationship with their employers. In France employment is deemed to be permanent. In the U.S., workers are employed at the whim of their employer. In a major shift of policy, France adopted legislation allowing parties to enter into voluntary employment separation agreements. To protect against abuse, all settlement agreements are subject to court review for approval of the separation terms and the amount of severance pay. This scheme parallels what happens in the U.S. in matrimonial actions. This paper argues that the workers in the United States should be afforded job security by requiring employers to have good cause for employment terminations. This would mean an end to at will employment and bring the United States in line with other industrialized nations.

Keywords: At will employment, ethics, employment termination, voluntary employment separation agreement.

Background

Although the American Revolution (1775-1783) and the French Revolution (1789-1799) occurred over two hundred years ago, they continue to impact the thoughts and beliefs of each country, their ethics and morals. Under the influence of John Locke the U.S. Constitution imbedded his belief that people have inalienable rights and that government's purpose is to protect those rights (Donaldson, 1999). Just a few years later, the citizens of France under the motto of "Liberty, Equality, Fraternity" began their revolution.

Over the past two hundred years both countries enacted labor laws to protect employers and employees and to develop equality in their bargaining powers. One area where the two countries and societies diverge in thought and practice is the area of employee termination. The United States and France are at opposite ends of the spectrum in their legal treatment and regulation of employee terminations.

Employment law in the United States follows the old English common law rules of master-servant and a doctrine known as "at will employment" (Wood, 1877). Under this legal principal the employment relationship can be terminated by either side at anytime without need to show good cause for the termination. As a result most U.S. workers are employed at the whim of their employer. In comparison, France is very protective of employees' rights to keep their jobs and has enacted comprehensive laws that regulate the termination process and has established specialized courts called employment tribunals to specifically address employee terminations (French Act January 18th, 1979 L.79-44). In France, good cause is not subjective; it is spelled out in detail in labor legislation (French labor Code L. 1232-6). Regardless of whether the termination is initiated by a voluntary resignation of the employee or forced by the employer, in France most employees are entitled to severance pay, called indemnity payments.

In an effort to reduce its high unemployment rates, France loosened its tight grip in this area by enacting a law in June 2008 that allows the parties to negotiate their own voluntary employment separation agreements (French Act June 25th, 2008). This is a departure from the very strictly regulated system of dismissal by the employer and introduces a more flexible method of separation. It reflects a major government policy shift, in which the intentions of both parties are weighted more than the framework set out by the law. This change is no doubt a reflection of current business needs and better suited to the volatility of the labor market that exists in today's Europe. Even with this change, France remains the leader in promoting employee protection.

In order to understand the magnitude of this shift, it is important to understand how encompassing and protective the previous French law was of employees and how this shift did not erode the government's scope of protection in the area of employment termination. Prior to this change, employers could only terminate for reasons permitted by law (French Act August 8th, 1989 L.89-549). In addition, employers were required to provide severance pay under all circumstances except terminations based on grave or gross misconduct of the employee. The severance amount is based on years of service and is required to be paid whether the termination was mutual or initiated solely by the employer. Unlike the U.S. standard for good cause, issues such as excessive absences and arguing with supervisors does not rise to the level of grave or gross under the French standard (French Labor Code Article L. 1232-1). To qualify for gross misconduct the employee's action must have been taken knowingly with intent to cause prejudice to the employer. The new law provides a more equitable process of separation from an employer when the parties mutually agree to a separation. This new law, however, does not change any rights provided employees in the case of terminations forced solely by the employer.

An employment relationship can sometimes end through an employee resignation. In France, resignation cannot be presumed or implied (French Act July 13th 1973 L. 73-680). An employer cannot insert a clause in an employment contract that implies resignation by an employee (e.g. irregular absences, refusal of a transfer to a new position, returning late from a paid leave). Nor is a resignation valid if an employee is coerced, angry, agitated, threatened, or intimidated. Even a resignation given by an employee who is under threat of legal action or dismissal for serious or gross professional misconduct is invalid (French Labor Code Article L. 1232-1). A resignation is not valid until it has been reviewed and determined that it is not a disguised termination. Under the French Act June 25th, 2008 the terms of the separation and the future obligations of the parties must be stated in writing. If an employee claims that the resignation was coerced, the burden is on the employee to provide proof that the consent is flawed in law. A resignation that does not meet the strict standards of the law is deemed invalid. Furthermore, a dismissal without genuine or serious grounds exacts a penalty on the employer. The employer must pay the employee compensation in the amount equal to the last six months of employment for violating the law. In addition the court must set the amount of compensatory damages actually suffered by the employee due to unjustified loss of employment.

A voluntary separation agreement becomes valid only after review by an established administrative authority that then has 15 business days from receipt to verify that the consent was freely given and the agreement complies with the law. The termination agreement is only valid if approved. If the authorities refuse to approve it within 15 days, either party (or both) can appeal against that refusal. In the event of a denial after appeal, the case is treated as a forced termination by the employer and indemnity payments are set according to law.

The strict review of the settlement agreement and setting of the indemnity amount parallels the process in the United States in divorce and separation proceedings. Decisions in matrimonial cases in the United States are subject to court review and approval (NY DRL236B(5)). The reasoning for each is the same. The parties may not be of equal strength in the bargaining process, whether it be the employer over the employee or one spouse, usually the husband, over the other, usually the wife. The Court's role is to insure equity and fairness in the process. In matrimonial action there are two issues the court must address: the separation of the parties and the equitable distribution of the marital property. Have the parties equitable dealt with each other fairly? Recognizing that the parties may not be equal and may not be in the right mental state of mind, property distributions and issues of marital support and child support require a judge's consent. Perhaps it is time for the United States to implement the same standard that is utilized in divorces to the area of employment termination.

From an ethical perspective, a strong argument can be made to provide some type of protection from the harsh consequences that at will employment agreements causes because there is no protection against employer initiated termination actions. An employee with no bargaining power and no protection under the law is vulnerable to an employer's exploits. In many cases, loss of a job can be more traumatic and financially devastating than a failed marriage. Challenging that status quo in the United States means challenging the doctrine of at will employment, one that is deeply imbedded in American culture.

The United States is unique among the industrialized countries with respect to the issue of at will employment. The issue of at will employment is rooted in our Constitution and ingrained in the fabric of our society. The individual who has had the greatest impact on this concept was John Locke, a 17th century British philosopher. Locke argued that people are born with "inalienable" rights, such as the right to "life, liberty, and property," and that the function of government is to protect those rights (Boatright, 2003). Locke believed that government interference on society should be minimal.

An at will employment relationship is a natural extension of the rights argument. It would violate the freedom and protected rights of the parties if the government were to interfere and require one party to that agreement to act contrary to their will. "If government regulation is inappropriate for personal, religious, or political activities, then what makes it intrinsically desirable for employment relations?" (Epstein, 1984). What basis would justify binding the hands of an employer? This is reinforced in the U.S. Constitution. John Locke's influence on rights even extended to the area of contracts. The Fifth Amendment to the U.S. Constitution protects society from unneeded governmental control or interference by declaring: "nor [shall any person] be deprived of life, liberty, or property without due process of law" and in Article I Section 10, "No state shall...pass any...law impairing the obligation of contracts." In an employment contract the parties are free to interject whatever terms to which they agree. Unless the parties specifically bargain away their rights to "at will" employment it would be unfair to either party to take away that right (Werhane , 1985).

In the U.S the employment relationship can be viewed as strictly an economic, and not a moral, one. The employer/capitalist is in need of the resource of labor and the employee has the resource of labor for sale. In economics there is no difference in the treatment of a machine and an employee, except that one resource is labeled capital and other labor (Bowie 2005). As long as the machine or the employee is generating profits it will be employed by the firm. Economics dictates that the firm owner will try to maximize profits. In economic terms, an employer will continue to hire workers until the marginal product of labor equals the wage or cost of that worker (McConnell, 1990).

When morality enters the debate, at will employment is difficult to justify. The concept of employment at will is not acceptable to a utilitarian (Werhane, 1985). According to Werhane, Utilitarians "would say that one cannot justify harming someone, in particular restraining their freedom, for the sake of some collective or corporate benefit" (Werhane, 1985 p.92). 17th –century philosopher Immanuel Kant's logic can be extended to the area of employment as well. Kant wrote that "Morality is a condition under which alone a rational being can be an end in himself because only through it is it possible to be a lawgiving member in the realm of ends. Thus morality, and humanity, in so far as it is capable of morality, alone have dignity" (Bowie, 2005 p. 44). "To treat a person simply as a cost is to violate Kant's respect for the persons principle" (Bowie, 2005 p. 45).

If we are to talk about the rights of man, then one can argue that by subjecting oneself to exclusive control of an employer they have subjected their ability to make a livelihood to that employer as well. In our rights oriented society in the United States, we recognize the right to a job, a right to a livelihood, but only for jobs in the government sector. Federal and State government employees have a right to their job and that right can only be taken away for good cause. These rights by government employees are protected by a process that places the burden on the government employer to prove good cause for termination.

Locke would argue that "at will" employment is fair to the employee since the parties entered into the employment relationship as equal partners and each was free to contract as they wished, and even free to refrain from contracting. Unfortunately, in reality we do not have perfect markets in the employment area. While employers in many cases face a perfectly competitive labor market, employees do not. In most cases, employees are not able to bargain effectively because the employer has a choice of many other labor resources available. Clearly this is so for unskilled labor. Employees with unique skills or high levels of education are better able to bargain with their employer and often enter into written employment agreements that negate at will employment. In such instances the labor market is not considered perfectly competitive for employers seeking to fill a specialized position.

Over fifty years ago, author Frank Tannenbaum insightfully wrote,

"We have become a nation of employees. We are dependent upon others for our means of livelihood, and most people have become completely dependent upon wages. If they lose their jobs they lose every resource, except for the relief supplied by various forms of social security. Such dependence of the mass of the people upon others for all of their income is something new in the world. For our generation, the substance of life is in another man's hands" (Tannenbaum, 1951 p. 9).

These words ring true today as well. Not only are unskilled employees unable to bargain effectively, they are often at a major financial loss once terminated from a job. If the market was perfectly competitive for the employee as well as the employer there would be no need for unions. Unions provide that collective clout to bargain effectively for its members. Union members are protected in their terminations by the collective bargaining agreement which, similar to government employment, requires that the employer show good cause for all employment terminations. Employees who do not have the benefit of such protections are at the mercy of their employer who has the legal right to terminate the employment relationship at any time without need for good cause. To these employees, termination is more than just a severing of the relationship; it is more than just a termination of the sale of the labor resource. It is the loss of financial security and a loss of the employee's livelihood, a loss of the ability to provide for the needs of one's family and is no different than the issues facing a couple in the termination of their marriage. To provide judicial protection for one and not the other cannot be justified.

Although at will employment is still deeply imbedded in the American culture, it is not uniformly applied. The State of Montana is the first and only state to enact legislation protecting all workers from at will termination of employment. In Montana an employer must have just cause for the termination. (MCA §903,904). Just cause includes employee wrongful conduct as well as termination by an employer for economic reasons.

Under the U.S. Constitution and Civil Service legislation termination of federal, state, and local government workers requires just cause as a basis for termination. (Constitution Fifth Amendment, CSRA 7513(a)). In addition, a hearing process is in place placing the burden on the government to prove just cause. Employees with bargaining power, such as executives and managers often bargain for protection by negotiating an employment contract that includes a clause allowing termination only for specified acts of wrongful conduct by the employee or some provision for guaranteed employment for a specific term of years. In firms where employees are represented by a union, the collective bargaining agreement always requires that an employer have good cause for an employee termination and a grievance procedure to challenge the termination. Regardless of the terms of employment, an employee cannot be terminated from employment if the sole basis for the termination violates a law, such as the Civil Rights Act of 1964 (CRA 2000(e)).

While every state provides parties with protection and oversight in marital property settlements, the same is not true of employment separations. This lack of equality in how employment terminations are regulated in the United States strengthens the argument to protect employees from the harshness of at will employment terminations. The State of Montana had the political will to enact such legislation. Moving from no protection to one requiring a showing of just cause for all employment terminations would be a major step in the right direction. That would open the courts for oversight of terminations for employees who believe that they were not fairly dealt with by their employer.

Clearly the two countries differ on their approach to employment contracts and terminations. While it is difficult for individuals in the U.S. to fathom a world where there is a legally protected expectation that your job will last a lifetime, or be entitled to severance pay for voluntary termination of your job, it is equally difficult for employees in France to even comprehend why so many workers in the U.S. have at will jobs with no protection except the good will of their employer. Ethical principles of equality dictate that the Unites States needs to move away from at will employment and begin treating all employees equally with dignity and respect.

REFERENCES

Boatright, John R.: 2003, *Ethics and the Conduct of Business*, 4th ed. (Prentice-Hall,

Englewood Cliffs, NJ), p. 59.

Bowie, Norman E. and Patricia H. Werhane.: 2005, *Management Ethics*, (Blackwell

Publishing, Malden, MA), pp. 41, 44-45.

Civil Rights Act of 1964 Title VII (CRA). 42 U.S.C. §2000(e)-23(a) (1964)

Civil Service Reform Act of 1978, 5 U.S.C. § 1101 et. seq., (1978).

Donaldson, Thomas and Patricia H. Werhane.: 1999, *Ethical Issues in Business: A*

Philosophical Approach, 6th ed., (Prentice-Hall, Englewood Cliffs, NJ), p. 131.

Epstein, Richard A.: 1984, 'In Defense of the Contract at Will', *University of Chicago Law*

Review 51, 947-982, p. 954.

French Act July 13th 1973 L.73-680

French Act January 18th, 1979 L.79-44

French Act August 8th, 1989 L.89-549

French Act January 18th, 2005 L. 2005-32

French Act June 25th, 2008 (and implementing decrees of July 18, 2008)

French Labor Agreement January, 11th 2008 (article 11)

French Labor Code Article L. 1232-1

French Labor Code Article L. 1232-6

McConnell, Campbell R. and Stanley L. Brue,: 1990, *Economics*, 11th ed., (McGraw Hill,

New York, NY), p. 578.

Montana Code Annotated Title 39 Chapter 2 (MCA) §901-915 Wrongful Discharge From

Employment

Tannenbaum, Frank.:1951, *A Philosophy of Labor,* (Alfred A. Knopf, New York, NY),

p. 9.

United States Constitution Article I Section 10.

United States Constitution 5th Amendment

Werhane, Patricia H.,: 1985, *Persons, Rights, and Corporations,* (Prentice-Hall, Englewood

Cliffs, NJ), pp. 81, 92.

Wood, H.G.: 1877, *A Treatise on the Law of Master and Servant,* (John D. Parsons, Jr.,

Albany, NY), §134.

.

Sustainable Revenue Generation System for Nonprofit Institutions of Higher Education

Graig P. Arcuri

Graig P. Arcuri, Ph.D. (graig.arcuri@oswego.edu) is a Visiting Assistant Professor of Finance at the State University of New York at Oswego, School of Business, Rich Hall, 7060 Route 104, Oswego, New York 13126-3599

Abstract

Social and individual spending on higher education has outpaced social and individual economic growth, resulting in nonprofit institutions of higher education (NIHEs) growing increasingly dependent upon unsustainable governmental subsidies and tuition increases. Congruent with the 3 research questions, the purpose of this study was to examine the interactions among components of the nonprofit university system existing revenue generation methods, and sustainability of revenue generation, thereby generating a new sustainable revenue theory for nonprofit universities within the United States. This qualitative grounded theory study used a multiphase design incorporating data from the literature review, historical documents, and phone interviews from a theoretical sampling of 10 NIHEs. Participants were 20 faculty, 40 students, 40 administrative staff, and 20 members of the business community. Analysis included open, focused, axial, and theoretical coding. The study's findings theorize that a sustainable revenue generation system must continually include, and respond to, the multidirectional interactions of all system components as they change over time, including businesses. The result of the multidirectional connectivity between all of the system components was increased revenue for NIHEs and reduced student and government-funded tuition. Additionally, an organizational culture that is incongruent with change has been identified in NIHEs and must be mitigated. The findings of this study could positively affect NIHEs by providing a sustainable and adaptable system for improving revenue generation while increasing affordability and accessibility for students of these institutions, which, in turn, may produce positive social change.

INTRODUCTION

For the purpose of disseminating of my research, this paper represents a synopsis of my research study with excerpts from the results section. My study resulted in the creation of a new and sustainable revenue generation theory for nonprofit institutions of higher education (NIHE) (Arcuri, 2014). This qualitative study used a grounded theory approach to examine the interactions among components of the NIHE system, existing revenue generation methods, organizational change, and sustainable revenue generation in an effort to generate a new sustainable revenue theory for NIHEs within the United States that is responsive to component interactions. For a new revenue generation theory for NIHEs to be sustainable, the system requires not only effectiveness and efficiency in the present time, but also continual adaptability in the future (Beinhocker, 2006). New revenue-generating systems for NIHEs must focus on connectivity, coevolution, reinforcing cycles, and self-organization (Luoma, 2006). The proactive nature of a sustainable revenue generation system is based on a constant flow of the "total capabilities and knowledge among all the fractals [components]. This integration of knowledge means that each fractal [component] must be kept constantly abreast of all significant events" (Shoham & Hasgall, 2005, p. 230). The findings of this qualitative grounded theory study theorize that a sustainable revenue generation system must continually include, and respond to, the multidirectional interactions of all system components as they change over time, including businesses. The result of the multidirectional connectivity between all of the system components was increased revenue for NIHEs and reduced student and government-funded tuition. Additionally, an organizational culture that is incongruent with change has been identified in NIHEs and must be mitigated.

The rationale for the study was that social and individual spending on higher education has outpaced social and individual economic growth, resulting in NIHEs growing increasingly dependent upon unsustainable governmental subsidies and tuition increases. The study fills a significant gap because current research into the interactions between the components of the NIHE system, as they relate to methods of sustainably generating revenue for NIHEs, is very limited. Specific qualitative research questions addressed the perceptions of the participants to determine their responses to various components of revenue generation. Current and scholarly literature on revenue generation models, revenue generation, historical financial data, and organizational change management provided the conceptual framework for the study. In addition to the literature review, this study included historical data and telephone interviews. Analysis included open, focused, axial, and theoretical coding. The findings of this study could positively affect NIHEs by providing a sustainable and adaptable system for improving revenue generation while increasing affordability and accessibility for students of these institutions, which in turn could produce positive social change.

RESEARCH QUESTIONS

The study explored the following research questions from a qualitative perspective.

1. What are the interactions between components of the NIHE system and revenue generation?

2. What are the interactions among components of the NIHE system, the current methods of revenue generation, and organizational change?

3. How can an analysis of the interactions identified in the first two questions be used to generate, inductively, a revenue generation theory, and how may this theory affect NIHEs?

DEFINITION OF TERMS

Throughout this study, the following key terms are used:

Administration personnel: Represents any current full-time member of the nonteaching staff of a NIHE.

Business leader: Represents any owner or senior manager of a business located within the United States.

Connectivity: Represents the quality, state, or capability of being connective or connected ("Connectivity," n.d.).

Existing revenue generation: Represents the major current methods of creating revenue for nonprofit institutions of higher education in the United States.

Faculty: Represents any current full-time member of the teaching staff of a NIHE.

Interaction: Represents the meaning set forth by Meltzer, Petras, and Reynolds (1975), who determined that human behavior must be analyzed from both overt and covert dimensions as a process that involves interpretative thought and observable action, as well as the two dimensions of interaction, namely the internal thought process and external action.

Nonprofit institution of higher education (NIHE): Represents the collection of all components of a private (not public) nonprofit institution of higher education (college or university) located within the United States, including both internal and external stakeholders.

Participant position: Represents the four strata of participants, namely student, faculty, administration personnel, and business leader.

Revenue: Represents the total amount of money received or recognized by a NIHE with one fiscal year.

Revenue generation: Represents the process of creating revenue.

Student: Represents any current full-time student of a NIHE who is 18 years of age or older.

Sustainability of revenue generation: Represents endurance and adaptability of revenue generation, over time measured in decades, as well as effective responsiveness to both internal and external environmental factors and stakeholders.

LITERATURE REVIEW SUMMARY

No studies emerged from the literature review that addressed the interactions among all of the components of the NIHE system as they relate to methods of sustainably generating revenue for NIHEs. Nor had a grounded theory study been conducted to inform a sustainable revenue generation model. Furthermore, the research into the interactions among some of the components of the NIHE system as they relate to methods of sustainably generating revenue for NIHEs is very limited and spread over a period of more than 5 years. Moreover, the literature review identified numerous calls for new and sustainable methods of revenue generations. Additionally, in an effort to clearly explore the gap and identify constructs, the components of the NIHE system as well as the current methods of revenue generation were identified.

The literature review focused on three main areas: (a) higher educational system and organizational change, (b) revenue generation, and (c) change management. In the end, the literature review identified a clear gap in empirical research between existing methods of revenue generation and the interactions among the components of the NIHE system as they relate to methods of generating revenue for NIHEs that are effective and sustainable in the current economic environment. Randall and Coakley (2007) determined that "leadership in today's academia should take into account the needs and demands of various stakeholders ... [and] ... for the institution to flourish in today's environment ... requires innovation and input from all relevant stakeholders" (p. 326). Furthermore, numerous calls for new and sustainable methods of revenue generation from researchers were identified such as Rollwagen (2010), who stated that higher education institutions must "diversify their sources of income in order to live up to their mission as purposeful institutions in the emerging knowledge economy" (p. 11), and Jones and Wellman (2010), who argued that the financial "problems affecting higher education are not short-term but structural. ... born of bad habits and an inattention to strategic financing and resource allocation" (p. 9). The research of Rollwagen (2010) as well as Jones and Wellman (2010) also supports the assertion of the literature review that a lack of current and relevant research into the interactions between the components of the NIHE system currently exists, as the components relate to methods of sustainably generating revenue for NIHEs, as well as methods of sustainably generating revenue for private nonprofit universities and colleges in the United States.

Organizational change, as suggested by Shah (2009), for higher educational institutions is difficult. As an example, Weisbrod and Asch (2010) showed how institutions of higher education have maintained decades-old linear and static revenue generation models which have left them vulnerable to the current "perfect storm of falling investments, credit tightening, declining private contributions from individuals and corporations, declining state funding, and increased student financial need leading to decreased tuition revenue" (p. 24). For Weisbrod and Asch this liner and static revenue generation model is comprised of three major components, tuition, donations, and governmental funding. All of which are being negatively affected by the current global economy.

The interactions among components of the traditional revenue generating model have also been depicted in equation form. As an example, Summers (2004), in an empirical analysis of historic quantitative data, identified several mathematical equations. The addition of quantifying interactions among components is significant, because by quantifying or weighting the value of inflows and outflows of system components, one can better determine the affects of change throughout the entire complex system of nonprofit higher education. From a perspective of special purpose nonprofit organizations (SPOs), Tucker, Cullen, Sinclair, and Wakeland (2005) examined systems thinking concepts in an effort to mitigate the financial challenges facing SPOs. As a result of their examination, as well as a case study, Tucker et al. (2005) created a dynamic model which leaders of SPOs can use to measure the impact of alternative strategies on financial health (p. 482). Similar to the model of Tucker et al. (2005), a new theory will show qualitative interactions similar to those identified in the stock and flow map in Figure 1.

The stock and flow map in Figure 1 has four main elements, namely stocks, flows, converters, and connectors. Adapted for Figure 1 from the definitions and descriptions of Forbes (1993), the four main elements are defined as follows:

- Stocks: Stocks represent an accumulation, either concrete or abstract, that increases or decreases over time. Figure 1 has six concrete stocks including, Annual Number of Students, which are displayed with a rectangle.

- Flows: Flows represent actions or processes; either concrete or abstract, that directly adds (inflow) to or takes away (outflow) from the accumulation in a stock. Figure 1 has 12 concrete flows including, the inflow of Adding Students to the stock of Annual Number of Students. Flows are displayed with a double line with an arrow at one end and a circle and cross mark in the center, with the intention of looking similar to a water valve.

- Converters: Represented by a circle, converters hold information or relationships that affect the rate of the flows. Converters also can affect the content of another converter. Figure 1 has many converters including, the converter of Poor Economy, which affects the content of converter Attrition Fraction, which in turn, affects the flow of Losing Donors.

- Connectors: Represented by curved lines with an arrow, connectors indicate that changes in one element causes changes in another element. Figure 1 has many connectors including, the connector between converters Poor Economy and Donation per Donor, which indicate that changes in converter Poor Economy causes changes in converter Donation per Donor.

The complex interactions among components in the stock and flow map of Figure 1 highlight specific interactions, such as the interactions between a reduction in tuition and an increase in the number of students. The interactions between governmental budget and incoming grants are also highlighted. Additionally, Figure 1 identifies the interactions among graduate partnerships (a potential partnership between graduates, NIHE, and employers) and jobs for graduates, students who become donors, and adding students. Figure 1 also responds to the work of Weisbrod and Asch (2010) who showed how institutions of higher education have maintained decades-old linear and static revenue generation models by having a character that is dynamic and focused on connectivity, co-evolution, reinforcing cycles, and self-organization as suggested by Luoma (2006).

A new revenue generation model for nonprofit institutions of higher education must also mitigate the financial vulnerability in nonprofit organizations as described by Trussel (2002). Trussel went on to identify "four financial indicators of financial vulnerability—the debt ratio, the revenue concentration index, the surplus margin, and the size of the organization—and control for the sector to which the organization belongs" (p. 11). For a new revenue generation theory for nonprofit institutions of higher education to be sustainable, the system not only requires effectiveness and efficiency in the present time, but also continual adaptability in the future (Beinhocker, 2006). Beinhocker determined that in order for organizations to improve their longevities as high performers they must find a way to adapt to the environment as change occurs in the future. Through a systems thinking approach, adaptability to a complex and chaotic future is enabled. This future is driven by the natural, universal, and constant force of change.

RESULTS

My study was composed of a multiphase design, which involved "both sequential and concurrent strands over a period of time" (Creswell & Plano Clark, 2010, p. 196). The first phase entailed the collection and broad analysis of historical data contained within publicly accessible financial reports of 10 NIHEs, namely IRS Form 990s. The second and final phase, partially in response to the data collected during the literature review and the first phase, involved the collection of qualitative data derived from 120 individual phone interviews. The data derived from the literature review, historical data, and phone interviews of the study were coded with either descriptive or analytical codes that identified an attribute, theme, category, explanation, or configuration regarding revenue generation in NIHEs, as well as each of the three research questions. The results of my data analysis include a new revenue theory for NIHEs within the United States, which states that a sustainable revenue generation system must continually include, and respond to, the multidirectional interactions of all system components as they change over time, including businesses, and that this connectivity resulted in both increased revenue and reduced student and government-funded tuition. This new revenue generation theory is depicted in Figure 2. Figure 2 highlights the results of a NIHE revenue generation system that continually includes, and responds to, the multidirectional interactions of all system components as they change over time.

Demographics

Phase 1 (historical data from IRS Form 990) participants were composed of 10 different most representative and typical NIHEs, stratified by region, highest degree awarded, tuition rate, and number of students. The 10 NIHEs were from three different geographical regions. I purposefully identified the regions as east (east of the Mississippi River), central (east of the Rocky Mountains, and west of the Mississippi River), and west (west of the Rocky Mountains). Six of the 10 NIHEs were from the east region, two were from the central region, and two were from the west region. Four of the 10 NIHEs had a highest degree awarded as doctorate, one had master's as the highest degree awarded, and five had bachelor's as the highest degree awarded. Annual tuition rates ranged from approximately $11,000 per year to approximately $53,000 per year. Student populations of the 10 NIHEs ranged from approximately 600 to approximately 10,000 students.

Phase 2 participants (phone interview) were composed of (a) 40 students, 20 faculty, and 40 administration personnel and (b) 20 different most representative and typical individual business leaders, stratified by region, industry, and number of employees. The students, faculty, and administrative personnel were from similar demographics as the Phase 1 population. The geographical demographics of the business leader participants were as follows: 12 were from the east region, four were from the central region, and four were from the west region.

Data Collection
I interviewed 120 individuals by phone during Phase 2 and collected IRS Form 990 for 10 NIHEs during Phase 1. As stated earlier, the study had a multiphase design. The design was sequential in the sense that I initially performed the literature review, then collected Phase 1 data (IRS Form 990) followed by Phase 2 data (phone interview). It was concurrent in the sense that while performing Phase 1, I went back and looked for more data from the literature review. Similarly, while performing Phase 2 data collection, I went back and looked for more data from both the literature review and Phase 1. NVivo, Excel, audio recordings of some of the phone interviews, and a research journal were used in an effort to collect data.

The first phase, which began upon IRB approval and continued until all data collection and analysis were complete (approximately 10 months), entailed the collection of historical data contained within publicly accessible financial reports of 10 NIHEs. These publicly accessible financial reports were IRS Form 990, as well as financial data published by each of the 10 individual NIHEs. IRS Form 990 from each NIHE was collected from the website http://www.guidestar.org/Home.aspx and downloaded onto my computer. Although data collection for the first phase lasted for approximately 10 months, I initially collected these data one NIHE at a time over a 2-week period. The data were then transferred into Excel and NVivo for data analysis. Data collection was based on an initial sample size of 10 different NIHEs, stratified by region, private or public, and size of student population. As concepts were identified and the theory began to develop, no further sampling was needed to achieve saturation. The sample was chosen from a list of NIHEs that were located within the United States from the National Center for Education Statistics website, http://nces.ed.gov/collegenavigator/?s=all&ct=2&ic=1+2. This theoretical sample was purposefully guided by constructs identified in the literature review and attributes such as region, highest degree awarded, tuition rate, and number of students. As an example, I made sure that I had an NIHE representing each region of the United States, as well as NIHEs that were diverse in terms of degrees awarded, range of tuition rate, and number of students. I also, in an effort to minimize bias, limited the number of NIHEs that, due to their public image, I had some preconceived perception of, to three.

During Phase 2 of my study, participants were asked to reflect upon their experiences as they were guided through open-ended interview questions during a 45-minute semi-structured phone interview. Largely due to the complexity of obtaining participants, the phone interviews were spread over approximately a 160-day period. Data collection was from (a) 40 students, 20 faculty, and 40 administration personnel and (b) 20 different most representative and typical individual business leaders, stratified by region, industry, and number of employees. My plan was initially to audio record all phone interviews directly into my password-protected computer during the phone interviews; however, I did not audio record all participants, as over 80% of the participants preferred not to be recorded. The lack of an audio recording did not affect my data analysis, as my field notes were very descriptive and detailed.

The data were then transferred into Excel and NVivo for data analysis on my password-protected computer. As concepts were identified and the theory began to develop, no further sampling was needed to meet theoretical saturation. Moreover, theoretical saturation was met well before 120 individuals were interviewed, and in retrospect, the sample size could have been smaller. The sample was chosen from a list of NIHEs from the National Center for Education Statistics website, http://nces.ed.gov/collegenavigator/?s=all&ct=2&ic=1+2.

Analysis of Literature Review

The analysis of the literature review focused on three main areas derived from my research questions, namely components of the NIHE system, revenue generation, and organizational change. My initial cycle of coding, an open coding analysis of the literature review, identified many components of the NIHE system, including the following: society, government, alumni, accreditation bodies, faculty, department leaders, students, boards, administrators, registrar, suppliers, tuition-paying students (and/or their parents), academic programs, majors, minors, employers, interdependency of student needing employer, employer needing student, university needing student, employer needing university, entrepreneurial activity students, donors, corporations, politicians, and governmental agencies. However, during a second pass at open coding, I reexamined my initial codes in an effort to minimize redundancy. I did not code the data from the literature review by themselves beyond the development of codes through open coding because this analysis would have been myopic and lacked the depth that the combination of the other data sources (historical and phone interview) would provide.

In addition, my initial cycle of an open-coding analysis of the literature review identified several methods of revenue generation that are currently being used in the general NIHE system, including the following: tuition, governmental funding, cost cutting, and philanthropy. During a second pass at open coding, I reexamined my initial codes in an effort to minimize redundancy. Again, I did not code these data from the literature review by themselves beyond the development of codes through open coding because this analysis would have been myopic and lacked the depth that the combination of the other data sources (historical IRS 990s and phone interview) would provide.

My initial cycle of an open coding analysis of the literature review also identified several perspectives regarding organizational change that are currently pervasive in the general NIHE system including the following: old linear and static methods, poor change management, and slow to change. During a second pass at open coding, I again reexamined my initial codes in an effort to minimize redundancy. I did not code this data from the literature review by itself beyond the development of codes through open coding because this analysis would be myopic and lack the depth that the combination of the other data sources (historic IRS 990s and phone interview) would provide

Analysis of Historical Data

During my initial cycle of coding (open coding) I was able to collect and analyze quantitative and qualitative data from IRS Form 990 and other financial data that were filed and publicly accessible by 10 NIHEs. During this cycle of coding certain revenue components of the NIHE revenue system with several preliminary relationships were identified. As an example, an inverse relationship in several NIHEs seems to exist between Tuition Fees and Sales and Services of Auxiliary Enterprises. This inverse relationship is most evident in the NIHE with a Tuition Rate of $42,852, as well as the NIHE with a Tuition Rate of $53,204. A similar inverse relationship was found between Program Services Revenue and Sales and Services of Auxiliary Enterprises, with particular attention to the NIHE with a Tuition Rate of $42,852, as well as the NIHE with a Tuition Rate of $53,204. Consistent with other how other sources of data were coded, I purposefully did not code those historic data by themselves beyond the development of initial open codes because this analysis would be myopic and lack the depth that the combination of the other data sources (literature review and phone interview) would provide.

Analysis of Phone Interviews with Literature Review and Historic Data

The analysis of the data that I collected during the phone interview (Phase 2) began with an open coding analysis of the data obtained during the phone interview phase of data collection without the influence of data from other data sources. My open coding analysis identified interactions and perspectives regarding organizational change, revenue generation, and system components.

During the second cycle of coding, I used focused coding in an effort to reexamine the level one codes and develop categories, which added focus to the interactions regarding methods of revenue generation, organizational change, and NIHE system components. The focus was enhanced by the inclusion of open coded data from both the literature review and historic data. In addition, I employed constant comparison and member checking throughout the coding process. During the third cycle of coding, I used pattern or axial coding, to identify emerging themes, configurations, explanations, or constructs. Coding continued until theoretical saturation was achieved. As a result of the first three levels of coding, Table 1, Table 2, and Table 3 represent important interactions and perceptions regarding methods of revenue generation, organizational change, and NIHE system components. These interactions were used during the fourth cycle of coding, theoretical coding, to develop theories from the saturated categories and themes. These theories are provided below, in response to each research question.

Findings - Research Question 1

In the context of the first exploratory research question (What are the interactions between components of the NIHE system and revenue generation?) and generated through the use of a grounded theory methodology, the results of my study were:

- Finding 1: My analysis of the data from all three data sources clearly indicated that significant, multifaceted, and comprehensive interactions between the components of the NIHE system and revenue generation exist.
- Finding 2: The interactions are all-inclusive between each component of the NIHE system and revenue generation.
- Finding 3: Many of the issues currently associated with revenue generation in NIHEs are related to a lack of recognition of the significance of the interactions between components of the NIHE system and revenue generation.

Congruent with the findings of Alstadsæter (2011), who found that the value of higher education to both individuals and society is significant and multifaceted, as higher education increases the skill level of both the individual, as well as society, these interactions are all-inclusive between each component of the NIHE system and revenue generation. As such, a lack of connectivity between system components and revenue generation systems has resulted in a dysfunctional revenue generation system that is not sustainable. Moreover, this dysfunctional revenue generation system has adversely affected components of the NIHE system. During the constant comparative process, I incorporated Glaser's (1992) advice to seek each participant's main concern and then to identify how this main concern can be resolved. The data of this study clearly indicate that both a lack of sustainability and adverse affect upon system components are currently occurring in NIHEs and their revenue generation system. As an example, the interactions and lack of a "systematic approach to assessing their environment, developing strategic plans, taking actions, and assessing their results" (Dew, 2009, p. 8), can have negative effects upon the entire system. A new revenue generation system is needed;

this new and sustainable revenue generation system must reflect the important, bidirectional, and dynamic relationship between revenue generation and system components.

These findings are congruent with data from the literature review and extend existing knowledge into NIHEs and revenue generation. Numerous pieces of literature support the finding that the interactions between components of the NIHE system and revenue generation are significant, multifaceted, and comprehensive, including the following statements and excerpts from the literature review: (a) new revenue generating systems for nonprofit institutions of higher education must focus on connectivity, coevolution, reinforcing cycles, and self-organization (Luoma, 2006); (b) Eastman (2006) suggested that because the components of revenue generation are so closely connected to the balance of the overall university system, a university's mission changes as the need for revenue generation increases; (c) Eastman also found that a strategy of raising revenue through increasing class size and student population resulted in a bifurcation of teaching and research where teaching received most human resources and research was minimized (p. 56); (d) Barrett (2010) concluded that "networks must have cross functionality and the institution must have in place systems that seek pertinent and relevant information from within and across their sectors" (p. 30); (e) Pathak and Pathak (2010) identified several components of the higher educational system as well as components of a revenue generation model in their paper regarding reconfiguring the education value chain. In their paper, Pathak and Pathak "proposed that the academic process can be unbundled into discrete components which have well developed measures" (p. 166); (f) Slaughter and Rhoades (2004) found "spheres of interactivity that had no boundaries" (p. 11). This interactivity has resulted in cost and revenue generation for higher education through entrepreneurial activity (Barrett, 2010; Slaughter & Rhoades, 2004); (g) The interconnection of system components and the importance of the corporate sector were further supported by Barrett (2010), who stated, "Kirp [2003] stressed that priorities in higher education were not necessarily determined by the institution but by external constituencies such as students, donors, corporations, and politicians" (p. 27); (h) the identification of a bidirectional interdependency of student needing employer, employer needing student, university needing student, and employer needing university, which clearly highlights the importance of the interactions between components of the nonprofit university system, as well as the importance of communication among stakeholders in institutions of higher education as identified by the research of Smith and Wolverton (2010); (i) McDevitt, Giapponi, and Solomon (2008) suggested that an attempt to get alumni involved in one aspect of the organization such as classroom activities could, with a systemic network approach, also provide an opportunity for scholarship or research initiatives; (j) McCuddy, Pinar, and Gingerich (2008) identified the interconnectivity of two important stakeholders, students and potential employers, when they concluded that "even though tuition-paying students (and/or their parents) consider themselves to be customers of the educational establishment, they are responding—through their selection of academic programs, majors, and minors—to the employment marketplace" (p. 630); (k) Nair, Bennett, and Mertova (2010) concluded that in order to effect positive change, student feedback must be collected and acted upon with ample support for academic staff (p. 553); and (l) Randall and Coakley (2007) determined that "leadership in today's academia should take into account the needs and demands of various stakeholders ... [and] ... for the institution to flourish in today's environment ... requires innovation and input from all relevant stakeholders" (p. 326).

Findings - Research Question 2

In the context of the second exploratory research question, which asked, , "What are the interactions among components of the NIHE system, the current methods of revenue generation, and organizational change", and generated through the use of a grounded theory methodology, the results for the second research question were:

- Finding 4: Consistent with my results for the first research question, my analysis of the data from all three data sources clearly indicated that significant, multifaceted, and comprehensive interactions among the components of the NIHE system, current methods of revenue generation, and organizational change are present.
- Finding 5: These interactions are all-inclusive among each component of the NIHE system, revenue generation, and organizational change.
- Finding 6: Many of the issues currently associated with revenue generation in NIHEs are related to a lack of recognition of the significance of the interactions among components of the NIHE system, revenue generation, and organizational change.

Moreover, the current industry culture and organizational culture are highly resistant to organizational change. As an example, Barrett (2010) concludes, "networks must have cross functionality and the institution must have in place systems that seek pertinent and relevant information from within and across their sectors. Innovation will be a cornerstone in these processes; resistance to change must be eliminated" (p. 30). The inability to adapt to the natural state of constant change has left NIHEs with a dysfunctional culture of change, an inability to change effectively, and an antiquated revenue generation system. Furthermore, the data of this study clearly indicate that the lack of an effective culture of change has negatively affected NIHEs as well as their components, including students, society, and faculty. A new and sustainable revenue generation system is affected by a NIHEs culture of change. Therefore, a new and sustainable revenue generation theory does include a clear connection between organizational change and revenue generation, as well as the negative and positive impacts of organizational change. Furthermore, this new and sustainable revenue generation system must reflect the important, bidirectional, and dynamic relationship among organizational change, revenue generation and system components.

These findings both, confirm the data from the literature review, and extend knowledge to specifically NIHEs components, revenue generation, and organizational change. As an example, numerous pieces of literature support the finding that the interactions between components of the NIHE system and revenue generation are significant, multifaceted, and comprehensive including the following statements and excerpts from the literature review: (a) Oliver and Hyun (2011) concluded that widespread collaboration between groups in institutions of higher education is incongruent with the current organizational culture of higher education institutions; (b) Nye, Brummel, and Drasgow (2010) confirm that history and indirectly human perception, not only affects change initiatives as Bordia, Restubog, Jimmieson, and Irmer (2011) determined, but the evaluation of change initiatives as well; (c) Bold (2011) stated "that change management is an attitude, rather than a set of tools and techniques and that the successful businesses in many areas of activity are strongly influenced by the ability to exploit moments of transformation, moments of change" (p. 12); (d) Becker (2010) found that prior knowledge and established mental models hinder change efforts, while unlearning was found to mitigate some resistance to organizational change; (e) an additional internal influence on change management was identified by Bordia et al. (2011) who found that a history of poor change management, and the subsequent perceptions of change, "… led to lower trust, job satisfaction and openness to change, and higher cynicism and turnover intentions" (p. 1); and (f) a case study by Oliver and Hyun (2011) examined how certain components of four-year institutions of higher education collaborate during the curriculum change process.

Findings - Research Question 3

In the context of the third exploratory research question, which asked, "How can an analysis of the interactions identified in the first two questions be used to generate, inductively, a revenue generation theory and how may this theory affect NIHEs", and generated through the use of a grounded theory methodology, resulted in a new revenue generation theory which is stated in finding 7.

- Finding 7: A sustainable revenue generation system must continually include, and respond to, the multidirectional interactions of all system components as they change over time, including businesses, and that the result of this connectivity is both increased revenue and reduced student and government-funded tuition.

The results reflect the fact that the proactive nature of a sustainable revenue generation system is based on a constant flow of the "total capabilities and knowledge among all the fractals [components]. This integration of knowledge means that each fractal [component] must be kept constantly abreast of all significant events" (Shoham & Hasgall, 2005, p. 230). The new revenue sustainable generation theory depicted in Figure 2, reflects a constant bidirectional and dynamic flow of the total capabilities and knowledge among all of the system components, from both a micro and macro perspective. As indicated in Figure 2, the theoretical affect of constant bidirectional and dynamic flow of the total capabilities and knowledge among all of the system components is positive among system components including, revenue generation, faculty, students, employers, and society. Furthermore, the theoretical affect of constant bidirectional and dynamic flow of the total capabilities and knowledge among all of the system components acts a positive agent of change as supported by Oliver and Hyun (2011) who concluded that, "the collaboration of various groups within the institution in the process promoted organizational change" (p. 2).

More specifically, the theoretical affect of the new revenue generation theory depicted in Figure 2 include, but are not limited to, the following findings:

- Finding 8: Increased revenue for NIHEs, which is a result of the sum of the interactions among system components, system converters, and system flows including those from (a) Investment Vehicle

Balance; (b) Donors and Foundations; (c) Faculty; (d) Net Tuition Total Balance; (e) increased revenue from alumni; (f) reduced tuition rate; and (g) total connectivity among components;

- Finding 9: Reduced dependency on student funded tuition, which is a result of the sum of the interactions among system components, system converters, and system flows including those from (a) Investment Vehicle Balance; (b) Net Tuition Total Balance; (c) increase in revenue for NIHEs; (d) low or no tuition; and (d) total connectivity among components;

- Finding 10: Reduced dependency on governmental funding, which is a result of the sum of the interactions among system components, system converters, and system flows including those from (a) Investment Vehicle Balance; (b) Net Tuition Total Balance; (c) increase in revenue for NIHEs; and (d) total connectivity among components;

- Finding11: Positive effect on the economy, which is a result of the sum of the interactions among system components, system converters, and system flows including those from (a) a decrease in the amount of outstanding student debt; (b) increase in high paying jobs; (c) increase in access to NIHEs by potential students; (d) an increase in the average wage rate, and (e) total connectivity among components;

- Finding 12: Increase in the number of students, which is a result of the sum of the interactions among system components, system converters, and system flows including those from (a) Investment Vehicle Balance; (b) referrals; (c) increase in revenue for NIHEs; (d) increase in the quality of education; and (e) total connectivity among components;

- Finding 13: Decrease in the barriers to entering a NIHE for students, which is a result of the sum of the interactions among system components, system converters, and system flows including those from (a) Investment Vehicle Balance; (b) low or no tuition; (c) increase in revenue for NIHEs; (d) increase in the quality of education; and (e) total connectivity among components;

- Finding 14: The potential for more effective academic programs, which is a result of the sum of the interactions among system components, system converters, and system flows including those from (a) Investment Vehicle Balance; (b) decrease in administrative resources focused on revenue generation; (c) increase in revenue for NIHEs; (d) increase in the quality of education; and (e) total connectivity among components;

- Finding 15: Increased revenue from companies/employers, which is a result of the sum of the interactions among system components, system converters, and system flows including those from (a) Investment Vehicle Balance; (b) increase in research; and (c) total connectivity among components;

- Finding 16: Decrease in the amount of student loans (lenders outstanding balance), which is a result of the sum of the interactions among system components, system converters, and system flows including those from (a) Investment Vehicle Balance; (b) low or no tuition; (c) increase in revenue for NIHEs; and (d) total connectivity among components;

- Finding 17: Decrease in the financial support from families, which is a result of the sum of the interactions among system components, system converters, and system flows including those from (a) low or no tuition; and (b) total connectivity among components;

- Finding 18: Increased opportunities for research, which is a result of the sum of the interactions among system components, system converters, and system flows including those from (a) Investment Vehicle Balance; (b) Net Tuition Total Balance; (c) increase in revenue for NIHEs; (d) low or no tuition; and (d) total connectivity among components;

- Finding 19: An increased focus on the mission of education, which is a result of the sum of the interactions among system components, system converters, and system flows including those from (a) Investment Vehicle Balance; (b) decrease in administrative resources focused on revenue generation; (c) increase in revenue for NIHEs; and (d) total connectivity among components.

These findings both, confirm the data from the literature review, and extend knowledge to specifically NIHEs components, revenue genera- tion, and organizational change. A further example of an extension of knowledge is the theoretical effect of the Investment Vehicle Balance depicted in Figure 2 and included above as a part of the theoretical affects of the new revenue generation theory. The *Investment Vehicle Balance* was informed through the data collection and analysis process. More particularly, this data includes quotes that informed the investment vehicle including, (a) participant's A2101 statement, "I can see how an investment vehicle for higher education [HEIT], similar to a real estate investment trust [REIT], could benefit both the student and the investor"; (b) participant's BL 2331 statement, "I guess many students would not end up returning the funds but if the pool of students was large enough, it should work out"; (c) the findings that over 95 percent of students were enthused about the possibility of what participant S1555 called an "angle investor group" or a fund such as a HEIT that is controlled by a single, or group of, NIHEs;(d) participant's A5303, statement, "Repayment models are very interesting and should be offered as an option to students" and "In a fully connected model students would find the path that best suits them".; and (e) Participant's FA4203, statement,

Basically instead of Jane Doe paying the tuition [as an example] the 3M Corporation pays it, is a mixed bag. On one hand, I love the idea, higher education being something that people don't have to think about the price tag of. That people should think of just what is the best match for them. Although getting some funding from private donors is something, I am of two minds about. On the one hand, if private donors can step- up that's great.... One issue is the nature of higher education is a public good so public sources should be the major source of funding. The other concern is whether the corporate interests would influence the type of education being offered by the school in terms of the types of classes being offered, what sorts of professors are hired, and tenured, etcetera. ... However, if there was a pool of organizations that provided funding, that would not be that different from corporations paying taxes and the taxes going to higher ed. (Participant FA4203)

Grounded Theory

As described earlier, a grounded theory for sustainably generating revenue for NIHEs in the United States has been emerged from the data. The new sustainable revenue generation theory in Figure 2 reflects a constant bidirectional and dynamic flow of the total capabilities and knowledge among all of the system components, from both a micro and macro perspective. As indicated in Figure 2, the theoretical affect of constant bidirectional and dynamic flow of the total capabilities and knowledge among all of the system components is positive, among system components including, revenue generation, faculty, students, employers, and society. Furthermore, the theoretical affect of constant bidirectional and dynamic flow of the total capabilities and knowledge among all of the system components acts as a positive agent of change as supported by Oliver and Hyun (2011) who concluded that, "the collaboration of various groups within the institution in the process promoted organizational change" (p. 2).

Important aspects of the findings of a grounded theory study are fit, workability, relevance, and modifiability. Glaser and Strauss (1967) stated that a grounded theory is not true or false, but has more or less fit, workability, relevance, and modifiability. Fit representing how closely concepts represent the data and realities of where the theory is to be applied (Glaser & Strauss, 1967). For this study, a close fit is present between the results of this study and both the data and functioning NIHEs. The relevance, or as Glaser and Strauss (1967) defined as the real concern of the participants, is also evident in this study, as the impact of current revenue generation methods and a concern regarding future revenue generation methods was found to a real concern of the participants. Similarly, workability was achieved during the data collection process when the participants identified how they are trying to solve problems associated with revenue generation in NIHEs (Glaser

& Strauss, 1967). Finally, modifiability, or indications that a theory can incorporate new data that causes variations in categories, is present as well. This is most evident by the fundamental nature of change that the theory itself incorporates.

SUMMARY

The objective of my study was to examine the interactions among components of the nonprofit university system, existing revenue generation methods, and sustainability of revenue generation, all in an effort to generate a new sustainable revenue theory for nonprofit universities within the United States. My study's findings suggest that significant, multifaceted, and comprehensive interactions between the components of the NIHE system and revenue generation exist. A further finding is that analysis of the data from all three data sources clearly indicates that significant, multifaceted, and comprehensive interactions among the components of the NIHE system, current methods of revenue generation, and organizational change are present. Furthermore, the findings of my study generated inductively, a new sustainable revenue theory for nonprofit universities within the United States, which states that a sustainable revenue generation system must continually include, and respond to, the multidirectional interactions of all system components as they change over time, including businesses, and that this connectivity resulted in both increased revenue and reduced student and government-funded tuition. This new theory is important because it indicates one potential method or system in which NIHEs can effectively and sustainably generate revenue in a fashion that reflects and supports all components of the system. It further suggests that system components such as students, family, employers, and society's economy can also benefit from the use of this theory by NIHEs.

References

Alstadsæter, A. (2011). Measuring the consumption value of higher education. *CESifo Economic Studies, 57*(3), 458-479. doi:10.1093/cesifo/ifq009

Arcuri, G. (2010, November). *Complex adaptive change plan: Revenue generation for a new nonprofit university*. A paper presentation at the Kenwood U of NY Campus Association's board meeting.

Arcuri, G. (2014). *Sustainable Revenue Generation System for Nonprofit Institutions of Higher Education* (Doctoral dissertation, WALDEN UNIVERSITY).

Barrett, S. E. (2010). Competitive intelligence: Significance in higher education. *World Future Review, 2*(4), 26-30.

Becker, K. (2010). Facilitating unlearning during implementation of new technology. *Journal of Organizational Change Management, 23*(3), 251–268. doi:10.1108/09534811011049590

Beinhocker, E. (2006). The adaptable corporation. *McKinsey Quarterly, 2*, 76-87. Retrieved from www.mckinsey.com/insights/mckinsey/quartlerly.

Bold, E. (2011). Instruments and techniques used in the design and implementation of change management. *Journal of Advanced Research in Management, 2*(1), 5-13. Retrieved from www.ceeol.com. (Document ID: 2443116071)

Bordia, P., Restubog, S. L. D., Jimmieson, N. L., & Irmer, B. E. (2011). Haunted by the past: Effects of poor change management history on employee attitudes and turnover. *Group Organization Management*, doi:10.1177/1059601110392990.

Connectivity. (n.d.). In *Merriam-Webster's online dictionary*. Retrieved July 2, 2014, from http://www.merriam-webster.com/dictionary/connectivity

Creswell, J. W., & Plano Clark, V. L. (2010). *Designing and conducting mixed methods research*. Thousand Oaks, CA: Sage.

Dew, J. R. (2009). Quality issues in higher education. *Journal for Quality and Participation, 32*(1), 4. Retrieved from http://asq.org.

Eastman, J. (2006). Revenue generation and organisational change in higher education: Insights from Canada. *Higher Education Management and Policy, 18*(3), 48-75. Retrieved from www1.oecd.org/edu/imhe/42348795.pdf#page=57

Forbes, J.L. (1993) *Externally driven growth: A system dynamics investigation* (Doctoral dissertation, Claremont Graduate University) UMI Number 9330342

Glaser, B. G. (1992). *Basics of grounded theory analysis: Emergence vs. forcing.* Mill Valley, CA: The Sociology Press.

Glaser, B., & Strauss A. (1967). *The discovery of grounded theory: Strategies for qualitative research.* Chicago: Aldine.

Jones, D., & Wellman, J. (2010). Breaking bad habits: Navigating the financial crisis. *Change: The Magazine of Higher Learning, 42*(3), 6-13. doi:10.1080/00091381003730169

Luoma, M. (2006). A play of four arenas how complexity can serve management development. *Management Learning, 37*(1), 101-123. doi:10.1177/1350507606058136

McCuddy, M. K., Pinar, M., & Gingerich, E. F. (2008). Using student feedback in designing student-focused curricula. *The International Journal of Educational Management, 22*(7), 611-637. doi:10.1108/09513540810908548

McDevitt, R., Giapponi, C., & Solomon, N. (2008). Strategy revitalization in academe: a balanced scorecard approach. *International Journal of Educational Management, 22*(1), 32-47. doi:10.1108/09513540810844549

Meltzer, B. N., Petras, J. W., & Reynolds, L. T. (1975). *Symbolic interactionism: Genesis, varieties and criticism.* Boston: Routledge & Kegan Paul

Nair, C. S., Bennett, L., & Mertova, P. (2010). Responding to the student voice: a case study of a systematic improvement strategy. *TQM Journal, 22*(5), 553-564. doi:10.1108/17542731011072883

Nye, C. D., Brummel, B. J., & Drasgow, F. (2010). Too good to be true? Understanding change in organizational outcomes. *Journal of Management, 36*(6), 1,555–1,577. doi:10.1177/0149206310376326

Oliver, S. L., & Hyun, E. (2011). Comprehensive curriculum reform in higher education: collaborative engagement of faculty and administrators. *Journal of Case Studies in Education, 2*(1), 1-20.Retrieved from ABI/INFORM Global. (Document ID: 2445056771).

Pathak, V., & Pathak, K. (2010). Reconfiguring the higher education value chain. *Management In Education, 24*(4), 166-171. doi:10.1177/0892020610376791

Randall, L. M., & Coakley, L. A. (2007). Applying adaptive leadership to successful change initiatives in academia. *Leadership & Organization Development Journal,* 28(4), 325-335. doi:10.1108/01437730710752201

Rollwagen, I. (2010). Project economy approaches for higher education: Diversifying the revenue base of German universities. *Higher Education Management And Policy, 22*(3), 9-29.

Shah, A. (2009). The impact of quality on satisfaction, revenue, and cost as perceived by providers of higher education. *Journal Of Marketing For Higher Education, 19*(2), 125-141. doi:10.1080/08841240903451324

Shoham, S., & Hasgall, A. (2005). Knowledge workers as fractals in a complex adaptive organization. *Knowledge and Process Management, 12*(3), 225-236. doi:10.1002/kpm.228

Slaughter, S., & G. Rhoades. (2004). *Academic capitalism and the new economy markets, state, and higher education.* Baltimore: The Johns Hopkins University Press.

Smith, Z. A., & Wolverton, M. (2010). Higher education leadership competencies: Quantitatively refining a qualitative model. *Journal of Leadership & Organizational Studies,* 17(1) 61-70. doi:10.1177/1548051809348018

Summers, J. A. (2004). Net tuition revenue generation at private liberal arts colleges. *Education Economics, 12*(3), 219-230. doi:10.1080/0964529042000258581

Trussel, J. (2002). Revisiting the Prediction of Financial Vulnerability. *Nonprofit Management & Leadership, 13*(1), 17. doi:10.1002/nml.13103

Tucker, J. S., Cullen, J. C., Sinclair, R. R., & Wakeland, W. W. (2005). Dynamic systems and organizational decision-making processes in nonprofits. *The Journal of Applied Behavioral Science, 41*(4), 482–502. doi:10.1177/0021886305279483

Weisbrod, B. A., & Asch, E. D. (2010). The truth about the "Crisis" in higher education finance. *Change: The Magazine of Higher Learning, 42*(1), 23-29. doi:10.1080/00091380903449086

WEB APPENDIX

A web appendix for this paper is available at:

http://www.businessresearchconsortium.org/pro/brcpro2015p2.pdf

Testing the Excess Return Hypothesis: The Canadian Case

Trevor W. Chamberlain and Abdul-Rahman Khokhar

Trevor W. Chamberlain
DeGroote School of Business, McMaster University
1280 Main Street
West Hamilton, ON, L8S 4M4.
Tel: (905) 525-9140, x23980. Fax: (905) 521-8995.
Email: chambert@mcmaster.ca

Abdul-Rahman Khokhar
Sobey School of Business
St. Mary's University
923 Robie Street
Halifax, NS, B3H 3C3
Tel: (962) 491-6371. Fax: (902) 496-8101.
Email: Rahman.Khokhar@smu.ca

Abstract

This study examines the relationship between stock returns and the term structure of interest rates in a Canadian setting. Following Zhou's study of the US market (Federal Reserve Board, 1996), the hypothesis tested is the excess return hypothesis, which states that expected returns move one-for-one with interest rates. This relationship is explored using nominal and real return data for Canadian stocks and bonds. In addition, given the close relationship between the Canadian and US economies, the study examines the ability of US interest rates to predict Canadian stock returns.

Using first differenced returns, the study finds that nominal Canadian interest rates have predictive power vis-à-vis nominal Canadian stock returns, but, unlike Zhou's (1996) results for the US, the relationship is negative. This is also true when real returns are used. As for US interest rates and Canadian stock returns, the relationship is of mixed sign and mainly insignificant for both nominal and real stock returns and interest rates. The only evidence supporting the excess return hypothesis occurs when two-stage least squares, using the short-term interest rate as an instrumental variable, are used to regress real Canadian stock returns on real US interest rates. Finally, tests to determine whether the results are dependent on the period studied indicate that they are not sample-dependent.

JEL Classification: G10

Keywords: Stock Returns, Interest Rates

Acknowledgements: The authors wish to thank session participants at the 9th Annual Conference of Business Research Consortium of Western New York held in Rochester, NY and the 77th IAES Conference held in Madrid for their helpful comments.

INTRODUCTION AND LITERATURE REVIEW

The relationship between stock prices and the term structure of interest rates has been examined in numerous studies utilizing US data. In an early study, Shiller (1981) explained the notion of efficient markets by attributing the volatility in stock prices to real interest rate changes. Subsequently, several attempts were made to predict stock returns using changes in the term structure. Flannery and James (1984) studied the effect of interest rate changes on the common stock returns of financial institutions. They used weekly stock return data for sixty-seven US commercial banks over the period January 1976 to November 1981 to find a correlation between common stock returns and interest rate changes. Likewise, Campbell (1987) used monthly US data between 1959 and 1983 to find that the term structure of interest rates predicts excess returns on stocks, bills and bonds. The study further examined simple asset pricing models and provided evidence that conditional variances of excess return change through time. Campbell also found a positive relationship between the conditional mean and the conditional variance at the short end of the term structure. Breen et al (1989) studied the economic significance of predictable variations in stock index returns and concluded that knowledge of the one-month interest rate is useful in forecasting the sign and variance of the excess return on stocks. This study documented a negative relationship between a stock index return and treasury bill interest rates using a value-weighted index. However, this relationship was not statistically or economically significant when an equally-weighted index was used. Ferson (1989) argued that the regression of security returns on treasury bill rates provides insights about the behaviour of risk in rational asset pricing models; that is, the changes in conditional betas, a measure of risk, are associated with interest rates.

A study by Jagadeesh (1990) rejected the hypothesis that stock prices follow a random walk and attributed predictability of stock returns either to market inefficiency or to systematic changes in expected stock returns. Campbell and Ammer (1993) used monthly postwar US data and a vector autoregression model to decompose excess stock returns and 10-year bond returns into changes in the expectation of future stock dividends, inflation, short-term real interest rates, and excess stock and bond returns. The study found that stock returns are driven by news about future excess stock returns, whereas real interest rates had little effect. In addition, real interest rates were found to affect short-term nominal interest rates and the slope of the term structure. Zhou (1996) used the term structure of interest rates to study the variation of stock prices and stock returns and found that interest rates had an important effect on long-horizon stock returns, especially for time horizons of twenty-four months or more. The paper supported the hypothesis that expected stock returns move one-for-one with *ex-ante* interest rates using real returns and long-horizon nominal returns.

In a more recent study, Domian and Reichenstein (2009) updated previous work and presented new evidence on the predictability of stock market returns. The study confirmed that stock returns are partially predictable while rejecting the random walk model. In another study, Czaja and Scholz (2009) examined the sensitivity of German stock returns to interest rate changes and concluded that the industry curvature and, to a lesser extent, the slope of the term structure, are useful in predicting variations in stock returns. The study also found that interest rate risk was of greater relevance for financial institutions than non-financial institutions.

One might expect to obtain results for Canada similar to those for the US, given the two countries geographic proximity and close economic relationship. Perhaps for these reasons, the relationship between Canadian stock returns and the term structure of interest rates does not appear to have been examined, with the exception of those studies which have examined momentum in Canadian stock returns. Cleary and Inglis (1998) argued that US and Canadian stock returns are predictable for short term horizons, and "abnormal profits have been generated by purchasing previous strong performers and selling previous poor performers" (p. 279). Similarly, Deaves and Miu (2007) concluded that "cross-section returns are predictable using both momentum and reversal strategies for Canadian financial markets," while testing "whether momentum profit in Canada could be improved on by conditioning on the term structure of prior returns" (p. 135).

The above notwithstanding, whether there is a relationship between Canadian stock returns and the term structure deserves to be empirically tested. This is the objective of the current study. Using an approach similar to that of Zhou (1996) we test the hypothesis that expected stock returns move one-for-one with *ex-ante* interest rates, which is also known as the excess return hypothesis. The relationship is explored using nominal and real data for stocks and the Canadian term structure. In addition, the paper examines the ability of the US term structure to predict changes in Canadian stock returns. Inasmuch as American monetary policy has been found to have a major influence on Canadian monetary policy and interest rates (Khoury and Melard, 1985), and conventional wisdom holds that Canadian stock prices are affected by US interest rate changes (see for example, Tilak, 2015), we would expect to obtain results similar to those of Zhou (1998).

The study contributes to the existing literature inasmuch as it appears to be the first attempt to test empirically the excess return hypothesis using Canadian data. The paper also appears to be the first attempt to explore the possibility of a relationship between the US term structure and Canadian stock returns.

METHODOLOGY

Data and Variables
Toronto Stock Exchange (TSX) data are sourced from the Canadian Financial Markets Research Centre (CFMRC) Summary Information Database. The S&P/TSX Monthly Price Index of stocks traded on the TSX is used to compute stock returns. Consistent with most empirical work in this area, log stock returns are calculated using equation 1 in Appendix 1, where variables are as defined in Exhibit 1. The S&P/TSX monthly price index data cover the period 1956:01 to 2008:06. Short and long horizon stock returns are estimated for six different periods, with n set equal to 3, 12, 24, 36, 60 and 84 months. These periodic returns are then transformed into annualized stock returns using equation 2 in Appendix 1.

The zero coupon bond yield for the matching maturity implied by the term structure (yield curve) for Canadian treasury securities is used as a proxy for the Canadian interest rate. Yield curve data are sourced from the Bank of Canada using 3, 12, 24, 36, 60 and 84 month maturity zero coupon Canadian treasury securities. The Canadian term structure data are only available since 1986:01, with the exception of the 3-month maturity zero coupon bond yield. The additional data for the 3-month maturity zero-coupon bond yield for the period 1956:01 to 1985:12 are sourced from the Canadian Socio-Economic Information Management System (CAMSIM) database.

To study the relationship between the US term structure and changes in Canadian stock returns, term structure data for US Treasury securities were also required. These data were sourced from two sources. Data for the period 1956:01 to 1991:02 were obtained from McCulloch and Kwon's (1993) dataset of zero-coupon bond yields implied by the yield curve of US treasury securities. Data for the period 1991:03 to 2009:01 were obtained from the Center for Research in Security Prices (CRSP) database through Wharton Research Data Services (WRDS).

To obtain real returns, the nominal data for each period were adjusted for, respectively, periodic US and Canadian inflation. Log inflation was computed using monthly Consumer Price Index (CPI) data and then annualized inflation for each month was computed using equation 3 in Appendix 1. Both Canadian and US CPI data were sourced through the CANSIM database for the period 1950:12 to 2008:06. Real stock returns and real interest rates were computed using equations 4 and 5 in Appendix 1.

Although the data for the S&P/TSX Monthly Price Index of stocks began on 1956:01, the return data series start later depending on the value of n. For example, for the 84 month return period, the first monthly observation starts on 1963:01. The summary of observations for each variable is shown in Table 1.

Since the number of available observations for the Canadian term structure is limited to 270, except for the 3-month rate for which 627 observations are available, the overall analysis uses 270 observations for all variables starting from 1986:01. However, an additional analysis is conducted for the short-horizon (3-month) using all 627 observations for the period 1956:04 to 2008:06, and these results are then compared with the short-horizon (3-months) results obtained using 270 observations in an effort to identify any effects arising as a result of differences in sample size. This is discussed in the next section.

Sample means and standard deviations for asset returns and inflation for all six maturities are provided in Table 2. Sample means and standard deviations for the larger sample using 627 observations, and for the small sample, using 270 observations, are compared in Table 3.

Overall, from Table 3, we see that the larger sample tends to have a higher standard deviation, not only for nominal stock returns and nominal interest rates, but also for real stock returns and real interest rates. This is true for both the Canadian and US samples.

Empirical Models
The methodology to analyze the co-movements of stocks and bonds is similar to that used in Zhou (1996). The paper investigates the predictive power of bond yields for stock returns and tests the hypothesis that expected stock returns move one-for-one with *ex-ante* interest rates – the so-called excess return hypothesis. The model in equation 6 (Appendix 1) is used to test the hypothesis.

The objective of the analysis is to determine for what value of n, if any, the excess return hypothesis holds. In other words, a value, b_1, equal or close to 1 will support the hypothesis that expected stock returns move one-for-one with *ex-ante* interest rates. The theoretical foundation of the excess return hypothesis is described in Zhou (1996).

Since the change in expected inflation has an effect on nominal asset returns, it might be argued that the co-movement of nominal stock returns and nominal interest rates could be due to changes in expected inflation. For this reason, after incorporating real variables, the model in equation 7 (Appendix 1) is employed to test the excess return hypothesis.

Ordinary least squares are used to examine the one-for-one relationship between stock returns and interest rates. We first examine if the data are trend stationary to the order $I(0)$ or $I(1)$ using the Phillips and Perron (1998) test and find they are trend stationary to the order $I(1)$. Consequently, we use first differencing to de-trend the data. Finally, to allow for probable autocorrelation in the return data, the standard errors are adjusted using Newey and West's (1987) approach with a maximum lag of 4. This lag value for regressions with Newey-West standard errors represents the optimal lag provided by the Phillips and Perron (1998) unit root test.

Since equations 6 and 7 in Appendix 1 assume that the relationship between stock returns and matching maturity bond yields is *ex-ante*, the regression of real stock returns on *ex-post* real interest rates could involve endogeneity, resulting in biased coefficient estimates. To address this problem, an instrumental variable (IV) approach is used to estimate unbiased coefficients. Consistent with most empirical work in this area and with Zhou (1996), the past real short-term interest rate, $z_t = y_{t-3,t}$, is used as an instrumental variable. A good instrumental variable must be highly correlated with the independent variable. The correlation between the chosen instrumental variable and independent variable is shown in Table 4. Finally, the two-stage least squares (2SLS) model is used for the regressions.

Finally, a test for any structural change was conducted to confirm if a smaller sample size for Canadian term structure data has any impact on the results. To this end, a monthly dummy variable was created, taking a value of 0 for months prior to 1986:01 and a value of 1 for months following 1985:12. Then an interaction variable was created using a monthly dummy and 3-month interest rates. 3-month stock returns were then regressed against 3-month interest rates, the monthly dummy variable and an interaction variable. An F-Test was conducted to determine if the coefficients on the monthly dummy and interaction variable are both equal to zero.

RESULTS

Canadian Stock Returns vs Canadian Term Structure

Stock Returns vs Interest Rates – Nominal

Consistent with existing empirical work, equation 6 (Appendix 1) is first used to explore the relationship between nominal 3 to 84 month stock returns and matching maturity zero coupon bond yields as a proxy for nominal interest rates. Table 5 provides the regression results for short to long term horizon nominal stock returns on the matching maturity interest rates for the period 1986:01 to 2008:06. The standard errors reported in brackets are adjusted for serial autocorrelation and hetroscedasticity using the Newey-West approach.

The coefficients for bond yield are consistently negative, tend to decline with increasing n, and are significant at the ten percent level for the three, thirty-six, and eighty-four month time horizons. The null hypothesis that the coefficient for interest rates is not significantly different from zero is thus rejected for some time horizons, but not for others. The results provide some evidence of a relationship between nominal Canadian stock returns and nominal Canadian interest rates for short, medium and long time horizons. However, they differ from the results reported by Zhou (1996) inasmuch as the indicated relationship is consistently negative in the Canadian case.

Stock Returns vs Interest Rates – Real

Equation 7 (Appendix 1) is used to investigate the relationship between real stock returns and matching maturity real interest rates for each of the six time horizons. The real data for stock return and interest rates are computed by deflating nominal data using periodic inflation. Table 6 shows the regression results using data for the period 1986:01 to 2008:06. The Newey-West approach is used to estimate the standard errors, adjusted for autocorrelation and hetroscedasticity.

The results using real data are similar to those obtained using nominal data inasmuch as the estimated coefficient for the interest rate is positive for the shortest time horizons - 12 months – but negative for all others. These results are, again, different than those of Zhou (1996), who reports a positive relationship using real data. However, only for the 84-month time horizon is the interest rate coefficient statistically significant and then only at the 10% level. Similarly, the R^2 values do not indicate significant predictive power of Canadian real interest rates for Canadian real stock returns.

Canadian Stock Returns vs US Term Structure

Canadian Stock Returns vs US Interest Rates – Nominal
Equation 6 (Appendix 1) is applied using Canadian nominal stock returns and matching maturity US nominal interest rates for the period 1986:01 to 2008:06. The regression results are presented in Table 7; the standard errors are adjusted for serial autocorrelation and hetroscedasticity using the Newey-West approach.

The coefficient estimates are both positive and negative across the various horizons considered, with no particular pattern indicated. These results suggest that the US term structure has little predictive ability for Canadian stock returns. None of the interest rate coefficients are statistically significant and, once again, the R^2 values are low indicating little predictive ability.

Canadian Stock Returns vs US Interest Rates – Real
The relationship between Canadian real stock returns and matching maturity US real interest rates is examined using equation 7 (Appendix 1) and data for the period 1986:01 to 2008:06. The nominal data for stock returns and bond yields are adjusted for inflation. Table 8 presents the regression results, with standard errors computed using the Newey-West approach.

With real US term structure data the estimated coefficients for real interest rates are, once again, both positive and negative with no particular pattern across time horizons. The coefficients are statistically insignificant, except for the 3-month horizon, which is positive and is significant at the 1% level. This suggests support for the excess return hypothesis, but only for the short horizon.

Stock Returns vs Term Structure using Instrumental Variable (IV)

The two-stage least squares (2SLS) model with an instrumental variable, as discussed in Section 2.2, is used to avoid potential endogeneity and to estimate consistent and unbiased coefficients. Canadian real stock returns are regressed first using Canadian real interest rates and, then, using US real interest rates, with the past short-term interest rate as the instrumental variable.

Canadian Stock Returns vs Canadian Interest Rates with Instrument

Canadian real stock returns and matching maturity Canadian real interest rates for the period 1986:01 to 2008:06 are regressed using the 2SLS approach with the results summarized in Table 9. In this case, there is no need to first difference the data.

The coefficient estimates for the interest rates are negative except for the 36 month time horizon, where it is positive but close to zero. However, only the coefficient for the 12 and 84-months time horizons are statistically significant, albeit in both cases at the 1% level. These results suggest that Canadian real interest rates may affect Canadian real stock returns, but unlike Zhou's (1996) results for the US, the relationship is negative.

Canadian Stock Returns vs US Interest Rates with Instrument

The relationship between Canadian real stock returns and matching maturity US real interest rates is examined through the 2SLS regression model as well. Table 10 provides the regression results with standard errors. Once again there is no need to first difference the data.

The coefficient on the interest rate for the short horizon of 3 months is negative but not significant. Most interestingly, we see strong support for the excess return hypothesis for the 24, 36, and 60 month time horizons, as coefficient estimates are close to 1 and significant at the 1% level. Unlike the relationship observed between real Canadian stock returns and real US interest rates using OLS regressions in section 3.2.2, the results here suggest that real Canadian stock returns move one-for-one with real US interest rates for medium to long time horizons.

Test for Sample Size-Related Effects:
As discussed earlier, Canadian term structure data are only available from 1986:01, except for the 3 month time horizon. The paper attempts to check for any structural change on account of this limitation. The comparative descriptive statistics for 3-month asset returns using large and small samples are reported in Table 3 in section 2.1. The regression results using large samples for the period 1956:04 to 2008:06 for 3-month Canadian stock returns with matching maturity interest rates are shown in Table 11. These results are similar to the results obtained earlier, when a smaller sample of 270 observations was used. The only notable change is in the coefficient on interest rates for the regression between Canadian real stock returns and US real interest rates, which is no longer statistically significant.

The question of interest is whether the availability of Canadian term structure data prior to 1986:01 would yield different results. If so, the conclusions indicated earlier in this paper would only apply to the period examined.

The approach described in section 2.2 is used to test for possible structural change through comparing the results obtained for the large 3-month asset return sample with those obtained for the small 3-month sample. The monthly dummy variable is interacted with 3-month interest rates to create an interaction variable. Canadian stock returns for a 3-month period are regressed against the 3-month interest rate, monthly dummy and interaction variable using the Newey-West approach with a maximum lag of 4. The regression is followed by a post estimation test for the null hypothesis that coefficients on the monthly dummy and interaction variable are jointly equal to zero. Rejection of this null hypothesis would provide support for the argument that there exists no structural change due to an increase in the period examined. The regression results are summarized in Table 12.

The regressions and post estimation tests for the null hypothesis described in the preceding paragraph were conducted using both nominal and real Canadian stock returns with nominal and real Canadian and US interest rates. The null hypothesis is not rejected for any of the four regressions, suggesting that the results do not depend on the sample size.

Conclusions

Canadian nominal interest rates represented by zero coupon yields on Canadian treasury bonds appear to have some predictive ability for Canadian nominal stock returns. Likewise, in contrast to results obtained by Zhou (1996) for the US, the relationship is negative. Canadian real interest rates are inversely related, except for the 3-month horizon, to bond yields, though only significantly for the 84 month time horizon. These findings generally hold using a 2SLS regression for Canadian real stock returns on Canadian real interest rates, where statistically significant (and negative) relationships are observed for both 12-month and 84-month time horizons.

On the other hand, the US term structure appears to have little relationship to Canadian stock returns. Regression results for Canadian stock returns and US nominal interest rate indicate coefficient signs that are both positive and negative, with no particular pattern across time horizons. Moreover, in all cases they lack statistical significance. The regression results for Canadian real stock returns and US real interest rates also have mixed signs, with the only significant relationship occurring in the short (3-month) horizon data. The two-stage least square regression results however indicate a one-for-one positive co-movement of Canadian real stock returns and US real interest rates, and for 24, 36, and 60 month time horizons. This relationship is quite unlike the one found between Canadian real stock returns and Canadian real interest rates, where the coefficients are negative in all cases except the 36-month time horizon. Finally, the test using the 3-month extended sample size suggests that there have not been any structural changes over the period studied.

References

Breen, William, Lawrence R. Glosten, and Ravi Jagannathan, 1989, Economic Significance of Predictable Variations in Stock Index Returns, *Journal of Finance* 44, 1177-1189. http://dx.doi.org/10.1111/j.1540-6261.1989.tb02649.x

Campbell, John H., and John Ammer, 1993, What Moves the Stock and Bond Markets? A Variance Decomposition for Long-Term Asset Returns, *Journal of Finance* 48, 3-37. http://dx.doi.org/10.1111/j.154 0-6261.1993.tb04700.x

Campbell, John Y., 1987, Stock returns and the term structure, *Journal of Financial Economics* 18, 373-399. http://dx.doi.org/10.1016/0304-4 05X(87)90045-6

Cleary, Sean, and Michael Inglis, 1998, Momentum in Canadian Stock Returns, *Canadian Journal of Administrative Sciences* 15, 279-291. http://dx.doi.org/10.1111/j.1936-4490.1998.tb00168.x

Czaja, Marc-Gregor, and Hendrik Scholz, 2009, Interest Rate Risk Rewards in Stock Returns of Financial Corporations: Evidence from Germany, *European Financial Management,* 16(1), 124-154. http://dx.doi.org/10 .1111/j.1468-036X.2008.00455.x

Deaves, Richard, and Peter Miu, 2007, Refining Momentum Strategies by Conditioning on Prior Long-term Returns: Canadian Evidence, *Canadian Journal of Administrative Sciences* 24, 135-145. http://dx.doi.org/10.1002/cjas.11

Domian, Dale L., and William Reichenstein, 2009, Long-Horizon Stock Predictability: Evidence and Application, *Journal of Investing* 18(3), 12-20. http://dx.doi.org/10.3905/JOI.2009.18.3.012

Ferson, Wayne E., 1989, Changes in Expected Security Returns, Risk, and the Level of Interest Rates, *Journal of Finance* 44, 1191-1217. http://dx.doi.org/10.1111/j.1540-6261.1989.tb02650.x

Flannery, Mark J., and Christopher M. James, 1984, The Effect of Interest Rate Changes on the Common Stock Returns of Financial Institutions, *Journal of Finance* 39, 1141-1153. http://dx.doi.org/10.1111/j.1540-6261.1984.tb03898.x

Jegadeesh, Narasimhan, 1990, Evidence of Predictable Behavior of Security Returns, *Journal of Finance* 45, 881-898. http://dx.doi.org/10.1111/j.1540-6261.1990.tb05110.x

Khoury, Nabil T., and Guy Melard, 1985, The Relationship between the Canadian Treasury-Bill Rate and Expected Inflation in Canada and in the United States, *Canadian Journal of Administrative Sciences* 2, 63-76.

McCulloch, John. H., and Heon-Chul Kwon, 1993, U.S. Term Structure Data, 1947-1991, Ohio State University Working Paper 93-6.

Newey, Whitney K., and Kenneth D. West, 1987, A Simple, Positive Semi-Definite, Heteroskedasticity and Autocorrelation Consistent Covariance Matrix, *Econometrica* 55, 703-708. http://dx.doi.org/10.2307/1913610

Phillips, P. C. B., and P. Perron, 1988, Testing for a unit root in time series regression. *Biometrika* 75, 335–346.

Shiller, Robert J., 1981, Do Stock Prices Move Too Much to be Justified by Subsequent Changes in Dividends? *American Economic Review* 71, 421-436.

Tilak, John, 2015, Canadian Stocks-TSX falls as US rate hike fears hit gold shares, Reuters, Feb 6, http://www.reuters.com/article/2015/02/06/markets-canada-stocks-idUSL1N0VG28A20150206

Zhou, Chunsheng, 1996, Stock Market Fluctuations and the Term Structure, *US Federal Reserve Board* 3, mimeo.

Web Appendix

A web appendix for this paper is available at:

http://www.businessresearchconsortium.org/pro/brcpro2015p3.pdf

Taxation Changes and the Cross-Border Pricing of REITs

Trevor W. Chamberlain and Hesam Shahriari

The authors would like to thank two anonymous reviewers of the *Journal* for their helpful comments. Please address correspondence to Trevor Chamberlain, DSB 304, DeGroote School of Business, McMaster University, 1280 Main Street West Hamilton, Ontario L8S 4M4.
Email: chambert@mcmaster.ca. Telephone: (905) 525-9140 x23980.
Fax: (905) 521-8995.

Abstract

On November 21, 2005 the Canadian government announced a reduction in the tax on dividends in an effort to neutralize the tax system's bias in favour of income trusts. Eleven months later, on October 31, 2006, a new government changed direction and eliminated the tax deductibility of income trust distributions altogether. Exempted from this change in policy was the real estate investment trust (REIT) sector.

This present study examines the return behaviour of both Canadian and U.S. REITs around the time of these announcements in an effort to inform the ongoing discussion about REIT taxation design in the United States and abroad. Ordinary least squares with dummy variables are used to estimate Canadian REIT returns using a variant of the market model on the event date and the day after. Both equally-weighted and value-weighted portfolios are created in order to check the robustness of the results. In addition, the relationships between Canadian REIT returns and U.S. REIT returns are examined for each event. Test results indicate statistically significant abnormal returns for the Canadian REITs relative to their U.S. counterparts on both dates.

Keywords: Asset Prices, REITs, Taxes

INTRODUCTION

In February 2014 Congressional Ways and Means Committee Chairman David Camp released the Tax Reform Act of 2014, a long-awaited plan for broad changes in the U.S. federal income tax. One aspect of the Camp bill that has received particular attention is a proposal to limit REIT-eligible assets and impose new taxes on companies that convert from corporations to REITs (Borden, 2015).[1]

The consequences for firms and investors of the draft legislation or an alternate proposal will not be known with certainty until such time as it is approved and markets react. However, the *raison d'être* for REITs is the premise that a competitive tax structure is necessary to attract funds into the high-risk real estate industry. Otherwise, investment capital earmarked for real estate would flow to other sectors or to other tax jurisdictions, particularly those with close economic ties.[2]

The cross-border effects of taxation changes are often acknowledged, but seldom studied. Slemrod (1992) suggests that the high level of integration between the U.S. and Canadian economies provides a natural setting for studying cross-border tax effects. The effects of Canadian tax changes on the United States are difficult to measure directly because of the vast difference in size between the two economies. However, the impact of Canadian REIT-related tax changes on the value of Canadian REITs relative to their US counterparts can be quantified. This is the goal of the present study, in an effort to contribute to the current discussion about REIT taxation in the United States and abroad.

BACKGROUND

Since 1971 the taxation of income received from Canadian corporations as dividends has been based on the principle of tax integration. That is, income taxed at the corporate level and then paid out to shareholders in dividends generates a tax credit intended to offset the tax paid by the corporation. When this provision was introduced, the integration was practically complete and double taxation of corporate income paid out in dividends was eliminated. However, over time, as the national debt ballooned, the value of the tax credit was reduced as subsequent governments sought to increase revenues.

In response, Canadian firms began to insert income trusts between the operating corporation and its owners. These entities would own up to one hundred percent of the equity of the corporation. Most of the cash flow generated by operations – interest, dividends and return of capital – would be distributed to trust unitholders. Interest payments would be paid out of pre-tax income, while dividends would be paid out of after-tax income. The income trust would recapitalize the corporation to ensure that its current tax liability was minimal, if not zero. Instead, the operating income earned at the corporate level would flow through the income trust to unitholders and be taxed at the relevant rate at the personal level. The net result is that income generated by operations at the corporate level would only be taxed once, as was originally contemplated by the Income Tax Act revisions in 1971.[3]

The proliferation of income trust conversions and new income trusts beginning in the 1990's represented a significant loss of tax revenue. In response, between November 2005 and October 2006, successive governments announced two very different changes in tax policy. The first announcement, on November 23, 2005, to take effect in taxation year 2006, proposed to lower the personal tax rate on dividend income to eliminate the advantage to individuals of receiving business income via an income trust. However, the policy announcement left unchanged the tax advantage of income trusts to foreign investors and nontaxable entities such as pension plans.[4] The second, by a new government, on October 31, 2006, proposed to eliminate the tax-deductibility of distributions by income trusts, except those of qualifying REITs,[5] to equalize the tax treatment between income trust distributions and corporate dividends for all investors. This proposal was to take effect in taxation year 2007 for new trusts and corporation-to-trust conversions and in 2011 for existing trusts.

Chamberlain and Shahriari (2012) examined the valuation consequences for Canadian REITs of the tax changes. They found that the November 2005 change, which followed a period of high return volatility and negative cumulative abnormal returns, had a positive and significant impact on the valuation of REITs. The October 2006 change had different implications for REITs than it did for non-REIT trusts. Nonetheless, like the rest of the income trust sector, REITs responded negatively on the day of the announcement and the day following. Cross-sectional tests, moreover, were unable to explain any cross-sectional variation in REIT values as a result of the two announcements, suggesting that they affected all REITs in the same way.

In an effort to inform the current discussion about REIT taxation, the present paper examines whether U.S. REITs behaved in the same way as their Canadian counterparts at the time of these announcements. Real estate companies of each country invest in the other country's real property and investors in each country invest in the other country's real estate companies, including REITs. Although the taxation of Canadian REITs did not change as a result of either of these tax announcements (and, thus, did not change relative to the taxation of their U.S. peers), on both dates REIT values changed significantly – positively on the first date and negatively on the second.

The reason given by the Minister of Finance in October 2006 for exempting REITs was that the Canadian government wanted to stay "in sync" with U.S. tax rules, which had exempted REITs from a clampdown on income trusts in the 1980s. The conventional wisdom, as reported in the media at the time, was that Canadian real estate assets would be "gobbled up" by U.S. REITs if Canadian REITs lost their tax exemption. Inasmuch as there is reportedly a significant cross-country component to real estate company returns (Ling and Naranjo, 2012), this raises the question of whether Canadian REITs got caught up in the overall market reaction to the two tax changes or investors were reacting to other conditions in the North American or international real estate market.

In the next section the empirical literature on the valuation effects of tax changes, with particular emphasis on Canadian income trusts, is examined briefly. This is followed by a description of the data and methodology employed in the present study. The fourth section describes and discusses the results of our tests. The paper concludes with a brief summary of the implications of our findings.

LITERATURE REVIEW

The taxation of corporate distributions is a longstanding topic of discussion among both academics and policymakers. From a public policy perspective, the debate has focused on the desirability of dividends for distributive reasons versus the potential efficiency costs (Poterba et al, 1995). At the level of the firm, the question, as described above, is whether taxes on dividends increase the firm's cost of capital, thereby negatively affecting its ability to create value through new investment. The traditional view is that dividends offer non-tax benefits to shareholders that offset their tax cost. The optimal dividend policy for the firm is that at which the marginal tax costs and non-tax benefits are equal (Zodrow, 1991). In addition, taxing dividends in the hands of investors may induce firms to retain earnings rather than pay dividends. Agency theory suggests that this will encourage overinvestment (Jensen, 1986).

An alternate view is that the firm's cost of capital is unaffected by the taxation of dividends inasmuch as dividends do not offer any benefits to investors relative to retained earnings. Dividends are only determined residually after all profitable investment opportunities have been undertaken. The tax paid on dividends can thus be viewed as a charge against the firm's equity (Auerbach, 1971).

The traditional view implies that if income trusts are taxed at lower rates than corporations, they will undertake investments that would be rejected by the latter. The literature on income trusts has largely focused on the role of taxes. Hayward (2002) observes that "by interposing a mutual fund trust between the public investors and the operating corporation, the corporation may substantially reduce or eliminate corporate tax at the operating level and pass these savings in the form of higher distributions to investors" (p.1531). Aggarwal and Mintz (2004) show that the double taxation of dividends arising from direct payments by the corporation to shareholders is eliminated by using an income trust. Edgar (2004) argues that income trusts are an example of tax-driven innovation in that they replicate existing securities and, as such, have no non-tax rationale. Halpern and Norli (2006) also describe income trusts as a vehicle whose sole purpose is to shield business income from corporate tax. As for non-tax factors, Aguerrevere et al (2005) offer evidence showing that firms using income trusts have tended to be smaller companies with growth opportunities, while Jog and Wang (2005) argue that the high payouts of income trusts relative to those of corporations reduce agency costs.

The valuation impact on income trusts of the November 2005 announcement of a dividend tax reduction was examined by Elayan et al (2009). Their results indicate that during the period leading up to the announcement, income trusts experienced significantly negative abnormal returns. This they attribute to an expectation that the government intended to tax income trusts at a level similar to that applied to corporations. The announcement period returns, in contrast, are positive and significant, suggesting investors revised their expectations or that the uncertainty about the government's plans was resolved.

In a closely related study, Amoako-Adu and Smith (2008) considered portfolios of income trusts as well as high dividend stocks, and for both the November 2005 and October 2006 announcements. They found that the 2005 announcement had a positive effect on the values of both groups during the announcement period. Amoako-Adu and Smith interpret their results as indicating that the reduced tax on dividends was favourable for dividend paying firms and that the government's willingness to maintain the non-taxable status of income trusts reassured investors.[6] As for the 2006 announcement, they found that the values of both groups fell during the announcement period. However, the impact on income trusts was larger. Moreover, the absolute value of the impact on high payout trusts was smaller than on low payout trusts, reflecting, perhaps, the government's decision to defer applying the tax to existing income trusts until 2011.

Finally, as noted above, Chamberlain and Shahriari (2012) found that the November 2005 change had a positive and significant effect on REIT values. The October 2006 change did not affect REITs in the way that it did non-REIT trusts. Nonetheless, like the rest of the trust sector, REITs responded negatively on the announcement date and the day following. However, within a short period REITs regained all of the value they had lost.

DATA DESCRIPTION AND METHODOLOGY

In order to examine the relationship between Canadian and U.S. REIT returns at the time of the tax change announcements, two portfolios were created. The Canadian portfolio comprised seventeen REITs listed on the Toronto Stock Exchange (TSX) with available data at the end of the 2004 fiscal year. The portfolio included all of the companies in the COMPUSTAT Canadian database in the "Real Estate Investment Trust" industry category, with additional data obtained from the Canadian Financial Markets Research Centre (CFMRC) summary information database (CFMRC/TSX Annual).[7] Table 1 lists the REITs included in the Canadian portfolio together with summary financial information.

The U.S. portfolio consisted of fifty-three REITs listed on the New York Stock Exchange (NYSE), the American Stock Exchange (AMEX) or NASDAQ with available data at the end of the 2004 fiscal year. Data were obtained from the Center for Security Prices (CRSP) Files for SIC codes 6798 and 6513. The REITs included in the U.S. portfolio appear in Table 2.

Summary statistics for both equally-weighted and value-weighted versions of the two portfolios appear in Table 3. Portfolios using both weighting schemes are used to check the robustness of the results. The sample comprises 468 return-days for each portfolio with a mean daily return of approximately 0.1 percent, with the Canadian returns being slightly higher and less volatile than the U.S. returns. The period covered by the sample is June 1, 2005 to January 31, 2007. Pearson correlation coefficients for the Canadian and U.S. portfolios are in the 0.31 to 0.34 range.

Event study methodology using a variant of the market model was used to examine the relationship between Canadian and U.S. REIT returns at the time of each of the tax change announcements. In the standard market model, the return of any individual security or portfolio of securities is regressed on the return of a market portfolio. In general, for any security or portfolio i we have (Campbell et al, 1997, Ch 4):

$$R_{it} = \alpha_i + \beta_i R_{mt} + \varepsilon_{it} \qquad (1)$$

$$E[\varepsilon_{it}] = 0, \ Var[\varepsilon_{it}] = \sigma^2(\varepsilon_i),$$

where R_{it} is the time-t return on security i; R_{mt} is the time-t return on the market portfolio; α_i, β_i, and σ^2 are model parameters; and ε_{it} is the mean-zero error term, which captures the abnormal return. Model parameters are often estimated over an estimation period before the event and then used to calculate the abnormal returns during the event period.

In the current study, both equally-weighted and value-weighted port-folios of Canadian REITs and U.S. REITs were created. Daily portfolio returns were then used to estimate the following time-series regression model for each event k:

$$CARET_t = b_0 + b_1 USRET_t + b_2 D_{kt} + e_t, \qquad (2)$$

where $CARET_t$ is the daily return on the Canadian REIT portfolio; $USRET_t$ is the daily return on the U.S. REIT portfolio; and D_{kt} is a dummy variable, which is set equal to 1 on the event day and the day following, and 0 otherwise. Equation (2) is estimated separately for each of the two announcement dates, November 23, 2005 and October 31, 2006, and for both equally- and value-weighted portfolios. Using a dummy variable in the regression allows us to isolate the differential effect, if any, of the announcements on Canadian REIT returns. That is, inasmuch as the long-term relationship between $CARET_t$ and $USRET_t$ is measured by b_1, any abnormal returns on days 0 and 1 are captured by the coefficient of the dummy variable. In addition, assuming that the market for REITs is liquid and efficient, prices would be expected to react to policy changes quickly. The coefficient b_2 should capture the differential effect of each announcement on the value of the REIT portfolios. None of the Canadian REITs are included in the U.S. REIT portfolio.

The November 23, 2005 announcement only affected the taxation of Canadian REITs slightly, as it did income trusts in general, and left their tax status unchanged for foreign investors. We would thus expect Canadian REIT returns to remain unchanged vis-à-vis U.S. REIT returns. As for the October 31, 2006 announcement, although it eliminated the tax advantage of non-REIT income trusts, it left the taxation of qualifying REITs unchanged. Thus, once again, one would not expect any decline in Canadian REIT values relative to their U.S. counterparts.

In so far as the first announcement changed the market's expectations about the Canadian government's tax policy intentions, the parameters of the estimation model would be expected to change from the first event to the second. In other words, the same estimation period cannot be used to calculate the abnormal returns for both announcements. Therefore, the valuation impact of each announcement is estimated with a separate regression over a period of 120 trading days before the announcement date to 60 trading days after the announcement date.

RESULTS AND DISCUSSION

The estimation results for equation (2) appear in Tables 4 through 7. Tables 4 and 5 show the equally-weighted and value-weighted portfolio results for the 2005 announcement and Tables 6 and 7 present the same information for the 2006 announcement. Figures 1 and 2 show the pattern of incremental returns and cumulative incremental returns, respectively, for the 2005 announcement, whereas Figures 3 and 4 show the corresponding patterns for the 2006 announcement. The patterns are similar for the value-weighted portfolios, which are not presented here.

RESULTS FOR THE NOVEMBER 23, 2005 ANNOUNCEMENT

As noted earlier, the November 23, 2005 announcement proposed a lower personal tax rate on dividend income to eliminate the advantage to individuals of receiving business income from an income trust, but left the tax advantage of income trusts to foreign investors unchanged. As stated earlier, Chamberlain and Shahriari (2012) found that the abnormal returns on both the announcement date and the next trading day were positive and significant at the one percent level. This was in line with the results of Amoako-Adu and Smith (2008) and Elayan et al (2009) for the trust sector in general, which were attributed by the latter to investors' prior expectation that the government intended to tax income trusts at the level at which it taxed corporations.

This inference is consistent with the results reported in Tables 4 and 5. In both cases the estimated coefficient for b_2 is positive and significant at the five percent level. That is, while b_1 (in both tables) indicates a positive and significant (at five percent) relationship between the Canadian and U.S. REIT portfolio returns, the return on the Canadian portfolio is significantly greater on the announcement date. This seems to confirm the hypothesis that the government's decision was not fully anticipated by the market and served as a positive signal to investors in Canadian REITs relative to their US counterparts. The possibility of increased taxes on income trusts had been part of the public discourse up until that time and the government's announcement dispelled those concerns, at least in the short run. It should also have resolved uncertainty in investors' minds as to how the government would proceed. This seems to be confirmed by the mean abnormal return and cumulative abnormal return patterns presented in Figures 1 and 2; the announcement window follows a period of high return volatility. As well, while the Canadian REIT portfolio experienced negative abnormal returns during the period leading up to the announcement, it regained most of its value in a short time.

RESULTS FOR THE OCTOBER 31, 2006 ANNOUNCEMENT

While the October 2006 announcement removed the tax advantage of most income trusts for all investors, the policy change excluded qualifying REITs (as described in Appendix II). Therefore, the negative effect of the tax change on the valuation of income trusts generally reported in Amoako-Adu and Smith (2008) would not necessarily affect the Canadian REIT portfolio. Nonetheless, Chamberlain and Shahriari (2012) found that the market reaction to the announcement on the first trading day following the announcement (November 1, 2006) was negative and statistically significant (at the one percent level). While the abnormal return on the day of the announcement was also negative, it was statistically insignificant, possibly because the announcement was made late in the trading day.

The relationship between the returns on the Canadian and U.S. REIT portfolios in this case is also positive and significant, at 0.01% for both the equally-weighted and value-weighted portfolios (see Tables 6 and 7). The coefficient for the event dummy is negative, but only significant for the equally-weighted portfolio (at approximately five percent). Though not strong evidence, it does suggest, once again, that Canadian REIT prices were caught up in the market response to the announcement impact on income trusts generally and, as a result, Canadian REITs became less attractive relative to their US counterparts. At the same time, referring to the Canadian REIT portfolio cumulative incremental returns shown in figure 4 (for the equally-weighted case), it is evident that while the market reacted negatively to the announcement when it occurred, the portfolio was able to recover most of its value in a short period after the event. In fact, after fifty days of trading, the REIT portfolio had regained all of the value it had lost during the period leading up to and including the first trading day. That is, as it became clear that the implications for the Canadian REIT sector were slight, the market corrected itself.

Conclusion

This study examined the implications for the REIT sector of two changes in tax policy introduced by successive Canadian governments in November 2005 and October 2006. The first change, on November 23, 2005, reduced the income tax on dividends, thus considerably narrowing, but not eliminating, the gap in the overall tax paid via the corporate versus income trust form of business organization. The second change, on October 31, 2006, removed the tax advantage of the income trust form, but excluded qualifying REITs.

While these results do not establish the presence of cross-border spillover effects between Canada and the United States, they do appear to confirm that the change in REIT values at the time of each announcement was attributable to the announcement itself. That is, in both cases, an abnormal return for the Canadian REIT portfolio was observed relative to that of its U.S. counterpart. Inasmuch as the returns on the Canadian and U.S. portfolios followed a similar pattern during the observation period, these abnormal returns are interesting in that as they are arguably not what one would have expected, especially in 2006. However, they are consistent with the premise that tax change announcements do affect security values in one country relative to those in another. An increase (decline) in REIT values implies a lower (higher) cost of capital and an increase (decline) in investment in real estate assets. While tax policy invariably has to balance a number of often competing objectives, our findings suggest that policymakers should proceed with caution as they consider the introduction or reform of taxes that influence investor behaviour.

REFERENCES

Aggarwal, L., & Mintz, J. (2004). Income trusts and shareholder taxation: Getting it right. *Canadian Tax Journal, 52*(3), 792-818.

Aguerrevere, F., Pazzaglia, F., & Ravi, R. (2005). Income trusts and the great conversion. *Canadian Investment Review, 18*(4), 8-12.

Amoako-Adu, B., & Smith, B. F. (2008). Valuation effects of recent corporate dividend and income trust distribution tax changes. *Canadian Journal of Administrative Sciences, 25*(1), 55-66. http://dx.doi.org/10.1002/cjas.49

Auerbach, A. J. (1979). Wealth maximization and the cost of capital. *The Quarterly Journal of Economics, 93*(3), 433-446. http://dx.doi.org/10.2307/1883167

Bernstein, J. (April 2007). Income trusts: Non-qualifying REITs. *Canadian Tax Highlights, 15,* Toronto, ON: Canadian Tax Foundation.

Borden B.T. (2015). Reforming REIT Taxation or Not. *Houston Law Review,* 53 (1), 1-102.

Campbell, J. Y., Lo, A. W., & MacKinlay, A. C. (1997). *The Econometrics of Financial Markets,* Princeton, NJ: Princeton University Press.

Chamberlain, T. W., & Shahriari, H. (2012). Asset prices and taxes: an empirical study. *BRC Academy Journal of Business, 2*(1), 1-25.

Edgar, T. (2004). The trouble with trusts. *Canadian Tax Journal, 52*(3), 819-852.

Elayan, F. A., Li, J., Donnelly, M. E., & Young, A. W. (2009). Changes to income trust taxation in Canada: investor reaction and dividend clientele theory. *Journal of Business Finance & Accounting, 36*(5-6), 725-753. http://dx.doi.org/10.1111/j.1468-5957.2009.02156.x

Halpern, P., & Norli, O. (2006). Canadian business trusts: A new organizational structure. *Journal of Applied Corporate Finance, 18*(3), 66-75. http://dx.doi.org/10.1111/j.1745-6622.2006.00099.x

Hayward, P. D. (2002). Income trusts: A "tax-efficient" product or the product of tax inefficiency? *Canadian Tax Journal, 50*(5), 1529-1568.

Jensen, M. C. (1986). Agency costs of free cash flow, corporate finance, and takeovers. *The American Economic Review, 76*(2), 323-329.

Jog, V., & Wang, L. (2004). The growth of income trusts in Canada and the economic consequences. *Canadian Tax Journal, 52*(3), 853-880.

Keenan C. (2015). Coming soon? REITs in India and China. *REIT Magazine*, Sept/Oct, 14-18.

Ling, D. C., & Naranjo, A. (2002). Commercial real estate returns performance: a cross-country analysis. *Journal of Real Estate Finance and Economics, 24*(1-2), 119-142. http://dx.doi.org/10.1023/A:101393 8506550

Poterba, J. M., & Summers, L. H. (1985). The economic effects of dividend taxation. In E. Altman, & M. Subrahmanyam (Eds.), *Recent Advances in Corporate Finance* (pp. 227-284), Homewood, IL: Irwin Professional Publishing. http://dx.doi.org/10.3386/w1353

Slemrod, J. (1992). The impact of U.S. tax reform on Canadian stock prices. Ch.7 in J. D. Shaven and J. Whaley (Eds.), *Canada-U.S. Tax Comparisons* (pp. 237-254), Chicago, IL: University of Chicago Press.

Zodrow, G. R. (1991). On the" traditional" and" new" views of dividend taxation. *National Tax Journal, 44*(4), 497-509.

WEB APPENDIX

A web appendix for this paper is available at:

   http://www.businessresearchconsortium.org/pro/brcpro2015p4.pdf

NOTES

1. REITs, or real estate investment trusts, are companies that own income-producing real estate. Their assets include hotels, nursing homes, shopping malls, office buildings and apartments. Originally created in 1960 in the United States, REITs have spread worldwide and have a significant presence in Canada.

2. Indeed, China and India are contending with this issue presently. In 2014 both countries approved regulations for REITs to be established, but so far neither has settled on a tax structure that would allow them to compete successfully with REITs in Hong Kong, Singapore and Malaysia (Keenan, 2015).

3. The mechanics of the taxation of dividends and distributions using the corporate and income trust in Canada are explained in more detail in Appendix 1.

4. The loss of revenue was acknowledged by the government when the change in tax policy was announced. However, it went on to say that "reducing the tax individuals pay on dividends will encourage savings and investments and will help establish a better balance between the tax treatment of large corporations and that of income trusts" (Canada, Department of Finance, November 23, 2005). Some commentators questioned the claim of equal treatment by pointing to differences between the tax treatments that still favoured income trusts (see Elayan et al, 2009).

5. The criteria for the REIT exemption in Canada are presented in Appendix 2.

6. Another interpretation of this result is that even when the personal and corporate taxes paid on dividend income are set equal to that paid on trust distributions, there are a number of other tax factors that favour the latter (see Elayan et al, 2009).

7. Canadian REITs are listed in the COMPUSTAT annual and quarterly databases under location "CAD" and Standard Industry Classification (SIC) code "6798". Boardwalk Real Estate Trust is an exception, and is classified under SIC code "6513" (the "operators apartment bldgs" industry category). However, it is included in the portfolio since it operates as a Canadian REIT.

Cost Accounting Variance: Blended Learning

R. Mithu Dey

R. Mithu Dey
Associate Professor of Accounting
School of Business
Howard University
Washington, DC
ratna.dey@howard.edu
Tel: (202)806-1500

I acknowledge a Rochester Institute of Technology Provost Learning and Innovation Grant in 2013 which provided resources for me to implement a blended and flipped classroom for my graduate Cost Management class.

Abstract

This paper is a personal account of how I teach a blended graduate accounting class, specifically Cost Management. I discuss my optimal combination of online course lectures regarding a cost accounting subject matter followed by in-class application of subject matter via Harvard business cases. Approximately half of the three hour per week class time was online while the remainder was an in-class meeting. My motivation for sharing my experience stems from the insight that many accounting faculty hesitate to teach blended classes and that my school has an excellent technology network that encourages me to introduce blended learning in a graduate class. Blended learning allows students to perform the passive learning with online material and active learning via in-class case discussions.

Albrecht and Sack (2000) recommend that we move away from our reliance on lectures and concentrate on cases that incorporate uncertainty to accompany the analytical skills, and to include group work. The Pathways Commission (2012) report was critical of the current teaching methods. It found that students are too often exposed to the technical material in a vocation-focused way that is disembodied from the complex, business-world environment. Based on this report and the findings of prior academic studies, I believe that using online lectures combined with in-class case discussions will be the wave of future accounting education.

Keywords: online education; course effectiveness; education technologies.

INTRODUCTION

This paper is a personal account of how I teach a blended graduate accounting class, specifically Cost Management. The motivation for sharing my experience stems from an AACSB Online Delivery Class where the participants complained that accounting faculty in general had more resistance to online classes than faculty from other business disciplines. I was asked by several participants to explain why I enjoyed blended learning and my strategies for success for both the student and professor. My three hour once a week class includes a combination of approximately half of the time online while the remainder is an in-class meeting.

Studies have found that students view accounting not only as boring but also as causing anxiety for the student (Ameen, Guffey, and Jackson 2002; Borja 2003). This anxiety can be decreased by modifying the presentation of accounting learning materials, introducing new ways of teaching, and identifying different methods of learning (Buckhaults and Fisher 2011). Albrecht and Sack (2000) recommend that we move away from our reliance on lectures and concentrate on cases that incorporate uncertainty to accompany the analytical skills, and to include group work in order to teach leadership and teamwork. The Pathways Commission Report (2012) by accounting leaders focuses on improving the accounting profession and its teaching, and is especially critical of the current teaching methods. It found that students are too often exposed to the technical material in a vocation-focused way that is disembodied from the complex, real-world settings. Based on this report and the findings of prior academic studies, I believe that using online lectures combined with in-class case discussions will be the wave of future accounting education.

In the next section, I focus on the literature regarding online classes and in-class case format discussions. Then, details regarding the online lectures, quizzes, exams and in-class cases are presented. Additionally, a discussion regarding choosing and grading cases follows. Finally, I discuss and present student feedback followed by limitations of the paper.

ONLINE CLASS BENEFITS

The motivation to prepare online lectures, homework problems, and quizzes stems from my students' needs. Students require flexibility as to when to listen to a lecture, how often to listen to a lecture, and what parts of the lecture to return to after completing the quiz and homework. Prior literature on online classes is mixed on their effectiveness. Some studies have found no difference in performance for online versus in-class courses while other studies have found higher performance for online classes (Dowling, Godfrey, and Gyles 2003; Keller, Hassell, Webber, and Johnson 2009; Klein, Noe, and Wang 2006; Krawiec, Salter, and Kay 2005; Rivera and Rice 2002; Utts, Sommer, Acredolo, Maher, and Matthews 2003; and Tang and Byrne 2007). The effectiveness of online principles accounting classes versus advanced cost accounting classes depends on the level of the course (Chen, Jones, and Moreland 2013). Chen et al. suggest that blended learning may be desirable, and the mix of face-to-face versus online instruction is important. This is consistent with Fortin and Legault (2010) who find that the blended teaching approach is useful in developing competencies set for their accounting students.

Additional benefits of online classes are that they are positively related to student participation rates and comfort in class, and they may improve student retention. Dallimore, Hertenstein, and Platt (2010) find that preparation is positively related to frequency of participation due to students' comfort in class, which should lead to increased student mastery of course content. Online classes provide students with several opportunities to prepare for class. Additionally, student preparation and attendance are also influenced by regular quizzes (Braun and Sellers 2012). Finally, Sargent, Borthick and Lederberg (2011) find that students using short online videos had significantly lower course drop rates and better pass rates. Thus, prior research documents several benefits to online course content.

IN-CLASS BENEFITS

Traditional in-class time with faculty and students provides opportunities to strengthen a student's skill set, especially when a student is not a passive participant. Active learning techniques can enhance students' learning by transforming them from passive receptors of information into information processors (Hermanson 1994). Active learning is defined "as any instructional method that engages students in the learning process. In short, active learning requires students to do meaningful learning activities and think about what they are doing" (Prince 2001, 1). Case discussions allow for students to actively participate in the learning process. Cases provide another benefit, writing in accounting, which is a skill imperative to success in accounting (Riley and Simons 2013). These benefits of case studies in the classroom appear to be echoed by students. Frecka and Reckers (2010) find that students in Master of Accountancy programs felt that the top three skills that should be emphasized in MA programs are critical thinking, written communication and oral communication. In addition to active learning in class, a student benefits from writing assignments.

Prior research reinforces/supports the techniques I have adopted in a blended classroom. The blended classroom allows the students to learn the material online at their pace and on their schedule. Reinforcement of the material is available through homework problems and testing via online quizzes. Once the material has been learned the student can apply the managerial accounting concepts to a case. Discussion with group members allows for exposure to various options for proceeding with the case. Final decisions related to the case are presented in the case write-up. The in-class meeting focuses solely on the case discussion. All students participate in the case discussion, and students must be able to support their answers clearly.

CLASS FORMAT

Online Lectures

The format of the class is designed to provide the student with basic knowledge during the online sessions and the opportunity to apply that knowledge during the in-class meeting. The online class allows students to learn the basic cost management material.

This learning process not only utilizes the tool of repetition but also learning via different techniques; thus, reinforcement is cultivated by way of various tools. Attempts to anchor the new knowledge are made. And understanding is gained through various avenues.

All online material is taped personally, without use of the publisher's material. This allows me to customize the material in order to reflect the way I understand and explain the cost accounting subject matter. It also allows me to use a system of introducing a topic, use a problem to expand the understanding of the topic, and then allow the students to solve a problem on their own. For instance, if the topic was break-even analysis, then I would introduce the topic, complete a problem with the student, and then have the student complete a problem from a textbook. The introduction, application, and repetition allow the student to begin learning the material. The online course management system that I have access to allows me to view who has accessed the lecture and for how long. This information allows me to determine if there is any correlation between time spent online and the weekly quiz results. I use Adobe Presenter for taping the lectures and Captivate or Snagit for solving the homework problems.

Weekly Online Quizzes and Online Exams

Both quizzes and exams are completed online and together are worth 50 percent of the grade. Even though the focus of the class is on the cases, I find that students need an objective measure of their progress. I provide weekly quizzes for three main reasons. First, quizzes ensure that a student is keeping up with the weekly reading. Cramming at the last minute is detrimental to a student's learning, especially in a subject that builds on itself. Second, the quizzes provide students with an incentive to complete the reading before starting work on the case. Third, quizzes allow students to preview types of exam questions. This diminishes some uncertainty related to the exam and hopefully provides more time for learning the material. My fixed cost for preparing the online material is extremely high: approximately fifteen to twenty hours per chapter for the customized PowerPoint presentation, taped Adobe Presenter, homework problems on Captivate, and the various versions of quizzes and exams on the course management system.

In-class Case Discussions

As a faculty member, I spend most of my time, once a course is up and running, on preparing for the case discussions in class. My variable cost for each class preparation is approximately six to ten hours, decreasing to three to four hours when repeating the case in future semesters. I spend a significant amount of time in thinking about what questions to ask my students and how to start the class, which influences the path I will go down. I rarely agree with the path recommended by the case teaching notes but do find them helpful as a starting point for my thought process. The class time for the case discussion is about two hours for a four-hour, once-a-week graduate class. The blended class format allows me the flexibility to adjust the case time as needed.

All cases are due the night before class. This ensures that I have an opportunity to review the cases quickly and that students have time to reflect on the material before class discussion, without the stress of having just completed the case and then reenergizing themselves to discuss it.

Each student's experience provides a different insight. I have name tents for all of my students and call on ALL of them by name, even the foreign students with the difficult-to-pronounce names and the students that want to "hide" in class. It is extremely important not to dominate the class and show my students how much I know. In fact, I take the approach of a novice in the subject matter and get my students to explain to me how they went about solving the case and why they chose their specific approach. I find that this structure empowers the students and contributes to their active participation in class. Overall, my strategy in class is to ask lots of questions that will guide my students to think about the case in a certain way. The biggest compliment I receive from my students as they exit the class door for the evening is that they thought they understood the case completely but they learned so much more during the class discussion.

CASES

Choosing Cases

I choose cases that relate directly to the material learnt. This provides another incentive for the students to learn the material available in the online lecture. This also provides the students a valuable resource to reference as they attempt to answer the case questions. If no reference material or valuable tools are made available to the student, then the student may not even attempt the case questions, leading to frustration. I try to remember that the students have not been exposed to this material before, and the purpose is to have them not only learn the material but also apply it in a case context.

I choose cases that follow the general path of the textbook. I start with product costing, traditional costing vs. activity-based costing, cost volume profit analysis, budgeting, variance analysis, transfer pricing, and then additional cases such as joint cost or process costing. I review online syllabi for the class at various universities and see what my peers use. I also use search tools available on case websites such as Ives or Harvard Publishing to search for cases for a specific topic. I choose cases that are of reasonable length for my students' schedule and relate to the material in the textbook used and online lectures. Also, I choose cases that may be of interest to my students. For instance, being in a northern climate, I chose a snow removal department cost variance analysis. Additionally, with the increase of job employment in healthcare, I include a couple of healthcare industry cases.

The first case that I use is a relatively simple case that can be viewed as a large homework problem. This allows the students to coordinate their team schedules, learn how to work together, purchase and read the textbook, and complete the online material and other new activities at the beginning of the semester. The next few cases start to build on the material learnt online yet provide a challenge. The last couple of cases such as the variance analysis and transfer pricing require the students to pull from more than just the assigned readings. At this point in the semester, they have developed enough basic knowledge to think creatively. These two cases are challenging when the students are pushed to answer additional questions. At the end of the semester, students' workloads tend to crescendo. Thus, I choose a couple of interesting but basic questions that students can complete easily, like joint costing and process costing. The choice and order of cases are important motivational tools for my students.

Grading Cases

I evaluate a student's understanding of the cost management material via case grading and class participation points. Immediately after class, I schedule approximately two hours for case grading and participation points. Time varies depending on the size of the class; mine is about 25 students. Also, if I attempt to save the grading to the next day, the time required multiplies to four to six hours. I complete the grading electronically using a course management system. First, I grade class participation. I start with the highest grades for the students that contributed the most insight to the case. Then, I grade the students that contributed to the case. Finally, I grade those that had minor or insignificant contributions to the case understanding. I keep this scale very simple with a grade of 2, 1 or 0.

I then grade each case that has been turned in by a group of 2-4 students. At the beginning of the semester, I assign students to groups, although I allow them to make membership changes during the first week. I assign groups based on gender, major, nationality, and other factors. I grade the cases using either my writing tablet or the editing software available on my course management system. This allows all students in the group to see my comments at the same time. It also allows me to go back and evaluate the progress of a group during the semester. I find that this immediate grading is important for the students so they can devise an effective strategy for the next case.

Personally, I find that spending this time on grading is extremely challenging. I'm usually drained from teaching the case and want to have nothing to do with the case until the next day. However, experience has shown me that my memory of the students' participation, arguments, and comments on the case versus what they wrote on the write-up is best after class, and not the next day when I'm fresh.

Setting a Schedule

In the syllabus, I include the required information such as contact information, textbook and cases, grading, and school policies. I also include, for each class date, items to complete before, during, and after the class. This provides a clear path for the many activities the student is required to complete each week, including the textbook readings, online lectures, online homework problem solving, and class objective, as well as case due date and quiz closing date. Additionally, for each case, I include all of the case questions because I generally do not keep the exact questions semester to semester, other than the first time around. I have two main reasons for not keeping the suggested questions. One, I may find that the question was confusing to students and can be improved. Second, with so many online solutions available, I like to change up the question.

STUDENT FEEDBACK

End of Class Discussion

Student feedback is vital to the success of my class. I ask students about the case at the end of each class. Then, I ask them to complete a questionnaire. I'm interested in knowing if the case was of interest and why, the level of difficulty and challenge, the number of hours spent on a case, if questions should be changed/deleted/added for future classes, what was valuable in my questioning during class, and what was confusing. I ask if there is anything else I should consider before assigning this case again. I note all of my students' comments on a case student feedback sheet that I maintain. I also update the syllabus for the next semester, while the information is fresh in my mind. As part of a grant provided by my academic institution, I conducted surveys to understand how the blended (in-class and online classes) contributed to my students success. Results are provided in table 1.

Survey Results

Based on the survey results, students generally found the process/routine of the class to be very helpful. All subject matter material was learnt online. In-class discussions were reserved for application of the cost management tools learnt. Based on a Likert scale of 1 to 5, 5 being highly effective, the students generally felt that the online material was effective. The students also felt that the online lecture helped them to prepare for the case. And, what was vital to me was that students felt that their knowledge of the material improved after the class discussion. In my mind, this validates the purpose of a flipped/blended class. Teaching of the material is reserved for online, while application of the material is reserved for the classroom.

LIMITATIONS

There are several limitations for others attempting to replicate the blended class in a graduate Cost Management class. My outcome may be impacted by class size, diversity of students, a strong and supportive IT department, an easy-to-use course management system, and an academic institution that is providing resources to faculty to implement technology in the classroom. First, class size may impact the outcome. My class size is generally between 20-25 students. I am unsure if a smaller or larger class will contribute to the same results. Second, diversity of the students may impact outcomes. Specifically, at least 50 percent of my students are international students and another 30 percent work full-time. My international students tend to prefer the online lectures due to language barriers; subject matter can be repeated several times when needed. However, my working students appreciate the flexibility of passive learning online while the active learning is reserved for the classroom. This design optimizes their available time. Third, technology access such as an easy-to-use online course management system, a strong faculty-oriented IT department, and reliable access to the online systems at the school may impact the outcome. This class was taught at a school that has extremely strong IT service, software and hardware. I never felt that I lacked any IT resource. When I attended an AACSB Online Class, in discussions with classmates, I noticed the IT shortcomings at several schools. None came close to what my school offered. There may be other limitations that impact the outcome.

I have found the blended class to be extremely satisfying since the focus on passive information is reserved for online classes while active learning occurs during in-class classes. The tremendous investment of time, both fixed and variable, is worthwhile as a faculty member.

REFERENCES

Albrecht, W., and R. Sack. 2000. *Accounting Education: Charting the Course Through a Perilous Future.* Sarasota, FL: The American Accounting Association.

Ameen, E., D. Guffey, and C. Jackson. 2002. Evidence of teaching anxiety among accounting educators. *Journal of Education for Business* 78 (1): 16-22.

Borja P.M. 2003. So you've been asked to teach principles of accounting. *Business Education Forum* 58 (2): 30–32.

Braun, K. W., and R. D. Sellers. 2012. Using a "daily motivational quiz" to increase student preparation, attendance, and participation. *Issues in Accounting Education* 27 (1): 267–279.

Buckhaults, J., and D. Fisher. 2011. Trends in accounting education: Decreasing accounting anxiety and promoting new methods. *Journal of Education for Business* 86 (1): 31-35.

Chen, C., K. Jones, and K. Moreland. 2013. Online accounting education versus in-class delivery: Does course level matter? *Issues in Accounting Education* 28 (1): 1-16.

Dallimore, E., J. Hertenstein, and M.Platt. 2010. Class participation in accounting courses: Factors that affect student comfort and learning. *Issues in Accounting Education* 25 (4): 613–629.

Dowling, C., J. Godfrey, and N. Gyles. 2003. Do hybrid flexible delivery teaching methods improve accounting students' learning outcomes? *Accounting Education* 4 (December): 373–391.

Fortin, A., and M. Legault. 2010. Development of generic competencies: Impact of a mixed teaching approach on students' perceptions. *Accounting Education: An International Journal* 19 (1–2): 93–122.

Frecka, T., and P.Reckers. 2010. Rekindling the debate: What's right and what's wrong with masters of accountancy programs: The staff auditor's perspective. *Issues in Accounting Education* 25 (2): 215–226.

Hermanson, D. 1994. The effect of self-generated elaboration on students' recall of tax and accounting material: Future evidence. *Issues in Accounting Education* 9 (2): 301–318.

Keller, J., J. Hassel, S. Webber, and J. Johnson. 2009 *Journal of Accounting Education* 27 (3): 147-154.

Klein, H., R Noe, & C. Wang, C. 2006. Motivation to learn and course outcomes: The impact of delivery mode, learning goal orientation, perceived barriers and enablers. *Personnel Psychology* 3 (Autumn): 665–702.

Krawiec, S., D. Salter, and E. Kay. 2005. A "hybrid" bacteriology course: The professor's design and expectations; the students' performance and assessment. *Microbiology Education* 6 (May): 8–13.

The Pathways Commission: Charting a National Strategy for the Next Generation of Accountants. 2012. Sponsored by AAA and AICPA

Prince, M. 2004. Does active learning work? A review of the research. *Journal of Engineering Education* 93 (3): 223–231.

Simons, K., T. Riley, and J. Tracey. 2013. Writing in the accounting curriculum: A review of the literature with conclusions for implementation and future research. *Issues in Accounting Education* 28 (4): 823-871.

Rivera, J., and M. Rice. 2002. A comparison of student outcomes and satisfaction between traditional and web based course offerings. *Online Journal of Distance Learning Administration* 5 (3). Available at: http://www.westga.edu/~distance/ojdla/fall53/rivera53.html (Last accessed May 10, 2015).

Sargent, C., A. Borthick, and A. Lederberg. 2011. Improving retention for principles of accounting students: Ultra-short online tutorials for motivating effort and improving performance. *Issues in Accounting Education* 26 (4): 657–679.

Tang, M., and R. Byrne. 2007. Regular versus online versus blended: A qualitative description of the advantages of the electronic modes and a quantitative evaluation. *International Journal on E-Learning* 6 (2): 257–266.

Utts, J., B. Sommer, C. Acredolo, M. Maher, and H. Matthews. 2003. A study comparing traditional and hybrid internetbased instruction in introductory statistics classes. *Journal of Statistics Education* 11(3). Available at: http://www.amstat.org/publications/jse/v11n3/utts.html (Last accessed May 10, 2015).

Web Appendix

A web appendix for this paper is available at:

http://www.businessresearchconsortium.org/pro/brcpro2015p5.pdf

Latent Employee Turnover and Prevention—When Job Creation Catches Up with Economic Recovery: An Employee Retention Model and Case Study

Barry A. Friedman* and Lisa M. Schnorr

Barry A. Friedman*
Professor, Organizational Behavior and Human Resource Management
State University of New York at Oswego
barry.friedman@oswego.edu

Lisa M. Schnorr
Senior Vice President, Finance and Controller
Constellation Brands, Inc.
Lisa.Schnorr@cbrands.com

*Corresponding author

Abstract

Most employees perform well, are solid organizational citizens, and possess valued intellectual capital. However, this critical mass of employees is at risk due to their experiences over the past two decades (e.g., reductions in force and developmental funding) and its associated reduction in organizational loyalty and commitment. Job creation lags behind economic recoveries. As the economy generates more jobs, more employees leave their organizations for better employment opportunities. We introduce the concept of *latent employee turnover*- the potential exodus of valued employees in the near future, and ways leaders can retain valued employees. An employee retention model is offered followed by an organizational case study, Constellation Brands, Inc., to illustrate effective employee retention practices.

Keywords: latent employee turnover, unemployment

INTRODUCTION

Most employees perform well, are solid organizational citizens, possess valued intellectual capital, and contribute to organizational effectiveness. This critical mass of employees is at risk due to their collective experience over the past two decades and negative lessons learned about their diminished value. These experiences include countless reductions in force, slashed training and development expenditures, reduced promotional opportunities brought about by flattened organizational structures, pay stagnation, and pay inequities (e.g., executives rewarded total compensation packages worth hundreds of times the value of average employees). Such experiences may reduce organizational loyalty and commitment. In the recent past, the employment psychological contract favored employers when unemployment was high, job openings were scarce, and employees believed that alternative external employment opportunities were few. The ultimate employee reaction to this psychological contract is to leave their organization and seek employment elsewhere; however, quitting is problematic if few external employment opportunities exist. Tekleab, Orvis and Taylor (2013) showed that adverse changes in employees' perceived psychological contracts had negative effects, including increased turnover intentions, reduced job satisfaction and organizational loyalty. However, the psychological contract leverage may shift towards employees as more jobs are created following economic recoveries. The loss of intellectual capital is a significant cost to organizations (Kraemer & Gouthier, 2014; Alexandrov, Babakus, & Yavas, 2007). This cost is increased when competitors hire employees that quit (Moreno, Torres & Vargas, 2015).

Job creation lags behind economic recovery as reflected in such indicators as major stock indices (e.g., DJA, S&P 500) and macroeconomic indicators (e.g., GDP). As recently as late 2013, the DJA reached record levels, but the unemployment rate stagnated and the number of new jobs generated failed to meet expectations. By 2015, new job creation increased over 200,000 monthly for 12 straight months and the unemployment rate fell to 5.5% in February, the lowest since May, 2008 (BLS, 2015; Maurer, 2015b). While the low unemployment rate is questionable (e.g., the rate doesn't comprehend underemployment or the unemployed that give up their job search), there exists a general consensus that unemployment is declining (Jackson, 2015). Jackson (2015) argues that there exist three signs of economic recovery: declining unemployment, strong job creation, and quit rates. When these three stars align, what will be the consequences of low organizational commitment and loyalty brought about by the negative organizational practices listed above?

As new jobs are created, it's likely that employees will perceive that external job opportunities exist. This perception may then result in active job searches. In their seminal work, March and Simon (1958) argued that employees seek and take alternative employment if they perceive that better jobs are available. A general myth is that employees don't test the job market in poor economies with fewer available jobs. This is only partly correct. The job market will always be better for top talent who are more marketable, more confident, have more employment alternatives than average employees, and are therefore more likely than their average counterparts to leave in any economy. This is true whether the economy is growing or contracting: there is typically a favorable market for excellent performers. The concept presented below, latent employee turnover, pertains to *all* employees that possess intellectual capital. That is, latent employee turnover pertains to all employees and not just top talent.

Latent Turnover

We introduce the concept of *latent employee turnover*- the potential exodus of valued employees in the near future, and ways leaders can retain valued employees. Employee adverse organizational practices such as layoffs may have resulted in employee beliefs that they are not valued, that the employment-at-will doctrine makes them expendable commodities, and that their psychological contracts have changed to their disadvantage. Employees may believe that they therefore must protect themselves and self-interest becomes paramount. These organizational practices may have eroded employee organizational commitment, decreased loyalty, and increased *latent employee turnover*. As early as 2012, the majority of employees was dissatisfied with their organizations and was already preparing to quit (Kelly, 2012).

We are still recovering from the toxic mortgage crisis that significantly damaged the economy. Undaunted by this lesson, economists warn that toxic auto and student loans present similar dangers. It seems that easy credit has migrated from home to auto and student loans. However, the emphasis on toxic loans has taken management's eye off another looming crisis that threatens organizations' ability to compete: latent turnover that is hidden and threatens organizational competitiveness. Like the iceberg that sunk the Titanic, latent employee turnover threatens organizations by lurking below the water line- hidden but dangerous.

Employee Turnover, Unemployment and GDP

Several models exist that emphasize the psychological antecedents of employee turnover (Price, 1977; Mobley, 1977; Mobley, Griffeth, Hand & Meglino, 1979). Recent research have explored the relationships among economic activity and turnover. Moreno, Torres and Vargas (2015) found that job turnover was positively correlated with Gross Domestic Product (GDP) and inversely correlated with unemployment. That is, increases in the economy are related to lower unemployment and more employees leaving their positions for better opportunities. Moreno, Torres and Vargas (2015, page 11) state that:

> "when the economy has a positive growth path, the turnover rate is higher at the prospect of finding work in companies that rehire or new establishments that initiate operations; in contrast, when the economy has a downturn, labor turnover rates decrease, given the shortage of vacancies in the market or the processes of layoffs"

Lazear and Spletzer (2012) distinguish between voluntary turnover (when employees quit) and churning, which occurs as employees move to other positions where they can add greater value and are replaced (i.e., no net new job growth). Drawing from the Job Openings and Labor Turnover Survey (JOLTS) microdata, Lazear and Spletzer (2012) state that

> "Churn declines during recessions because separations, which during good times would have been associated with a replacement hire, are allowed to go unfilled during recessions. As a result, employment declines. Churn also declines during recessions because workers become reluctant to quit their jobs, and in response businesses reduce their hiring. Hiring declines during recessions. During the 2007–09 recession, four-fifths of hiring reductions were associated with reduced churn, not with reductions in job creation" (page 575).

The cost of churn is high in that employee movement to more productive uses of their intellectual capital slows during recessions and high unemployment. Conversely, churning increases during economic recoveries and GDP growth as employees leave their positions for better opportunities.

Leamer (2008) argued that economic downturns lead to loss of jobs, higher unemployment in the short term, and adversely impact the long term supply of certain occupations. With respect to nursing jobs in the healthcare industry, Alameddine, Baumann, Laporte and Deber (2012) propose that economic downturns decrease demand, increase supply, freeze or decrease salaries, and decrease turnover.

Conversely, economic recoveries may be associated with job creation and reduction in layoffs (Maurer, 2015a). While most research suggests that increases in job creation following economic recoveries, a minority of researchers argues that new job creation is volatile (Abo-Zaid, 2014). Moscarini and Postel-Vinay (2009) report that many employees terminated by large organizations during recessions are subsequently hired by small organizations during economic recoveries. Camacho, Quiros and Mendizabal (2011) argue that intense job creation followed economic recoveries during the eighties, but slower job creation followed recoveries since that time. Summers (2010) also finds that job creation will follow recovery, albeit slowly. There appears a general consensus that job creation follows economic recoveries, only slower than in previous recoveries.

EMPLOYEE RETENTION MODEL

Retention of valued employees in the face of latent employee turnover requires strategic leadership and strategic human resource management. While latent turnover threatens to decrease organizational competitiveness, leaders can take steps to reduce the threat. Figure 1 contains a model of employee retention (i.e., latent turnover prevention). Human resource systems such as staffing and employee development exist within a macro-organizational context. The model's outer ring contains four contextual elements: organizational culture and values, total rewards, mentoring, and retention tracking. Organizational culture has been shown to be related to employee intention to leave and retention (Vafeas, 2015; Fleig-Palmer and Rathert, 2015; Timms et al., 2015; Ahmed, Pavani, and Kumar, 2014; Inabinett and Ballaro, 2014; Santora, 2009). Total rewards, including financial and non-financial rewards, are also associated with employee retention (Giannetti and Metzger, 2015; Korsakiene, Stankeviciene, Simelyte & Talackiene, 2015; Treuren, and Frankish, 2014; Milman and Dickson, 2014; Singh and Natasha, 2010). Mentoring refers to the process by which experienced employees assist less experienced employees. Mentoring with respect to job performance, career planning and mobility is associated with employee retention (Flynn, Mathis, Jackson and Valentine, 2016; Wang, Hu, Hurst, and Yang, 2014; Reinstein, Sinason, and Fogarty, 2012). While not a contextual element, retention tracking, as part of a larger Human Resource Management System (HRIS), is a sound management practice that can identify turnover risks and help plan organizational responses.

Within the contextual variables described above, Figure 1 contains human resource management practices that occur during employees' life cycle. That is, employees' organizational lives begin with recruitment and selection, experience various onboarding activities (e.g., new employee orientation), complete training and development processes, progress through their careers, and finally leave the organization.

Effective human resource initiatives that are aligned with organizational objectives and effectively implemented have been linked to positive employee job commitment, low turnover intent, and organizational effectiveness (Kim, Wehbi, DelliFraine & Brannon, 2014; Wheeler, Halbesleben, & Harris, 2012; Friedman, 2009; Friedman, 2007; Becker, Huselid, & Ulrich, 2001; Urlich, 1997). Figure 2 contains specific effective human resource management suggestions intended to decrease latent employee turnover at each stage of the employee life cycle.

RECRUITMENT

Recruitment refers to establishing a pool of qualified and diverse job applicants. Best practices for recruitment include identifying effective recruitment sources, establishing networks within these sources, and establishing effective recruiting messages and methods (e.g., job fairs,

Internet, social media). In order to reduce short term turnover, Wanous (1992, 1980) introduced realistic job previews to the recruiting process. Realistic job previews provide applicants with information needed to make an informed job acceptance decision (Earnest, Allen, & Landis, 2011). Baur, Buckley, Bagdasarov and Dharmasiri (2014) maintain that realistic job previews add value to worker socialization programs.

The use of e-recruiting has recently increased (e.g., Facebook and LinkedIn). After reviewing the use of e-recruiting, Melanthiou, Pavlou, and Constantinou (2015, page 31) concluded that a "well-designed system and strategic utilization of available information about potential candidates may significantly assist the recruitment of employees with the most suitable skills and competencies."

SELECTION

Selection refers to the process of selecting individuals from the applicant pool. Following a period of time where organizations were concerned about bias and discrimination, tests are commonly used in the selection process (Halzack, 2014). The literature is replete with effective selection techniques, including job information inventories, interviews (Maurer & Solamon, 2006; Huffcutt & Woehr, 1999; Schmidt & Rader, 1999), written tests (e.g., cognitive, aptitude, personality), and simulations (e.g., assessment centers). Of special note is the use of effective job analysis, job relatedness of employment tests, and empirical test validation (i.e., test validity and reliability) of all techniques used by decision makers to make an employment decision.

ONBOARDING

Onboarding is the process of socializing new employees to organizational expectations and culture. Onboarding represents an opportunity for the organization and the new employee to make positive first impressions.

Graybill, Hudson Carpenter, Offord, Piorun, and Shaffer (2013) reported that typical onboarding activities include company overviews (e.g., mission, vision and objectives), introduction to key personnel, and initial training. Cable, Gino, and Staats (2013) argue that organizations should encourage new employees to express their unique job perspectives and strengths early in the onboarding process. Smith et al. (2013) found that positive feedback from peers and supervisors early in the onboarding process was related to positive new employee coping strategies and reduced turnover intentions.

TRAINING AND DEVELOPMENT

Training and development refer to short term job specific skill building and long term career competency building, respectively. Best practices in this domain include effective needs assessment, selection and delivery of effective and efficient methods, and evaluation of training results. Alignment of training and organizational objectives is very important, as well as reinforcement of learning outcomes in the workplace that promote transfer of learning, especially with respect to training conducted off the job. Peter and Eunice (2014) demonstrated that effective training and development practices are associated with such positive outcomes as increased organizational commitment. Yean and Yahya (2013) reported a positive relationship between training and development practices and career satisfaction.

CAREER MANAGEMENT

Career management refers to the programs and activities that facilitate the progression of employees through careers. Such programs and activities include career pathing, mentoring, developmental action plans, and succession plans. The long term nature of career planning sends a message to employees that organizations value them, invest in their long term employee development, and promote from within. The deployment of a human resource management system as a tool in the planning process is also important to identify internal candidates for internal promotion. Baek-Kyoo and Ready (2012) found that employee goal orientation, perceived organizational learning culture, and favorable supervisory relationships were associated with career satisfaction.

EXIT PLANNING

The final stage of the employee life cycle occurs as employees leave the organization. Organizations often ignore the process by which valued employees leave. Exit planning include conducting and analyzing exit interviews and retirement planning. Causes of turnover and actions to increase retention can be gleamed during exit interviews of employees that voluntarily leave (Neal, 1989). Retirement plans may include goal setting, financial advice concerning relocation, savings, employee benefits, investment, and budgeting. The psychological challenges associated with retirement may also be addressed, such as establishing new networks, social support, and time use. Employees may believe that such activities and assistance may be indicative of a long term organizational concern for their valued employees, and hence may increase organizational commitment and reduce latent employee turnover. A case study of one organization's concerted efforts to retain its valued employees is offered below.

CASE STUDY –CONSTELLATION BRANDS, INC.

Constellation Brands (NYSE: STZ and STZ.B) is a leading international producer and marketer of beer, wine and spirits with operations in the U.S., Canada, Mexico, New Zealand and Italy. In 2015, Constellation was one of the top performing stocks in the S&P 500 Consumer Staples Index. Constellation is the number three beer company in the U.S. with high-end, iconic imported brands including Corona Extra, Corona Light, Modelo Especial, Negra Modelo and Pacifico. Constellation is also the world's leader in premium wine selling great brands that people love including Robert Mondavi, Clos du Bois, Kim Crawford, Meiomi, Mark West, Franciscan Estate, Ruffino and Jackson-Triggs. The company's premium spirits brands include SVEDKA Vodka and Black Velvet Canadian Whisky (Constellation Brands, 2016).

Constellation Brands' voluntary employee turnover is well below the average for Consumer Packaged Goods (CPG) industrial sector. According to recent survey data, the average annual voluntary turnover within the U.S. consumer products sector was 8% for 2011-2014 (Elkjaer & Filmer, 2015), while the Constellation Brands' average U.S. turnover was just under 6% for the same time period. What accounts for Constellation Brands' employee retention effectiveness?

CONTEXTUAL FACTORS

Using the Employee Retention model presented earlier (Figures 1 & 2), several contextual factors drive employee retention (the model's outer ring). Constellation's market performance is a significant factor in attracting and retaining employees. STZ has outperformed the S&P 500 in 12 of the last 15 years. Constellation Brands operates within the dynamic, fast-paced beverage and alcohol industry (beer, wine and spirits). The U.S. beverage alcohol industry is growing at more than twice the rate of other CPG companies. During the 52 weeks ended Jan 4, 2015, the U.S. beverage alcohol sector dollar value grew 3-4%, while the overall CPG sector dollar value grew approximately 1.4% (Information Resources, Inc., 2015).

Constellation Brands' organizational culture and ownership structure also contribute to employees' desire to remain with the company. The company has a high percentage of family ownership and family manage-ment involvement. Constellation was founded 70 years ago by Marvin Sands and throughout its 70-year history, there have been only three Chief Executive Officers, all of whom are Sands family members. Marvin Sands served as President and CEO until 1994; his son, Richard Sands served as President and CEO from 1994 until 2007 and in 2007, Richard's brother, Robert Sands, was appointed President and CEO and continues to serve in that role today. Despite growth and leadership succession, Constellation Brands' works to remain a small company culture and feel despite its growth to more than 8,000 employees worldwide.

Corporate social responsibility, employee engagement and employee retention are closely related (Slack, Corlett & Morris, 2015; Kusuma & Sukanya, 2013; Turker, 2009; Berger, Cunningham, & Drumwright, 2006). Constellation Brands and the Sands family have a long and generous philanthropic history and encourage company employees to give back to the communities in which they live and work. Employees are proud to work for such a giving company. Corporate social responsibility is highly valued as evidenced by the Constellation Brands' active support of the community, including significant contributions to The V Foundation for Cancer Research, F.F. Thompson Hospital and Rochester General Hospital in New York, the Heart and Stroke Foundation of Canada and the Ride to Conquer Cancer in Canada, the American Diabetes Association's Tour de Cure, Constellation Marvin Sands Performing Arts Center (CMAC), the New York Wine & Culinary Center, Haiti earthquake relief efforts, Habitat for Humanity, United Way, and many others institutions and causes.

Another important contextual factor driving employee retention is Constellation Brands' Total Rewards program is designed to attract, motivate and retain employees. The company base salaries are competitive and generally targeted at the market median; high performing employees and those considered to be "experts in their fields" have the opportunity to earn salaries toward the high end of the salary range and well above market median.

The company also offers competitive short-term cash incentives with the ability to earn higher payouts for higher levels of company and individual performance and an equity compensation program goes deep in the company. During times of high growth and/or strong performance, the equity compensation program has been a significant differentiator in the marketplace, as it has resulted in significant wealth creation for many employees. Most equity awards vest over a four-year period, and has significantly contributed to long-term employee retention. There exists a significant disincentive to leave before awards become fully vested.

Other marketplace differentiators include an attractive Employee Stock Purchase Plan (ESPP) that offers the maximum allowable discount (15%), and an annual allowance to purchase company products for purposes of promoting the company's brands with friends and family.

Performance-based equity awards are often used as a means of rewarding key employees for completion of large, strategic projects. The value of such awards can be significant, often as high as 0.5x – 1x base salary, as these need to be meaningful enough to keep employees focused on the project objectives and timeline. The company also provides a web-based employee recognition program that allows employees to publicly recognize another employee for going above and beyond to solve a business problem or assist other employees and customers.

Lastly, the company offers competitive employee benefits that some researchers claim contribute to attracting and retaining valued employees (Mrkvicka, 2015). Constellation Brands offers employees a wide range of employee benefits, including medical, dental, vision, and 401k retirement options. While not a significant driver of employee motivation, the lack of competitive employee benefits may contribute to attrition.

The contextual factors of family ownership and stability, strong phil-anthropic orientation, sense of corporate social responsibility, small company feel, a comprehensive Total Rewards program, and strong financial performance are intended to retain employees. The company has also proactively invested in numerous programs intended to increase employee retention and improve engagement. For example, recognizing the link between employee engagement and retention (Swarnalatha & Prasanna, 2013), Constellation Brands conducts periodic employee surveys to assess employee engagement and to identify action plans to improve employee engagement and retention. Using the Employee Retention Model, several other Constellation Brands programs are described below (Figure 3).

Recruit

The contextual factors described above combined with Constellation Brands' public profile has made the company an employer of choice with access to a growing candidate pool over the past several years. Constellation Brands can therefore be very selective when hiring candidates for open positions. This growing candidate pool can be evidenced in the growth of the company's summer internship program over the past four years. In 2012, there were 33 applicants for 17 summer internships. In 2013, the applicant pool grew to 137 and by 2015, 1,359 applicants competed for 40 internship positions.

To support its performance management programs and help ensure the right candidates are selected for open positions, the company recently developed a competency-based model that is used throughout the various stages in the employee lifecycle (recruiting, selection, performance management, career planning, etc.). Recruiters identify candidates with the right competencies to narrow down the field of candidates and interview those exhibiting the required competencies for the role. Competencies include communication, working with others and taking initiative as well as technical competencies required to be successful in a given role.

Select

To foster retention, employees are selected and later evaluated on their ability to recognize development needs, provide challenging work assignments and develop others for more responsibility. Candidates are screened and those with the required competencies are identified using resume reviews, telephone screenings, online evaluations, and interviews.

The competency-based model helps improve the probability for a high quality hire that will remain with the company.

ONBOARD

Constellation's new hire on-boarding class is an instructor-led comprehensive introduction to the company's industry and business, functional departments, product education and Brand Ambassadorship. During Salute, employees learn about Constellation's rich culture and history as well as the company's vision, mission, strategic imperatives and core values. The program is designed to assist employees in their assimilation into Constellation and to provide information about the company's products to give employees a comfort level with being a Constellation Brand Ambassador.

DEVELOP

Valued employees desire development opportunities, growth, increased responsibilities and promotional opportunities. Constellation Brands established an infrastructure that allows for developmental growth and career progression. A comprehensive employee, management and leadership curriculum supports employee growth needs. Classroom or online training programs are available to employees to build specific skills in many areas, including self-development, management development, leadership development, team development, and competency development. These programs target individual contributors as they develop functional competencies and other skills development; managers as they coach and manage others' performance, and leaders as they develop skills to motivate and direct large groups of employees. The company also offers support for continuing professional education programs (e.g., CPAs, attorneys, etc.), system skills training and industry-specific certifications (e.g., the Wine & Spirits Education Trust provides employees the opportunity to grow their knowledge of the wine & spirits industry).

About every two years, Constellation Brands nominates approximately 30 of its high potential company leaders to participate in a formal Executive Development Program (EDP). EDP consists of a week-long classroom program conducted at Harvard University followed by participation in Action Learning Projects whereby groups of 5-6 employees work on some of the company's greatest strategic initiatives. The teams develop recommendations which are then presented to the senior leadership team for consideration. To date, more than half of the recommendations have been adopted by the company, and have resulted in new product ideas, technology solutions, or other investment ideas to grow the company. Not counting employee departures due to divestitures or reorganizations, 114 employees have participated in the EDP since 2007, and only 3 have voluntarily left the organizations. In addition to working on and addressing real business issues, participants benefit from building valuable working relationships with employees throughout the organization.

Developmental opportunities and tools exist outside the classroom. For example, informal mentor programs match employees with mentors that provide coaching, in such areas as leadership and career development.

Career Management

The company recently introduced a new Talent Management process and will complete its first cycle during Spring 2016. The purpose of this process is to assess "Bench" readiness (replacements for key positions); to identify talent gaps in the organization; and to plan for development opportunities (internal) and investments (new hires). The process involves first identifying the most critical roles in the organization and then identifying the company's key talent/high potential employees. The next step is to ensure that the most critical roles are staffed with key talent. Where this is not the case, job rotations can be planned to move key talent into critical roles. Where there is not a clear match within the organization, the company can either develop the talent internally by moving a high potential employee into a critical role "stretch" assignment to develop their skills; or recruit the necessary talent into the organization. The results of the talent review process can be used for deliberate, planned job rotations or when an employee vacates a critical role unexpectedly- the company can refer to its key talent roster to identify a suitable successor.

EXIT PLAN

The company routinely conducts exit interviews for employees that leave voluntarily. These exit interviews have provided valuable information that reinforces several of the initiatives described above.

DISCUSSION AND CONCLUSION

Economists point out that the current economic recovery is not unique in that job creation typically lags economic indicators. Employers often delay filling job vacancies because of market uncertainty and an emphasis on increased productivity in lieu of adding staff. Of course, people need income to buy products and use services which in turn drive demand and the economy. Jobs are critical for long term sustainable economic growth, Job growth will eventually increase, albeit at a slow pace. When employees perceive employment opportunities outside their organization, will latent turnover manifest itself, or will valued employees be retained? The most obvious employer consideration is to place greater emphasis on the long term impact on employees of all employment actions.

Future research should explore the implications of psychological contract as employees gain more leverage and latent turnover becomes actual turnover. An important variable is employee intention to leave their organizations. Turnover intent is the process of thinking, planning, and desiring to leave a job (Wheeler, Harris, & Harvey, 2010; Steel & Ovalle, 1984; Mobley, Griffeth, Hand, & Meglino, 1979). Research suggests that intent to leave is a predictor of turnover (Udechukwu & Mujtaba,

2007) and should be studied as they relate to the turnover model presented here (Lambert, 2012).

The model depicted here lists specific programs organizations can employ to retain their most valued employees, such as those implemented by Constellation Brands. The model also suggests avenues for future research. For example, wages have not increased in proportion to the economic recovery (Jackson, 2015; Coombs, 2015). Contributing further to a climate of income inequality, executive compensation has increased disproportionally more than the average workforce (typically averaging 3% over the last few years). Pay has recently become the most important factor contributing to employee dissatisfaction (SHRM, 2013a, SHRM, 2013b). The impact of pay, size of pay increases, perceived inequity, and income inequality on turnover intentions when external opportunities are believed to exist is but one avenue of study. Similar avenues for future research include the impact of latent employee turnover for staffing, career pathing, leadership, motivation and other human resource practices.

Figure 1. Employee Retention Model

Figure 2. Effective Human Resource Practices that Promote Employee Retention

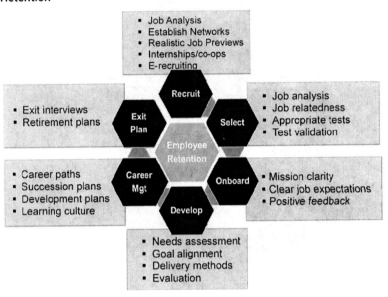

Figure 3. Case Study: Constellation Brands, Inc. Employee Retention Resource Practices

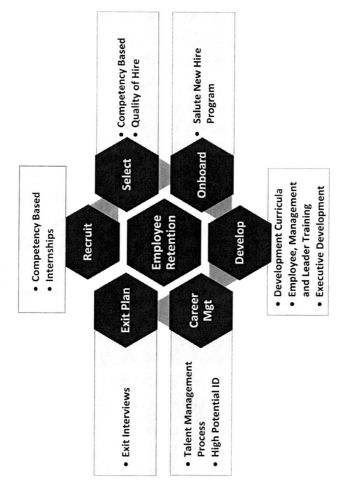

REFERENCES

Abo-Zaid, S. (2014). Net job creation in the US economy: Lessons from monthly data, 1950-2011. *Applied Economics,* 46(22), 2623-2638.

Ahmed, S. F., Pavani, K. L., & Kumar, S. C. (2014). A study on employee commitment in private banking sector. *International Journal of Organizational Behavior & Management Perspectives,* 3(4), 1227-1233.

Alameddine, M., Baumann, A., Laporte, A., & Deber, R. (2012). A narrative review on the effect of economic downturns on the nursing labor market: Implications for policy and planning. *Human Resources for Health,* 10, 23-30. doi:http://dx.doi.org/10.1186/1478-4491-10-23.

Alexandrov, A., Babakus, E. & Yavas, U. (2007), "The effects of perceived management concern for frontline employees and customers on turnover intentions". *Journal of Service Research,* 9(4), 356-371.

Baek-Kyoo, J., & Ready, K. J. (2012). Career satisfaction. *Career Development International,* 17(3), 276-295. doi:http://dx.doi.org/10.1108/13620431211241090.

Baur, J. E., Buckley, M. R., Bagdasarov, Z., & Dharmasiri, A. S. (2014). A historical approach to realistic job previews. *Journal of Management History,* 20(2), 200-223. doi:http://dx.doi.org/10.1108/JMH-06-2012-0046.

Becker, B.E., Huselid, M.A., & Ulrich, D. *The HR Scorecard: Linking People, Strategy and Performance.* Boston, Ma: Harvard Business School Press, 2001.

Berger, I. E., Cunningham, P. M., & Drumwright, M. E. (2006). Identity identification and relationship through social alliances. Journal of the Academy of Marketing Sciences, 34(2), 128–137.

Bureau of Labor Statistics (2015). January jobless rates down in 24 states, up in 8; payroll jobs up in 39 states, down in 10. Retrieved March 17, 2005 from http://www.bls.gov/.

Cable, D. M., Gino, F., & Staats, B. R. (2013). Reinventing employee onboarding. *MIT Sloan Management Review,* 54(3), 23-28.

Camacho, M., Quiros, G. P., & Mendizabal, H. R. (2011). High-growth recoveries, inventories and the great moderation. *Journal of Economic Dynamics & Control*, 35(8), 1322-1339.

Constellation Brands (2016). About Constellation Brands, Inc. Retrieved January 6, 2016 from http://www.cbrands.com/investors.

Coombs, J. (2015). Wages Stagnate Despite Thriving Job Market. *SHRM HR Week*, Retrieved March 10, 2015 from https://www.shrm.org/hrdisciplines/staffingmanagement/articles/pages/wages-stagnate-thriving-job-market.aspx.

Earnest, D. R., Allen, D. G., & Landis, R. S. (2011). Mechanisms linking realistic job previews with turnover: a meta-analytic path analysis. *Personnel Psychology*, 64(4), 865-897.

Fleig-Palmer, M., & Rathert, C. (2015). Interpersonal mentoring and its influence on retention of valued health care workers: The moderating role of affective commitment. *Health Care Management Review*, 40(1), 56-64.

Flynn, W.J., Mathis, R.L., Jackson, J.H. & Valentine, S.R. (2016). *Healthcare Human Resource Management.* Cengage Learning, Boston, Mass.

Friedman, B.A. (2009). Human Resource Management Role Implications for Corporate Reputation. *Corporate Reputation Review.* 12(3), 229-244.

Friedman, B.A. (2007). Globalization Implications for Human Resource Roles. *Employee Responsibilities and Rights Journal*, 19, 157-171.

Giannetti, M., & Metzger, D. (2015). Compensation and competition for talent: Evidence from the financial industry. *Finance Research Letters*, 12, 11-16.

Graybill, J. O., Hudson Carpenter, M. T., Offord, J., Piorun, M., & Shaffer, G. (2013). Employee onboarding: Identification of best practices in ACRL libraries. *Library Management*, 34(3), 200-218. doi:http://dx.doi.org/10.1108/01435121311310897.

Halzack, S. (2014, May 09). Online tests are the latest gateway to landing a new job (posted 2014-05-09 02:05:17). *The Washington Post.* Retrieved

on March 10, 2015 from http://ezproxy.oswego.edu:2048/login?url=
http://search.proquest.com/docview/1522647137?accountid=13025.

Huffcutt, A. I., & Woehr, D. J. (1999). Further analysis of employment interview validity: A quantitative evaluation of interviewer-re-
lated structuring methods. *Journal of Organizational Behavior, 20*(4),
549-560.

Inabinett, J.M. & Ballaro, J. M. (2014). Developing an organization by
predicting employee retention by matching corporate culture with
employee's values: A correlation study. *Organization Development
Journal, 32*(1), 55-74.

Information Resources Incorporated (2015). Confidential CPG sector
analysis. Retrieved on Jan 5, 2016 from https://www.iriworldwide.
com/en-US/solutions/market-performance-and-strategy/market-
measurement.

Kelly (2012). Acquisition and retention in the war for talent.
Kelly Global Workforce Report. Retrieved on March 5, 2015
from http://www.kellyocg.com/uploadedFiles/Content/ Knowledge/
Kelly_Global_Workforce_Index_Content/Acquisition%20and
%20Retention%20in%20the%20War%20for%20Talent%20Report.pdf.

Kim, J., Wehbi, N., DelliFraine, J.L. & Brannon, D. (2014). The joint relationship between organizational design factors and HR practice
factors on direct care workers' job satisfaction and turnover intent. *Health Care Management Review,* 39(2), 174-184. DOI: 10.1097/
HMR.0b013e31828c8b8f.

Korsakiene, R., Stankeviciene, A., Simelyte, A., & Talackiene, M. (2015).
Factors driving turnover and retention of information technology
professionals. *Journal of Business Economics and Management,* 16(1),
DOI 1. 10.3846/16111699.2015.984492.

Kraemer, T., & Matthias H.J. Gouthier. (2014). How organizational
pride and emotional exhaustion explain turnover intentions in call
centers. *Journal of Service Management, 25*(1), 125-148. doi:http://
dx.doi.org/10.1108/JOSM-07-2013-0173.

Kusuma, P. G., & Sukanya, M. (2013). Research synthesis on employee
engagement strategies. *International Journal of Organizational*

Behavior & Management Perspectives, 2(4), 661-666. Retrieved from http://search.proquest.com/openview/3ed081b89cf60f0f86ec7d7684 dd11da/1?pq-origsite=gscholar&cbl=2032284

Jackson, H.G. (2015). Three signs of economic recovery. *HR Magazine*, 60(2), 8.

Lambert, E.G., Cluse-tolar, T., Pasupuleti, S., Prior, M. & Allen, R.I. (2012). A Test of a Turnover Intent Model. *Administration in Social Work*, 36, 67–84, DOI: 10.1080/03643107.2010.551494.

Lazear, E. P., & Spletzer, J. R. (2012). Hiring, churn, and the business cycle. *The American Economic Review*, 102(3), 575-579.

Leamer E: What's a Recession, Anyway? National Bureau of Economic Research Working Paper Series 2008, 14221:1-36.

March, J., & Simon, H. (1958). *Organizations*. New York: Wiley.

Maurer R. (2015a). Planned layoffs off 5%. *SHRM HR Week*. Retrieved on March 10, 2015 from https://www.shrm.org/hrdisciplines/ staffingmanagement/articles/pages/payrolls-forecast-unemployment-dips.aspx.

Maurer R. (2015b). Payrolls Exceed Forecast, Unemployment Dips to 5.5%. *SHRM HR Week*. Retrieved on March 10, 2015 from http://www.shrm.org/hrdisciplines/ staffingmanagement/articles/pages/payrolls-forecast-unemployment-dips.aspx?utm_ source=HR%20Week%20March %209%202015%20(1)&utm_medium=email&utm_content=March % 2 0 0 9 , %202015&spMailingID=22259705&spUserID=ODY2OTYwMDc3MDAS1&spJobID=!

Maurer, T.J., & Solamon, J.M. (2006). The science and practice of a structured employment interview coaching program. *Personnel Psychology*, 59(2), 433-456.

Melanthiou, Y., Pavlou, F., & Constantinou, E. (2015). The use of social network sites as an E-recruitment tool. *Journal of Transnational Management, 20*(1), 31. DOI: 10.1080/15475778.2015.998141.

Elkjaer, D., & Filmer, S. (2015). Trends and drivers of workforce turnover. Mercer Consulting. Retrieved January 12, 2016 from http://www.mercer.com/content/dam/mercer/attachments/global/

webcasts/trends-and-drivers-of-workforce-turnover-results-from-mercers-2014-turnover-survey.pdf.

Milman, A., & Dickson, D. (2014). Employment characteristics and retention predictors among hourly employees in large US theme parks and attractions. *International Journal of Contemporary Hospitality Management, 26*(3), 447-469.

Mrkvicka, N. (2015, 01). 2014 benefits benchmarking. *Benefits Magazine, 52,* 12. Retrieved from http://ezproxy.oswego.edu:2048/login?url=http://search.proquest.com.ezproxy. oswego.edu:2048/docview/1651468517? accountid=13025

Mobley, W. H. (1977). Intermediate linkages in the relationship between job satisfaction and employee turnover. Journal of Applied Psychology, 62, 237-240.

Mobley, W., Griffeth, R., Hand, H., & Meglino, B. (1979). Review and conceptual analysis of the employee turnover process. *Psychological Bulletin, 86,* 493–522.

Moreno, L. R. M., Torres, V. G. L., & Vargas, M. E. M. (2015). Comportamiento de la tasa de rotación laboral en la industria maquiladora en Mexicali, Baja California, 2009-2013/behavior of labor turnover rate at the maquila industry in Mexicali, Baja California, 2009-2013. *Revista Global De Negocios, 3*(4), 11-26.

Moscarini, G., & Postel-Vinay, F. (2012). The Contribution of Large and Small Employers to Job Creation in Times of High and Low Unemployment. *American Economic Review, 102*(6), 2509–2539. http://dx.doi.org/10.1257/aer.102.6.2509.

Neal, J. G. (1989). Employee turnover and the exit interview. *Library Trends, 38*(1), 32.

Peter, I. A., & Eunice, A. E. (2014). The link between human resource management practices and organizational commitment. *Indian Journal of Management Science, 4*(1), 10-18.

Price, J. L. (1977). The study of turnover. Ames: Iowa State University Press, Coral Springs, Florida.

Reinstein, A., Sinason, D. H., & Fogarty, T. J. (2012). Examining mentoring in public accounting organizations. *Review of Business,* 33(1), 40-49.

Santora, J. (2009). Quality management and manufacturing performance: Does success depend on firm culture? *Academy of Management Perspectives,* 23(2), 103-105.

Schmidt, F. L., & Rader, M. (1999). Exploring the boundary conditions for interview validity: Meta-analytic validity findings for a new interview type. *Personnel Psychology, 52*(2), 445-464.

Singh, P., & Natasha, L. (2010). Pay Satisfaction, Job Satisfaction and Turnover Intent. *Relations Industrielles,* 65(3), 470-490.

SHRM (2013a). *Future Insights: The top trends for 2012 according to SHRM's HR subject matter expert panels.* Retrieved January 1, 2013 from http://www.shrm.org/ Research/FutureWorkplaceTrends/Documents/11-0622%20Workplace%20 panel_trends_symp%20v4.pdf.

SHRM (2013b). *HR Benchmarks Trendbook.* Retrieved January 1, 2013 from http://online.qmags.com/HRM1212T#pg1&mode2.

Slack, R. E., Corlett, S., & Morris, R. (2015). Exploring employee engagement with (corporate) social responsibility: A social exchange perspective on organizational participation. *Journal of Business Ethics, 127*(3), 537-548. doi:http://dx.doi.org.ezproxy.oswego.edu:2048/10.1007/s10551-014-2057-3

Smith, L. G. E., Amiot, C. E., Smith, J. R., Callan, V. J., & Terry, D. J. (2013). The social validation and coping model of organizational identity development: A longitudinal test. *Journal of Management, 39*(7), 1952-1978. doi:http://dx.doi.org/10.1177 /0149206313488212.

Steel, R., & Ovalle, N. (1984). A review and meta-analysis of research on the relationship between behavioral intentions and employee turnover. *Journal of Applied Psychology,* 69, 673–686.

Summary Annual Report (2015). *The sky is the limit Constellation Summary Annual Report.* Retrieved December 28, 2015 from http://www.cbrands.com/sites/default/files/2015%20Annual%20Report%20.pdf.pdf

Summers, L. H. (2010). Principles for economic recovery and renewal. *Business Economics, 45*(1), 3-7. doi:http://dx.doi.org/10.1057/be.2009.41.

Swarnalatha, C., & Prasanna, T. S. (2013). Leveraging employee engagement for competitive advantage: Strategic role of HR. *Review of HRM, 2,* 139-148. Retrieved from http://ezproxy.oswego.edu:20 48/login?url=http://search.proquest.com.ezproxy.oswego.edu:2048/ docview/1655997743?accountid=13025

Tekleab, A. G., Orvis, K. A., & Taylor, M. S. (2013). Deleterious consequences of change in newcomers' employer-based psychological contract obligations. *Journal of Business and Psychology, 28*(3), 361-374. doi:http://dx.doi.org/10.1007/s10869-012-9277-2.

Timms, C., Brough, P., O'Driscoll, M., Kalliath, T., Siu, O. L., Sit, C., & Lo, D. (2015). Flexible work arrangements, work engagement, turnover intentions and psychological health. *Asia Pacific Journal of Human Resources, 53*(1), 83.

Treuren, G. J. M., & Frankish, E. (2014). Pay dissatisfaction and intention to leave: The moderating role of personal care worker client embeddedness. *Nonprofit Management and Leadership, 25*(1), 5.

Turker, D. (2009b). How corporate social responsibility influences organizational commitment. Journal of Business Ethics, 89(2), 189–204.

Udechukwu, I. I., & Mujtaba, B. G. (2007). Determining the probability that an employee will stay or leave the organization: A mathematical and theoretical model for organizations. *Human Resource Development Review,* 6(2), 164-184.

Urlich, D. *HR Champions.* Boston, Ma: Harvard Business Press, 1997.

Vafeas, M. (2015). Account manager turnover and the influence of context: An exploratory study. *The Journal of Business & Industrial Marketing,* 30(1), 72-82.

Wang, Y., Hu, C., Hurst, C. S., & Yang, C. (2014). Antecedents and outcomes of career plateaus: The roles of mentoring others and proactive personality. *Journal of Vocational Behavior,* 85(3), 319-328.

Wanous J.P., (1980). *Organizational entry: Recruitment, selection and socialization of newcomers.* Reading MA: Addison-Wesley.

Wanous J.P., Poland, T.D., Premack, S.L., Davis, K.S. (1992). The effects of met expectations on newcomer attitudes and behaviors: A review and meta-analysis. *Journal of Applied Psychology*, 77, 288–297.

Wheeler, A.R., Harris, K.J., & Harvey, P. (2010). Moderating and Mediating the HRM Effectiveness - Intent to Turnover. *Journal of Managerial Issues*, 22(2), 182-196.

Wheeler, A.R., Halbesleben, J.R.B., & Harris, K.J. (2012). How job-level HRM effectiveness influences employee intent to turnover and workarounds in hospitals. *Journal of Business Research*, 65, 547-554. doi:10.1016/j.jbusres.2011.02.020.

Yean, T. F., & Yahya, K. K. (2013). The influence of human resource management practices and career strategy on career satisfaction of insurance agents. *International Journal of Business and Society*, 14(2), 193-206.

Recommendations for Implementing Sustainability in New Product Development for Supply Chain Management

Lynn Fish

Lynn Fish, Ph.D.
Associate Professor of Management
Wehle School of Business
Canisius College. 2001 Main St., Buffalo, NY 14208.
Email: fishl@canisius.edu. Telephone: (716) 888-2642.

Abstract

Six recommendations remain relevant to incorporate sustainability into New Product Development for Supply Chain Management. With respect to sustainability and the Triple Bottom Line, the current literature highlights economic sustainability issues, with a growing wealth of knowledge in the environmental area, and a significant lack of research in social sustainability for New Product Development–Supply Chain Management. Research continues to highlight the importance of evaluating the end customers' sustainability requirements and what the end customer is willing to pay for with respect to sustainability. Areas for future research are highlighted.

Keywords: Sustainability, New Product Development, Supply Chain Management

LITERATURE REVIEW

A thorough literature review of the New Product Development (NPD) process as it is coupled with Supply Chain Management (SCM) and transitioned through the quality, lean, time reduction and globalization movements highlight six critical recommendations that positively impact upon a successful product (Authors, 2002, 2003, 2008; Author, 2015 a,b). As the sustainability trend continues to add complexity to the NPD process, these six recommendations remain as critical advice to today's managers. Why address sustainability in NPD-SCM? NPD is the processes from design and development through sourcing and production planning. Without new products or service, companies will eventually cease to exist. SCM is the integration of processes that procure materials, transform them into intermediate and final products and deliver them to the end customer. In today's competitive environment, competition is supply-chain versus supply-chain, and companies must integrate NPD with SCM to survive (Simchi-Levi et al., 2013). Carefully matching product characteristics to the appropriate supply chain strategy is critical to being competitive (Fisher, 1997), and product characteristics must be aligned with end customer requirements (Aitken, Childerhouse & Towill, 2003).

Sustainability is a conceptual framework for aligning economic, environmental and social dimensions – also known as, the 'triple bottom line' (Asby, Leat & Hudson-Smith, 2012) or 'people, planet, profits'. Without economic sustainability, which refers to the profitability aspect of any product, businesses will cease to exist, and thus, at a minimum, is an order qualifier for any product. Environmental sustainability, which refers to the 'green' aspects, includes the impact the product and its associated processes have on the environment in such areas as global warming and pollution. The key with environmental sustainability is for the natural resource consumption to be below the natural reproduction for products and processes. Since industrial activities in the United States account for about a third of carbon dioxide emissions and 40% occur due to transportation, supply chain activities are a primary factor in environmental sustainability (Gupta & Palsule-Desai, 2011). In recent years, research in environmental sustainability has increased significantly. The third element of sustainability – the social aspect is the least researched (Gmelin & Seuring, 2014a, Mu et al., 2011; Beske et al., 2014). Social sustainability can be divided into internal (the motivation, skills and loyalty of employees and supply chain business partners) and external (the value that is added to the community that the company operates in). While many businesses view the social aspect as less tangible and difficult to measure (Hutchins & Sutherland, 2008), many people view these as trade-off's and not necessarily 'win-win' situations. For example, while environmental regulations provide social benefits, private costs for prevention and clean-up increase, which reduces competitiveness (Porter & van der Linde, 1995).

Why address sustainability today? Today's business leaders are confronting resource depletion, responding to stakeholder demands (for example, shareholders, employees, environmental, government organizations and citizens) and recognizing new roles for businesses in economic and social change (CEOForumGroup, 2009). There is increasing pressure from government and society to address issues of global warming, raw material scarcity, and the deterioration of human rights (Seuring, 2004), consumer's concerns, legal requirements and company's intrinsic motivations (Beske et al., 2014). Today, roughly half of top executives view sustainability as a source of innovation and new business opportunity (Sroufe & Melnyk, 201.

Sustainable Supply Chain Management (SSCM) can be defined as "the strategic, transparent integration and achievement of an organisation's social, environmental and economic goals in the systemic coordination of key inter-organisational business processes for improving the long term economic performance of the individual company and its supply chains" (Carter & Rogers, 2008, p. 368). SSCM is the management of material, information and capital flows as well as the cooperation among companies along the supply chain, while addressing all three dimensions of sustainable development (economic, environmental and social) and are derived from customer and stakeholder requirements (Seuring & Muller, 2008b). SSCM includes evaluation of the environmental impact, a multi-disciplinary perspective of the entire product life-cycle, and considerations for all stages of the entire product value chain (Gupta & Palsule-Desai, 2011). Competitive advantages may be achieved through incorporating sustainability (Campbell, 2007).

Therefore, in order to remain competitive in today's marketplace, SSCM must be integrated with NPD. Doing so significantly increases the product design complexity (Gmelin & Seuring, 2014a). However, incorporating sustainability decision-making in the NPD-SCM processes can significantly impact upon all sustainability aspects over the entire product life cycles. Unfortunately, as recently as 2010, there was little knowledge on why and how companies integrate environmental sustainability into NPD (Dangelico & Pujari, 2010). Fortunately, research over the past 15 years has shown six key recommendations are paramount to new product success and remain relevant to incorporating sustainability into New Product Development (Author, 2015a, b): top management support and development of an integrated NPD-SCM strategy, resource allocation, financial support and support for a common, shared information system; a focus on marketing demands; supplier/customer integration; integrated physical networks, processes and information technology (IT) networks; a coordinated, cross-functional team; and a clear product vision. The intent of this article is to review the current state of sustainability – economic, environmental and social, with respect to these six recommendations and highlight various research areas that remain. The literature review focused on peer-reviewed articles in the decision sciences subject area.

Recommendation #1: Top Management Support: Development of an Integrated Sustainable NPD-SSCM Strategy, Resource Allocation, Financial Support and Common, Shared Information System

Top management support is one of the most critical aspects of developing NPD with SSCM (Gmelin & Seuring, 2014a, 2014b; Griffin, 1997; Cooper, 2001; Marion et al., 2012) and includes strategy development, resource allocation, financial support and support for a common, shared information system. In general, the NPD process with sustainability is generally the same as traditional NPD; however, the underlying features and mechanisms needed to address the increased complexity require specific managerial skills and coordination (Driessen et al., 2013).

In general - and to meet economic or 'order qualifier' requirements for any product, top management develops the sustainable vision, mission, scope goals and explicit targets that direct NPD decisions towards sustainable products (Alblas, Peters & Wortmann, 2014). In mature, sustainable NPD processes and organizations, sustainability scope and targets are clear and operational; customized tools, databases, design for sustainability methods, and supply chain tools exist; process definitions include sustainability issues; roles and responsibilities are clear; and NPD designers are experts in sustainability and are active in knowledge networks (Allen et al., 2012). It is imperative that top management develop a cohesive strategy (Alblas et al., 2014) that aligns the firm and its associated supply chains toward delivering sustainable products and services. Corporations that are beginning to address sustainability should focus on what sustainability means for their business and products through defining a sustainability strategy, scope, targets, and processes first, and worry less at the beginning about the metrics (Allen et al., 2012). A recent KPMG global survey showed that roughly two-thirds of companies have a corporate sustainability strategy with a quarter developing one (Sroufe & Melnyk, 2013). Upper management needs to use different performance metrics for different types of NPD, particularly radical versus incremental product development (Driessen et al., 2013).

Management must accept a certain amount of uncertainty in sustainable NPD, and encourage proactive capabilities through exploration, experimentation, double-loop learning, creativity and entrepreneurship (Allen et al., 2012). Top management drives process management through establishing processes with supply chain development partners that encourage design team competence and remove process issues (Gmelin & Seuring, 2014a). Top Management needs to articulate that sustainability is critical to the company's future and important in all buyer-supplier relationships (and a 'shared focus') as well as proliferating resources to support sustainability efforts (Allen et al., 2012). For example, top management can create a management-level sustainability position and train employees and other supply chain member employees in sustainability, innovation and entrepreneurship. Similarly, top management can provide the resources and funds to establish a common, shared database, and although expensive, can reduce development costs, shorten time to market, improve consistency and data flexibility (Gmelin & Seuring, 2014a). Additionally, to achieve economic goals, management needs to understand that the corporate reputation on green leadership may compensate for low financial and customer performance of green products (Driessen et al., 2013). Technology leadership reputation is directly related to green leadership as very green product innovations generally require advanced technology development (Seebode et al., 2012).

With respect to environmental sustainability, top management must align the strategic objectives of the firm with green initiatives (Gupta & Palsule-Desai, 2011). Alignment may be accomplished through a green company policy (Driessen et al., 2013), which in the past has shown a significant impact upon green product innovation (Dangelico & Pujari, 2010). In the green company policy, top management conveys the company's commitment to sustainability through its values, norms and practices (Driessen et al., 2013). Top management should also use environmental benchmarking to guide their strategy development (Pujari, Peattie & Wright, 2004). With respect to performance outcomes, use different performance metrics for green and non-green products (Driessen et al., 2013). It is recommended that management establish specific sustainability targets for energy efficiency, carbon dioxide footprint, product weight, materials (recyclables and recycling), sustainable packaging, and hazardous substances (Allen et al., 2012). As an example, IBM, a leader in balancing economic performance and environmental sustainability, embeds sustainability concepts in its NPD processes and its internal continuous improvement processes, aligns its business and sustainability strategy, integrates its operations and sustainability initiatives, maintains its sustainability culture, and develops systems that execute operational and sustainability goals (Peters et al., 2011).

While companies are starting to recognize the need to address social sustainability and the concept of social sustainability is growing (Vachon & Mao, 2008), social sustainability issues are difficult to incorporate into NPD-SSCM as they are difficult to measure and results may be intangible. By addressing the social sustainability issues in the corporate sustainability policy and training NPD designers throughout the supply chain in social sustainability (Allen et al, 2012; Nawrocka et al., 2009), top management positively encourages designers to incorporate social sustainability issues in their decision-making. Additional top management encourages social sustainability through improving supply chain transparency and encouraging fair trade practices (Vacho & Mao, 2008). For example, Walmart pledged to broaden its sustainability efforts to all functions within the company, to all parts of the world where it does business, and to work with suppliers (for example, Unilever and Proctor & Gamble) and with non-governmental organizations (for example, the China Green Foundation) (Anonymous, 2009, April 13).

In general, top management needs to foster a sustainability culture that creates an innovative, collaborative, integrative supply chain lead by a systems view of NPD-SSCM through resource and financial support through a common, shared information system. Without top management support, the new product is doomed to failure. Unfortunately, due to differences between global markets, industries, and cultures, research into this is more complex as factors will certainly interact. Some potential research streams for this recommendation include:

- Which company in the supply chain oversees and decides upon the final processes and product?
- How to resolve differences between sustainability visions and practices between partners?
- How to encourage a corporate and supply chain strategy to fully incorporate all three dimensions of sustainability into NPD?
- What level of financial and resource support are recommended to support NPD-SSCM?
- How to design an information system to encourage sustainability in NPD-SCM?
- How to manage global differences in sustainability perspectives and incorporation into NPD-SSCM?
- What performance metrics are recommended for environmental and social sustainability NPD? Do these differ between incremental and radical NPD (Driessen et al., 2013)?

Recommendation #2: Focus on Marketing Demands

In today's customer-oriented environment where consumers are increasingly aware of environmental and social responsibility issues (Cohen et al., 2009), NPD-SSCM strategy needs to seamlessly incorporate critical market information into these processes and focus on the end customer (Gmelin & Seuring, 2014a). Management needs to carefully analyze the end customers' sustainability requirements. A structured process bridges the gap between market planning and process management (Gmelin & Seuring, 2014a). Some companies demonstrate their engagement in sustainability by seeking certifications such as ISO-14000 (for environmental standards) or following ISO-26000 (for social responsibility standards) (Gmelin & Seuring, 2014b). As the sustainability trend continues, companies that lack certification or fewer then their competitors may trigger a loss of trust or a negative image to the customer (Gmelin & Seuring, 2014b).

Consumer market strategies focus on bringing environmental and socially responsive products to market by concentrating on the key stages of the product life cycle (Cohen et al., 2009). Product Lifecycle Management (PLM) assesses the impact on the end customer as well as operational benefits such as cost reduction and risk management, and may increase revenues and market share (Cohen et al., 2009). PLM supports current best practices in NPD- SSCM including incorporating sustainability into NPD by evaluating product safety for the end-user, detecting marketing needs for ecological and social demands and restrictions, evaluating market changes to comply with company goals, resources and capabilities, and analyzing the market for sustainable needs and capabilities (Gmelin & Seuring, 2014a). Designers need to balance the perceived trade-offs between product performance and sustainability (Luchs, Brower & Chitturi, 2012). Strategist must also consider how much consumers are willing to pay to support sustainability efforts (Cohen et al., 2009). Unfortunately, until product sustainability is unequivocally positive for the end consumer, companies will struggle with sustainability efforts and marketing sustainable products (Luchs et al., 2012).

To encourage 'green' NPD, management recognizes that products' environmental impacts over their lifecycles can best be managed through goal-oriented and market-based mechanisms that provide flexibility (Gupta & Palsule-Desai, 2011). While managers should implement procedures and rules that encourage green NPD, many companies struggle with reconciling greenness with costs (Driessen et al., 2013). Companies need to educate and convince customers to purchase its green products, which may cost more (Hassini et al., 2012). Marketing green new products is very complex due to several factors, such as product 'greenness' and industry factors. Important drivers of a successful product innovation strategy include the proposed marked orientation, associated processes to acquire information about customers and competitors, and research on sustainable NPD that includes information on non-market stakeholders (such as regulators or special interest groups) (Driessen et al., 2013). Strategies to introduce green NPD into the market are characterized by green targeting and green positioning. Green targeting, which is the degree to which a customer values green attributes, extends from niche to mass marketing; while green positioning, which is the degree to which green attributes are used to communicate to the market about how the product differs from existing products, may position green attributes at the core or not at all (Driessen et al., 2013). Greenness and industry type affect green targeting, and while green niches are emerging in some markets, market demand for green products in many industries is still low (Driessen et al., 2013).

Unfortunately, other than noting that marketing needs to detect, plan and manage for social sustainability, very little research on marketing and social sustainability for NPD-SCM exists (Gmelin & Seuring, 2014a).

With respect to a focus on marketing demands, potential avenues for future research include:

- How to assess and address customer perceived trade-offs between the three sustainability dimensions?
- How to align the marketing strategy with the overall company and supply chain sustainability strategies?
- How to align the marketing strategy with specific product contextual attributes?
- How to assess social sustainability requirements in the end consumer market and align these with specific product contextual attributes?
- What is the relationship between green targeting and green positioning and product attributes?

Recommendation #3: Supplier/Customer Integration
Sustainable supply chains differ from conventional supply chains with respect to the critical nature of selecting supply chain partners that

match sustainability concerns (Beske et al., 2014). A critical challenge is to find suppliers that follow the same guiding principles with respect to sustainability as the company, and to extend this throughout the entire supply chain (Hutchins & Sutherland, 2008; Allen et al., 2012). Joint sustainability initiatives emphasize supplier/buyer relationships in NPD-SCM; however, many suppliers - particularly those further from the end customer, have little to no interest in sustainability (Allen et al., 2012). Successful sustainable product implementations depend upon suppliers' willingness to cooperate in this effort and to implement changes.

Supplier selection is critical to NPD-SSCM development and may include co-evolving, collaboration, and joint product and process development. Co-evolving evolves by improved relationships amongst members through activities that encourage joint growth in knowledge and partner development. Collaboration including both internal and external interactions is critical in sustainable NPD development (Tan & Tracey, 2007). To support sustainability, supplier selection criteria includes a willingness to engage in sustainable practices (Wiskerke & Roep, 2007), and technical superiority and cooperativeness (Ellram et al., 2007). Potential partners may demonstrate their commitment to sustainability through attaining environmental certifications (such as ISO14000) or following social sustainability standards (such as ISO26000) (Gmelin & Seuring, 2014b) or being certified to SA8000 (Waage et al., 2005). (SA8000 is a standard that covers child labor, forced labor, health & safety, right to collective bargaining, discrimination, disciplinary procedures, working hours, and compensation, and requires a social management system prior to certification (Waage et al., 2005)). Significant challenges in developing these relationships arise due to a lack of trust, data management issues, interoperability and communication issues (Gmelin & Seuring, 2014a). Best practices to improve the buyer-supplier relationship include jointly implementing a code of conduct focused on all aspects of sustainability, holding regular meetings for enhanced communication, joint participation in activities that develop trust, developing joint decision-making procedures, assisting partners to learn new methods and sustainability, and potentially, providing financial support (Beske et al., 2014). Economically, practitioners need to analyze all relationships within the supply chain and pay particular attention to monetary and non-monetary costs to implement NPD practices that may outweigh the benefits (Homburg & Kuehnl, 2014).

Since roughly 60% of the product's cost may be attributed to purchased materials (Monczka et al., 2009) green purchasing can significantly impact upon sustainability efforts. Therefore, it is not surprising to find a significant amount of research in green purchasing exists (Driessen & Hillebrand, 2012) as suppliers play a significant role in green innovations (Lee & Kim, 2011). Within green purchasing research, specific issues addressed include cooperation and communication between supply chain members to achieve a proactive sustainability approach, risk management to identify environmental and social problems prior to public exposure, and total life cycle product analysis (Seuring & Muller, 2008a).

The need for strong, collaborative, cooperative relationships between supply chain members toward developing environmental products and using innovative, environmental technologies in processes exists in several studies (Vachon & Klassen, 2006; Vachon & Mao, 2008; Nawrocka et al., 2009). To select and evaluate suppliers for sustainable practices, use specific environmental requirements and environmental audits (Nawrocka et al., 2009). Companies, such as IKEA, Sony, Ericsson and Volvo, established their own detailed environmental sustainability qualification schemes (Nawrocka et al., 2009). Managers should be cautious about environmental compliance in different countries as legislative compliance may carry different meanings (Nawrocka et al., 2009).

Life Cycle Analysis (LCA) , a pro-active technique, emphasizes the physical substance flow and chemical changes and can analyze the 'global' aspects in environmental supply chain relationships (Beske et al., 2014). LCA is a comprehensive approach to addresses the environmental impact at every supply chain stage from raw material extraction through disposal and focuses on supply chain partnerships (Bras, 2009). Current research indicates a gap and need for more holistic, relational research in this area (Ashby et al., 2012). LCA looks at all phases of a product's life cycle (Gmelin & Seuring, 2014b) and assumes a significant amount of detailed information on products and processes (Allen et al., 2012). Therefore, LCA is limited in early product design (Sousa & Wallace, 2006) and provides limited guidance to immature NPD organizations due to methodological problems, lack of knowledge and data (Allen et al., 2012).

Evaluating partner's social sustainability can be difficult as many indicators are dependent upon the economic resources of the family (poverty, nutritional status, healthcare, life expectancy and living conditions). Social sustainability efforts may be encouraged through green purchasing efforts (Seuring & Muller, 2008b), and as mentioned previously, by encouraging supply chain members to incorporate social sustainability efforts – such as ISO26000 or SA8000, in NPD-SCM. Purchasing managers may also use social sustainability indicators such as equity, healthcare, education, housing, security and population (UNDSD, 2001). They should also be expected to engage in fair trade practices; however, fair trade practices may result in higher prices for the end consumer, who may prove unwilling to pay extra to support this practice (Hassini et al., 2012). In the United States, partner selection measures may include the average wages versus the cost of living in the region, wage equity, gender and minority wage equity, healthcare benefits, philanthropic activities, educational initiatives and workforce job safety; however, many indicators are dependent upon the economic resources available to the family and difficult to incorporate into decision-making (Hutchins & Sutherland, 2008). Companies may encourage decent working conditions at suppliers by providing training and expert knowledge (Nawrocka et al., 2009).

Potential research streams with respect to supplier/customer NPD-SSCM integration include:

- How to resolve differences between sustainability visions and practices between partners?
- How to extend LCA to address NPD (Sousa & Wallace, 2006)?

- How to address the gap and need for more holistic, relationship research in LCA – particularly in NPD (Ashby et al. 2012)?
- What are the significant factors that encourage and discourage supplier-customer relationships toward developing sustainable new products?
- How to gather and disseminate relevant knowledge and data to encourage sustainable NPD (Allen et al, 2012)?
- What are the best practices to incorporate and monitor social sustainability (e.g. indices) for supplier-customer interaction (Nawrocka et al., 2012)?
- How should managers extend sustainability efforts up the supply chain (Allen et al., 2012)?
- What measures should be used to select partners that foster sustainability in NPD?

Recommendation#4: Integrated Networks (Physical Network, Processes & IT Management)

As previously discussed, integrated supplier-customer relationships are critical to successful NPD-SSCM. Related to this are decisions which impact upon the development of this integrated network, from a physical network, process integration, and IT management perspectives. For example, decisions on how to technically and logistically integrate supply chain partners, the quality of information integration and exchange, and the operational processes used to integrate partners can impact upon the success of NPD in a supply chain (Beske et al., 2014). Formalized, streamlined processes between supply chain members support doing the NPD correctly (Marion et al., 2012).

The physical network design for sustainable new products includes decisions on location and transportation. However, there is a definitive link between product characteristics and supply chain structure (Fine, 1998), and channel structure plays a critical role in product success (Ellram et al., 2007). Innovative products are best delivered through responsive supply chains, while functional products are better served through efficient supply chains (Fisher, 1997). By continuing to use this product/process approach, managers can avoid un-necessary steps that do not support sustainability efforts (Gmelin & Seuring, 2014a).

Best practices to develop streamline processes and coordination across globally-dispersed companies include product data management, process improvement management and engineering project management that extend across departments, companies and international borders (Gmelin & Seuring, 2014a). Product data management enables data acquisition on environmental and social sourcing (Gmelin & Seuring, 2014a). Companies that are more mature when it comes to sustainability use structured process management to guide projects, align targets and management sustainability targets (Allen et al., 2012). In strong collaborative relationships, data management is defined and controlled jointly (Gmelin & Seuring, 2014a). Recommendations call for a common product development platform that balances economic product development with environmental and social sustainability along with project and program goals (Gmelin & Seuring, 2014a). As previously discussed, PLM is a technique that may assist in the required information integration through all product phases including NPD to every supply chain member (Sudarsan et al., 2005). Relevant to this recommendation for integrated networks, PLM assists in reducing product data inconsistencies and improves coordination and control (Cantemessa et al., 2012) as information on revenues, costs, time, energy and materials may be exchanged across and within organizations (Gmelin & Seuring, 2014b). Sustainable NPD success factors supported by PLM include process formalization (including product-focused sustainable data handling processes, process flexibility improvement, common change management processes for economic and environmental success, and workflow management for economic process execution) and cross-functional work (including cross-company and cross-functional sustainable process alignment) (Gmelin & Seuring, 2014a).

With respect to IT management, recommendations call for a central location for data management and storage, which reduces data duplication and data inconsistencies (Gmelin & Seuring, 2014a). Security concerns across informational boundaries increase with SCM; however, through utilizing procedures previously discussed to improve collaboration and encourage trust-building, concerns may be alleviated.

Environmental sustainability and integrated networks are related. For example, from a NPD and supply chain perspective, as product complexity increases with a larger number of target components, the value of short lead times increases and the environmental impact due to shorter distances decreases (Ferrer & Ketzenberg, 2004). Similarly, partners located physically closer to the end customer are more likely to be aware of environmental issues (Nawrocka et al, 2009). As previously mentioned, partners are encouraged to manage physical network aspects through an environmental management system (Nawrocka et al, 2009).

Similar to other recommendations, no specific research was uncovered specifically related to social sustainability and this recommendation – whether related to a physical network, processes or IT. Therefore, *any research* that explores the relationships between social sustainability and the processes/practices, physical network and IT will be beneficial. Additionally, within integrated networks, potential avenues for research include:

- What are the relationships between product complexity, lead time and environmental impact (Ferrer & Ketzenberg, 2004)?
- What data management practices and characteristics should a product development platform have to encourage information exchange in PLM?
- What is the relationship between, and what factors impact upon, the channel structure, sustainability (all three areas) and NPD?
- What is the relationship between efficient and responsible supply chains, and the three areas of sustainability – economic, environmental and social?

Recommendation #5: Coordinated, Cross-functional Team

Departmental cross-functional collaboration is a success factor for sustainability in NPD (Petala et al., 2010). As noted previously, top management must support cross-functional NPD work (Marion et al., 2012). In today's business environment, cross-functional development may include internal organizational integration as well as inter-firm (external) collaboration (Homburg & Kuehnl, 2014). Engineering collaboration across company boundaries is essential to developing innovative, sustainable products. As a first step towards collaboration, companies need to remove functional silos and adopt a product/process approach (Lambert et al., 1998). Collaboration improves through sharing information that focuses on the organization's common goals, sharing resources, improving communication, creating knowledge, trusting and making joint decisions (Beske et al., 2014), and it is dependent upon technology and organized processes (Johnson et al, 2010). Cross-functional teams reflect the core values of sustainable NPD (Sarin & McDermott, 2003). To facilitate collaboration, the development team needs well-defined roles and functions (Zhang, 2011), and include experts with sustainability capabilities (Gmelin & Seuring, 2014a). Specific to sustainability, the team should use a resource-based view that reviews the inter-firm resources that are valuable for increased competitiveness (Gmelin & Seuring, 2014a).

The coordination between environment, R&D and purchasing departments significantly influences product improvement activities, particularly with respect to the environmental supply chain, and is an important feature of environmental supply chain cooperation (Green, Morton & New, 1998). PLM supports NPD success factors related to teams including cross-functional and cross-company environmental and social data provisioning, avoiding silo thinking – particularly one solely focused on economic development, and managing key sustainability resources (Gmelin & Seuring, 2014a).

Sustainable innovation is founded upon a sustainable culture in the firm and supply chain that encourages every employee to participate on a daily basis in sustainability efforts. Cross-functional, coordinated teams build upon this culture toward sustainable products and sustainable supply chain processes.

In today's business environment, coordinated, cross-functional teams, operating within and across cultural and global boundaries to develop NPD in supply chains, are expected. While the review here is not comprehensive, the available literature with respect to coordinated, cross-functional teams highlights sustainability in general, and does not address specific environmental or social sustainability issues in NPD-SCM. Addressing cultural, global issues and different perspectives with respect to sustainability are areas ripe for research.

Recommendation #6: A Clear Product Vision
As with any NPD in order to be competitive, the product and its associated supply chain must match market requirements and value stream objectives (Fisher, 1997). Designers must understand the product definitions and work with manufacturing to develop a seamless product delivery process. As previously mentioned to encourage sustainability in NPD, top management needs to provide specific sustainability scope and targets, and educate and encourage NPD designers in sustainability. Designers must have clearly defined roles and responsibilities, build active knowledge networks, and must be capable of using customized tools, databases, and design for sustainability methods and tools.

From an economic standpoint, designers need to monitor NPD and costs through all NPD phases and realize that as more information is gathered, it is easier to estimate NPD costs (Chwastynk & Kolosowski, 2014). Unfortunately, the gap between consumers articulated support of sustainability and actual sustainable consumption is very wide (UNEP, 2005), which implies that there is a minimum threshold of performance that sustainable products must meet (Luchs et al., 2012). In one case study, results show that customers tend to stick to conventional products instead of buying eco-products – even if price, quality and functionality are the same (Allen et al., 2012). Therefore, to promote sustainable products, it is important to improve consumer's confidence toward these products. Researchers continue to explore the perceived trade-off between product performance and sustainability, and results show that superior aesthetic design has a disproportionately positive effect on the likelihood of a successful sustainability-advantaged (versus performance-advantaged) product (Luchs et al, 2012). Therefore, a key recommendation for a company interested in sustainable products is to develop product aesthetic design capabilities (Luchs et al., 2012).

In recent years, green product innovation activities are growing (Driessen et al, 2013) as designers incorporate green into NPD through techniques such as Design for Environment (DfE), design-oriented work for green operations and green supply chain management (Sarkis et al., 2011; Seuring & Muller, 2008a, b), and metrics focused on sustainability (Waage et al, 2005). The antecedents of product characteristics (greenness, relative advantage, costs and newness) and introduction characteristics (green targeting and green positioning) must be established and balanced (Driessen et al., 2013). NPD designers need to consider all supply chain management processes for all product lifecycle phases in the product's design including using environmentally-conscious methods in manufacturing, material selection, delivery to the end consumer and end-of-life product management (Gungor & Gupta, 1999). Designers must consider green versus non-green characteristics for materials, energy and pollution across all supply chain processes (Dangelico & Pontrandolfo, 2010). Unfortunately, many designers today are unfamiliar with the associated manufacturing processes, which create additional supply chain issues, and designers need guidance on aligning specific product contextual factors with an appropriate strategy (Ashby et al., 2012).

Designers need to develop a better understanding of the reverse value chain processes (reuse, repair, recycling, remanufacturing or redesign of returned products). For example, designers need to understand remanufacturing design concerns, such as product/component durability, level of product re-manufacturability, return stream processes, relationship between new and re-manufactured products, and consumer preferences between new and re-manufacturing products (Gupta & Palsule-Desai, 2011). Design decisions on the timing and volume of product returns, re-manufacturability, and specific component re-usability also exist (Gupta & Palsule-Desai, 2011). The reverse supply chain, product characteristics and strategy need to be appropriately aligned to encourage product success (Guide et al, 2006).

In recent years, Extended Producer Responsibility (EPR) policies shifted responsibility toward producers and away from local municipalities through incentives to incorporate environmental considerations into the design of products (Gupta & Palsule-Desai, 2011). EPR examples include product take-back and recovery targets (such as home appliance recycling in Japan), disposal fees and material taxes (such as tire disposal in some U.S. states) and design/performance standards (such as U.S. fuel efficiency laws). Strategies to address EPR that impact upon NPD include: changing product design to incorporate end-of-life take back, disassembly and reuse; rationalizing parts and components to decrease material usage, eliminate hazardous substances, and facilitate remanufacturing; and choosing optimal product durability to include planned obsolescence, take-backs and replacements (Gupta & Palsule-Desai, 2011).

While current research supports the recommendation for a clear, product vision in NPD-SSCM, research in the social sustainability arena is again lacking. However, research to integrate economic and NPD-SCM exist for over two decades. A potential avenue for economic research is to focus on the trade-offs and complex factors between end product and component performance and sustainability (Luchs et al., 2012). Similarly, research in NPD and environmental sustainability exists as well. Current questions within environmental sustainability to address include:

- How do carbon prices affect product line design decisions when different products require different capacities and have different levels of emissions during production (Gupta & Palsule-Desai, 2011)?

- How do different regulatory regimes affect a firms' technology choice (Gupta & Palsule-Desai, 2011)?
- What are the best practices to align DfE, product contextual factors and strategy alignment (Ashby et al., 2012)?
- How to address different global regulatory issues?
- How to address different technology choices for NPD-SSCM?
- How to balance emissions rights within a supply chain to optimize the value chain?

Within a clear product vision, research on the reverse supply chain alignment and sustainability is lacking. Potential research streams include:

- What is the relationship between specific product characteristics (contextual factors) and the reverse supply chain (Gupta & Palsule-Desai, 2011)?
- With respect to specific components, which components should be reused in their original functionality, which components should be modified for re-use, and how many times should a particular component be reused (Gupta & Palsule-Desai, 2011)?

DISCUSSION

The thorough, but not comprehensive, literature review reveals that the NPD-SCM recommendations (Authors, 2002, 2003, 2008; Author, 2015 a, b) continue to be relevant today in light of the increasing demand for sustainability in products and processes. These recommendations are not separate recommendations that may be implemented separately from one another; rather, they need to be integrated and jointly implemented in order to achieve a successful NPD. A single, specific NPD-SSCM strategy does not exist as managers must consider the specific product, industry and country factors relevant to their end market and supply chains in strategy development.

Economic sustainability is paramount to any NPD-SCM development as products that do not meet the needs of the end customer will cease to be demanded and therefore, its supply chain will ultimately cease to exist. With respect to each recommendation, the discussion highlights key suggestions to develop new products and encourage overall sustainability development. However, as was highlighted at several points in the literature review (for example, Luchs et al, 2012), new products that do not meet the cost-value proposition of the end customer will fail. It is imperative that designers understand the trade-off between sustainability and performance as economic sustainability is an order qualifier for any new product. Methods, such as green targeting and green positioning, can assist to align the end market with financial and operational objectives of supply chains. Research in this area is still evolving.

Since Earth Day in 1970 in the U.S., efforts to incorporate environmental sustainability into decision-making increased. However, as noted in the literature review, research focused on incorporating environmental sustainability increased significantly in the past 5 years in NPD-SCM. PLM, DfE, and LCA are some of the techniques designers can use to address environmental concerns in NPD. Unfortunately, as noted previously, consumers do not fully understand the value of environmentally friendly products – nor are they ready to pay more for these attributes. So while designers struggle with incorporating and addressing environmental issues in product design, a significant hurdle is to bridge the gap between what consumers truly want from products with respect to the environment, and what they are willing to pay for.

Social sustainability research tends to focus on existing practices of firms with respect to treatment of their labor force, sourcing practices and community environmental impact. However, while corporate social responsibility has gained momentum in the past decade, as the literature review highlighted, research into social sustainability in NPD-SCM is extremely lacking. Current recommendations for NPD-SSCM development emphasize selecting and fostering relationships with similar socially sustainable values through trust-building and communication. Managers need to assist designers to overcome the complexity that is added by considering social sustainability issues in the product and process design through support, processes, and knowledge. It is critically important to understand the end customer's specific product requirements and what they are willing to pay for with respect to social sustainability. Management can encourage social sustainability in new products through leveraging their brand image to foster positive customer perceptions. Obviously there is a significant need for research specific to social sustainability in NPD-SCM.

CONCLUSIONS

Six recommendations are still relevant to incorporating sustainability into NPD for SCM. These six recommendations are: (1) Top management support to develop an integrated strategy support through resource and financial support through a common, shared information system is vital to developing a new product; (2) A focus on marketing demands; (3) Supplier/Customer integration; (4) Integrated networks (Physical Network, Processes & IT Management); (5) Coordinated, cross-functional team; and (6) A clear product vision. In general, the underlying recommendation for NPD-SSCM is a focus on the end-customer. Research into economic sustainability in NPD-SCM is on-going as every product must be economically viable or it will disappear from the marketplace, environmental sustainability research is on the rise, but social sustainability research is extremely lacking. The issue for today's managers is to appropriately address environment and social sustainability issues through focusing on the end customer. Limitations to this research include the lack of specific data and test cases and difficulties in testing interactions due to the significant number of factors that may impact upon NPD-SSCM (such as industry, quality, cost, timing, and global issues). Fortunately, for researchers, potential research avenues in NPD-SSCM abound.

REFERENCES

Aitken, J. Childerhouse, P. & Towill, D. (2003). The impact of product life cycle on supply chain strategy. *International Journal of Production Economics*, 85, pp. 127-140. doi:10.1016/S0925-5273[03]00105-1

Alblas, A.A., Peters, K. & Wortman, J.C. (2014). Fuzzy sustainability incentives in new product development: An empirical exploration of sustainability challenges in manufacturing companies. *International Journal of Operations & Production Management*, 34(4), pp. 513-545. doi:10.1108/IJOPM-10-2012-0461

Allen, M.W., Walker, K.L.,& Brady, R. (2012). Sustainability Discourse within a Supply Chain Relationship: Mapping Convergence and Divergence *Journal of Business Communication*. 49(3), pp. 210-236. doi:10.1177/0021943612446732

Anonymous (2009, April 13). Wal-Mart' earth month efforts circle the globe: Retailer unveils eco-friendly products, mobilizes workforce and engages global communities. *PR Newswire*. Retrieved from http://www.prnewswire.com/news-releases/wal-marts-earth-month-efforts-circle-the-globe-61799172.html.

Ashby, A., Leat, M. & Hudson-Smith, M. (2012). Making connections: A review of supply chain management and sustainability literature. *Supply Chain Management*,17(5), pp. 497-516. doi:10.1108/13598541211258573

Barratt, M. (2004). Understanding the meaning of collaboration in the supply chain. *Supply Chain Management: International Journal.* 9(1), 30-42. doi:10.1108/13598540410517566

Beske, P., Land, A., & Seuring, S. (2014). Sustainable supply chain management practices and dynamic capabilities in the food industry: A critical analysis of the literature. *International Journal of Production Economics*, 152, pp. 131-143. doi:10.1016/j.ijpe.2013.12.026

Bras, B. (2009). Sustainability and product life cycle management – issues and healthy emissions – a strategy for eco-effective product and system design. *International Journal of Product Lifecycle Management*, 4(1/2/3), 23-47. doi:10.1504/IJPLM.2009.031665

Campbell, J. L. (2007). Why would corporations behave in socially responsible ways? An institutional theory of corporate social responsibility. *Academic Management Review*, 32(3), pp. 946-967. doi:10.5465/AMR.2007.25275684

Cantamessa, M., Montagna, F.,& Neirotti, P. (2012). Understanding the organizational impact of PLM systems: evidence from an aerospace company. *International Journal of Operations & Production Management*, 32(2), 191-215. http://dx.doi.org/10.1108/01443571211208623

Carter, C.R. & Rogers, D.S. (2008). A framework for sustainable supply chain management: moving toward new theory. *International Journal of Physical Distribution & Logistics Management*, 38, pp. 360-387. doi:10.1108/09600030810882816

CEOForumGroup (2009). Engaging external stakeholders: Sustainability performance. Retried from http://www.ceoforum.com.au/article-detail.cfm?cid=8981&t=/Rob-Hogarth-KPMG/Sustainability-performance/

Chwastyk, P. & Kolosowski, M. (2014). Estimating the Cost of the New Product in Development Process. 24th *DAAAM International Symposium on Intelligent Manufacturing and Automation, 2013*. *Procedia Engineering*, 69, pp. 351-360. http://dx.doi.org/10.1016/j.proeng.2014.02.243

Cohen, S., Wilkos, D., Garon, A, & Gownder, J.P. (2009). Environmental and social responsibility in consumer product strategies: How central is environmental and social responsibility to your product? April 9, 2009. Accessed from Forrester Research, Inc. on Sept. 22, 2014 from https://www.forrester.com/Environmental+And+Social+Responsibility+In+Consumer+Product+Strategies/fulltext/-/E-RES53747

Cooper, A. C. (2001). *Winning at New Products*. Perseus Publishing, Cambridge, MA.

Dangelico, R.M. & Pujari, D. (2010). Mainstreaming green production innovation: Why and how companies integrate environmental sustainability. *Journal of Business Ethics*, 95(3), pp. 471-486. doi:10.1007/s10551-010-0434-0

Dangelico, R.M. & Pontrandolfo, P. (2010). From green product definitions and classifications to the green options matrix. *Journal of Cleaner Production*, 18(16-17), pp. 1608-1628. http://dx.doi.org/10.1016/j.jclepro.2010.07.007

Driessen, P.H., Hillebrand, B., Kok, R.A.W. & Verhallen, T.M.M. (2013). Green New Product Development: The Pivotal Role of Product Greenness. *IEEE Transactions on Engineering Management*, 60(2), pp. 315-326. doi:10.1109/TEM.2013.2246792

Driessen, P.H., & Hillebrand, B. (2012). Integrating multiple stakeholder issues in new product development: an exploration. *Journal of Product Innovation Management*, 30(2), 364-379. doi:10.1111/j.1540-5885.2012.01004.x

Ellram, L.M., Tate, W.L. & Carter, C.R. (2007). Product-process-supply chain: an integrative approach to three-dimensional concurrent engineering, *International Journal of Physical Distribution & Logistics Management*, 37(4), pp. 305-330. doi:10.1108/09600030710752523

Ferrer, G. & Ketzenberg, M.E. (2004).Value of information in remanufacturing complex products. *IIE Transactions*, 36(3), pp. 265-277. doi:10.1080/07408170490274223

Fine, C. (1998). *Clockspeed*, Perseus Books, New York, NY.

Author (2015a). Sustainable Supply Chain Management & New Product Development. *Applications of Contemporary Management Approaches in Supply Chains*. ISBN 978-953-51-4197-6, Croatia: InTech. 83-115.

Author. (2015b). New Product Development and Supply Chain Management: A Literature Review of the Past 15 Years. *Proceedings of the North East Decisions Sciences Institute*, Cambridge, MA, March 20-22, 2015.

Authors (2008). A Literature Review and Areas for Future Academic Research in New Product Development in Supply Chain Management. *Proceedings of the Decision Sciences Institute Annual Meeting*, Baltimore, MD, Nov. 2008, pp. 2291-6.

Authors (2003). New Product Development in Supply Chain Management: Recommendations for Practitioners and Future Academic Research. *2003 Northeast Decision Sciences Institute Conference*, Providence, RI, March 2003, pp. 264-6.

Authors (2002). A Discussion of Managerial Issues in New Product Development for Supply Chain Management. *2002 International Conference on Industry, Engineering, and Management Systems Proceedings*, Cocoa Beach, FL, March 13-15, 2002.

Fisher, M. (1997). What is the right supply chain for your product? *Harvard Business Review*, March/April, 105-116.

Gmelin, H. & Seuring, S. (2014a). Achieving sustainable new product development by integrating product life-cycle management capabilities. *International Journal of Production Economics*, 154, pp. 166-177. doi:10.1016/j.ijpe.2014.04.023

Gmelin, H. & Seuring, S. (2014b). Determinants of a sustainable new product development. *Journal of Cleaner Production*, 69, pp. 1-9. doi:10.1016/j.jclepro.2014.01.053

Green, K. Morton, BG. & New, S. (1998). Green purchasing and supply policies: do they improve companies' environmental performance? *Supply Chain Management*, 3(2), pp. 89-95. doi:10.1108/13598549810215405

Griffin, A. (1997). PDMA research on new product development practices: updating trends and benchmarking best practices. *Journal of Product Innovation Management*, 14(6), 429-458. doi:10.1016/S0737-6782(97)00061-1

Guide, V.D.R., Jr., Souza, G.C., van Wassenhove, L.N. & Blackburn, J.D. (2006). The time value of commercial product returns. *Management Science*, 52(8), pp. 1200-1214. doi:10.1287/mnsc.1060.0522

Gungor, A. & Gupta, S. (1999). Issues in environmentally conscious manufacturing and product recover: a survey. *Computers and Industrial Engineering*, 36(44), pp. 811-853. doi:10.1016/S0360-8352[106]00167-9

Gupta, S.& Palsule-Desai, O.D. (2011). Sustainable supply chain management: Review and research opportunities. *Indian Institute of Management Bangalore Management Review*, 23, pp. 234-245.

Hassini, E., Surti, C. & Searcy, C. (2012). A literature review and a case study of sustainable supply chains with a focus on metrics.

International Journal of Production Economics, 140, 69-82. http://dx.doi.org/10.1016/j.ijpe.2012.01.042

Homburg, C., & Kuehnl, C. (2014).Is the more always better? A comparative study of internal and external integration practices in new product and new service development. *Journal of Business Research*, 67, 1360-1367. http://dx.doi.org/10.1016/j.jbusres.2013.08.017.

Hutchins, M.J. & Sutherland, J.W. (2008). An exploration of measure of social sustainability and their application to supply chain decisions. *Journal of Cleaner Production*, 16, pp, 1688-1698. doi:10.1016/j.jclepro.2008.06.001

Johnson, M.E., Cochran, J.J., Cox, L.A., Keskinocak, P. Kharougeh, J.P., & Smith, J.C. (2010). Product/service design collaboration. *Managing the Product Life Cycle*, pp. 1.

Lambert, D.M., Coooper, M.C., & Pagh, J.D. (1998). Supply chain management: implementation issues and research opportunities. *International Journal of Logistics Management*, 9(2), 1-19. doi:10.1108/09574099810805807

Lee, K-H.,& Kim, J-W. (2011). Integrating suppliers into green product innovation development: an empirical case study in the semiconductor industry. *Business Strategy Environment*, 20(8), 527-538. doi:10.1002/bse.714

Luchs, M.G., Brower, J. & Chitturi, R. (2012). Product choice and the importance of aesthetic design given the emotion-laden trade-off between sustainability and functional performance. *Journal of Product Innovation Management*, 29(6), pp. 903-916. doi:10.1111/j.1540-5885.2012.00970.x

Marion, T.J., Friar, J.H., & Simpson, T.W. (2012). New product development practices and early-stage firms: two in-depth case studies. *Journal of Product Innovation Management*, 29(4), 639-654. doi:10.1111/j.1540-5885.2012.00930.x

Monczka, R.M., Handfield, R.B., Giunipero, L.C. & Patterson, J.L. (2009). *Purchasing and Supply Chain Management, Fourth Edition*. South-Western Cengage, Mason, OH.

Mu, J., Zhang, G. & MacLachlan, D.L., (2011). Social competency and new product development performance, IEEE Trans. Eng. Management, 58(2), 363-376. http://dx.doi.org/10.1109/TEM.2010.2099231

Nawrocka, D., Brorson, T. & Lindhqvist, T. (2009). ISO14001 in environmental supply chain practices. *Journal of Cleaner Production*, 17, pp. 1435-1443. doi:10.1016/j.jclepro.2009.05.004

Petala, E., Wever, R., Dutilh, C., & Brezet, H.C. (2010). The role of new product development briefs in implementing sustainability: a case study. *Journal of Engineering Technology Management*, 27(3-4), 172-182. doi:10.1016/j.jengtecman.2010.06.004

Peters, A., Moore, C. & Margarie, A. (2011). IBM's Approach To Sustainability Provides A Model For Long-Lasting Competitive Edge. *Forrester Research*. Accessed on Sept. 22, 2014 from https://www.forrester.com/IBMs+Approach+To+Sustainability+Provides+A+Model+For+LongLasting+Competitive+Edge/fulltext/-/E-RES58152

Porter, M. & van der Linde, C. (1995). Green and competitive: ending the stalemate. *Harvard Business Review*, 73(5), pp. 120-134.

Pujari, D., Peattie, K. & Wright, G. (2004). Organizational antecedents of environmental responsiveness in industrial new product development. Industrial Marketing Management, 33(5), 381-391. doi:10.1016/j.indmarman.2003.09.001

Sarin, S. & McDermott, C. (2003). The effect of team leader characteristics on learning, knowledge application, and performance of cross-functional new product development teams. *Decision Science*, 34 (4), 707-739. doi:10.1111/j.1540-5414.2003.02350.x

Sarkis, J., Zhu, Q. & Lai, K. (2011). An organizational theoretic review of green supply chain management literature. *International Journal of Production Economics*, 130(1), pp.1-15. doi:10.1016/j.ijpe.2010.11.010

Seebode, D., Jeanrenaud, S. & Bessant, J. (2012). Managing innovation for sustainability. *R&D Manage.*, 42(3), pp. 195-206.

Seuring, D. (2004). Industrial ecology, life cycles, supply chains – differences and interrelations. *Business Strategy and the Environment*, 3(5), pp. 306-319. doi:10.1002/bse.418

Seuring, D. & Muller, M. (2008a). Core issues in sustainable supply chain management: a Delphi study. *Business Strategy and the Environment*, 17, pp. 455-466. doi:10.1002/bse.607

Seuring, D. & Muller, M. (2008b). From a literature review to a conceptual framework for sustainable supply chain management. *Journal of Cleaner Production*, 16(15), pp.1699-1710. doi:10.1016/ j.jclepro.2008.04.020

Simchi-Levi, D., Kaminsky, P. & Simchi-Levi, E. (2013). *Designing & Managing the Supply Chain: Concepts, Strategies & Case Studies, Third Edition*, McGraw-Hill, Irwin, NY, NY.

Sousa, I. & Wallace, D. (2006). Product classification to support approximate life-cycle assessment of design concepts. *Technological Forecasting & Social Change*, 73, pp. 228-249. doi:10.1016/ j.techfore.2004.03.007

Sroufe, R.P. & Melnyk, S.A. (2013). Developing Sustainable Supply Chains to Drive Value: Management Issues, Insights, Concepts and Tools. *Business Expert Press*. ISBN-13:978-1-60649-372-4.

Tan, C. L. & Tracey, M. (2007). Collaborative new product development environments: Implications for supply chain management. *Journal of Supply Chain Management*, 43(3), 2-15. http://dx.doi.org/10.1111/ j.1745-493X.2007.00031.x

United Nations Environment Programme (UNEP) (2005). Talk the walk: Advancing sustainable lifestyles through marketing and communications. New York: UN Global Compact and Utopies.

UNDSD (United Nations Division for Sustainable Development) (2001). Indicators of sustainable development, guidelines and methodologies. http://sustainabledevelopment.un.org/content/documents/indisd-mg2001.pdf. Accessed on 9/19/14.

Vachon, S., & Klasen, R.D. (2006), Extending green practices across the supply chain: the impact of upstream and downstream integration. *International Journal of Operations & Production Management*, 26(7), pp. 795-821. doi:10.1108/01443570610672248

Vachon, S. & Mao, Z. (2008). Linking supply chain strength to sustainable development: a country-level analysis. *Journal of Cleaner Production*, 16(15), pp. 1552-1560. doi:10.1016/j.jclepro.2008.04.012

Waage, S.A., Geiser, K. Irwin, F, Weissman, A.B., Bertolucci, M.D., Fisk, P. Basile, G., Cowan, S. , Cauley, H. & McPherson, A. (2005). Fitting together the building blocks for sustainability: a revised model for integrating ecological, social and financial factors into business decision-making. *Journal of Cleaner Production.* 13, pp. 1145-1163. http://dx.doi.org/10.1016/j.jclepro.2004.06.003

Wiskerke, J. & Roep, D. (2007). Constructing a sustainable pork supply chain: a case of techno-institutional innovation. *Journal of Environment Policy Plan.*, 9(1), pp. 53-74. doi:10.1080/15239080701254982

Zhang, D.Z. (2011). Towards theory building in agile manufacturing strategies – case studies of an agility taxonomy. *International Journal of Production Economics*, 131(1), pp.303-312. doi:10.1016/j.ijpe.2010.08.010

Using TQM to Implement Sustainability in Supply Chain Management

Lynn A. Fish

Lynn A. Fish, Ph.D.
Associate Professor of Management
Wehle School of Business
Canisius College. 2001 Main St., Buffalo, NY 14208.
Email: fishl@canisius.edu. Telephone: (716) 888-2642.

Abstract

Through a literature review, research supports using Total Quality Management (TQM) as a potential framework to implement sustainability in Supply Chain Management (SCM). The research highlights Total Quality Management (TQM) philosophies of a customer focus, continuous improvement and cultural shift necessary to implement sustainability. The relationship between sustainability and Quality gurus' philosophies, TQM approaches and tools are developed. This framework offers practitioners best practices and known tools and techniques to implement sustainability and avenues for future research for academics.

Keywords: Sustainability, Total Quality Management, Supply Chain Management

INTRODUCTION

Throughout history, in order to remain in business managers have met customer's requirements. Following World War II, the Japanese incorporated quality management into their systems. By the 1980's, due to the Japanese influence, quality was the competitive priority demanded in the marketplace. U.S. and European managers adopted quality management systems and the concept of Total Quality Management (TQM) to address this need. By the 1990's, companies needed to address time competition and waste reduction, and the Just-In-Time (JIT) and lean production philosophies assisted managers to meet these requirements. As the 21st century began competition was no longer company versus company, but rather, supply chain versus supply chain. Managers needed to address the integration aspects demanded by Supply Chain Management (SCM) – and more specifically the complex, global SCM. Today, global environment and humanitarian concerns are highlighted in news headlines, and managers must address sustainability issues with their products and processes. Since companies that do not develop new products or services will ultimately cease to exist, managers always need to manage the development chain as well. In short, today's managers need to simultaneously address SCM, TQM, JIT, globalization, the development chain – and now, sustainability. This is a complex undertaking!

What frameworks, tools and techniques can managers use to address sustainability? Research highlights the lack of management systems or frameworks to support organizations to achieve their sustainability objectives in a systematic and continuous way (Delai & Takahashi, 2013). However, as the literature review below demonstrates, the philosophy, tools and techniques of TQM have been used to address sustainability requirements in SCM. In the discussion, we propose using TQM more fully as a framework to support sustainability in SCM.

DEFINITIONS AND RELATIONSHIPS

Since various definitions exist for key concepts, we begin by defining key terms and concepts. The development chain includes idea generation, market research, product design and development phase, sourcing decisions, and production plans. During the plan/design phase, decisions on the product architecture, make versus buy and early supplier involvement are made. The sourcing phase follows and addresses supplier selection and contracts, and potential strategic partnerships. In order to remain competitive, supply chains must continuously develop and deliver new products and services to the marketplace (Simchi-Levi, Kaminsky & Simchi-Levi, 2013).

Simply put, quality can be defined as meeting or exceeding customer expectations (Evans & Lindsay, 2002). Total Quality Management (TQM) is a management philosophy whereby all management principles and practices can develop from the belief that the continual improvement of quality is the key to success (Deming, 1986). TQM is a philosophy that stresses three principles for achieving high levels of process performance and quality: customer satisfaction, employee involvement and continuous improvement (Krajewski, Ritzman & Malhotra, 2013). Employee involvement, which encompasses changing the organizational culture, encouraging teamwork and empowering employees, and continuous improvement through various techniques to continually improve processes, support the critical focus on customer satisfaction. Quality leaders, such as Philip B. Crosby, W. Edwards Deming, Joseph M. Juran, Armand Feigenbaum, and Genichi Taguchi, developed methods to improve quality throughout the organization and build a culture of continuous improvement focused on the customer (APICS, 2010). Key TQM concepts include continuous improvement through the Deming Wheel, Six Sigma Quality and DMAIC, employee empowerment, benchmarking, JIT, Taguchi Concepts, and various TQM tools (Heizer & Render, 2014). Quality tools exist and include, but are not limited to: cause analysis tools (cause-and-effect diagrams, Pareto charts, and scatter diagram), evaluation and decision-making tools (decision matrix and multi-voting), process analysis tools (flowchart, failure modes and effects analysis, mistake-proofing, and spaghetti diagrams), data collection and analysis tools (box and whisker plot, check sheet, control chart, design of experiments, histogram, scatter diagram, stratification, and surveys), idea creation tools (affinity diagram, benchmarking, brainstorming, and nominal group technique), an project management tools (Gantt chart and Plan-Do-Check-Act continuous improvement model), and other process management tools (relations diagram, tree diagram, matrix diagram, L-shaped matrix, arrow diagram, and process decision program chart) (Tague, 2004).

SCM is the design, planning, execution, control and monitoring of the global network used to delivery products and services from raw materials to end customers through engineered flows of information, physical distribution and cash (APICS, 2010). The objective of SCM is to create net value, build a competitive infrastructure, leverage worldwide logistics, synchronize supply and demand, and measure global performance. SCM is an approach to integrating suppliers, manufacturers, distributors and retailers, such that products are produced and distributed at the right quantities, to the right location, at the right time, with the mutual goals of minimizing system wide costs and satisfying customer service require-ments (Simchi-Levi et al., 2008). Key supply chain processes include product design, production, delivery, support, supplier-customer rela-tionship management, and reverse logistics. Supply chains compete based upon cost, quality, time and responsiveness. Supply chain improvement tools include, but are not limited to process improvement tools of flow charting, flow diagrams, service blueprints, process analysis, process re-engineering, link charts, multi-activity analysis, backward chaining, and Gantt charts.

SCM and TQM are integrated through Supply Chain Quality Manage-ment (SCQM), which is a systems-based approach to performance improvement that integrates supply chain partners and leverages oppor-tunities created by upstream and downstream linkages with a focus on creating value and achieving satisfaction of intermediate and final customers (Foster, 2008; Robinson & Malhotra, 2005). SCQM combines TQM practices (particularly top management commitment, customer focus, training and education, continuous improvement and innovation, supplier management, and employee involvement (Talib, Rahman & Quereeshi, 2010; Talib & Rahman, 2010) with SCM practices: customer relationship, material management, strategic supplier partnerships, information and communication technologies, corporate culture and close supplier partnerships (Tan, 2001; Koh et al., 2007). In SCQM, the six TQM areas that are related to supply chain performance are leadership, strategic planning, human resources management, supplier quality management, customer focus, and process management (Azar, Kahnali & Taghavi 2010). Several cases to support supply chain improvement through SCQM exist (Fish, 2011).

The Brundtland's Report defines sustainability as 'a development that meets the needs of the present without compromising the ability of future generations to meet their own needs' (World Commission on Environment and Development, 1987, p. 43). Sustainability is often conceptualized as a framework for aligning the 'triple bottom line' (TBL) – environment, social and economic dimensions (Asby, Leat & Hudson-Smith, 2012), also referred to as 'people, planet, profits'. Environmental sustainability, which includes pollution and global warming (that can be attributed to 6 greenhouse gases), is the most recognized dimension of sustainability as corporations seek to reduce the natural resource consumption below the natural reproduction for the products that are produced and processes that are used. Social sustainability addresses companies' relationship with their main stakeholders: employees, community, public sector, suppliers and customers (Delai & Takahashi, 2013), and can be divided into internal (motivation, skills, and loyalty of employees and business partners in the supply chain) and external (value that is added to the community that the company operates in). Social sustainability is the least researched and developed dimension (Gmelin & Seuring, 2014; Beske, Land & Seuring, 2014). While companies are starting to recognize the need to address social sustainability and the concept of social sustainability is growing (Vachon & Mao, 2008), many managers feel that social sustainability efforts are more difficult to measure and results may be intangible. Economic sustainability refers to the profitability of the sustainable efforts. Without economic sustainability, businesses will cease to exist, and therefore, economic viability is a requirement in order to remain in business. Many business theories view the three dimensions as trade-offs and not necessarily 'win-win' situations (Porter & van der Linde, 1995). Most sustainability studies focus on environmental factors over social factors and examples of corporations and associated supply chains demonstrating integration of all three extremely rare (Asby et al., 2012; Ozcelik & AvciOzturk, 2014).

SCM and sustainability have been integrated through a field known as Sustainable Supply Chain Management (SSCM). SSCM can be defined as the management of material, information and capital flows through coop-eration among companies along the supply chain while addressing goals from all three dimensions of sustainable development (economic, envi-ronmental and social), which are derived from customer and stakeholder requirements (Seuring & Muller, 2008). Companies can gain competi-tive advantage through sustainability (Campbell, 2007). SSCM includes evaluation of the environmental impact, a multi-disciplinary perspec-tive of the entire product life-cycle, and considerations for all stages across the entire value chain for each product (Gupta & Palsule-Desai, 2011). Top management commitment, a supportive culture, employee involvement, cross-functional teams, enhanced communication, adopting environmental management systems, and cooperation with suppliers enable SSCM (Ozcelik & AvciOzturk, 2014).

In another integration of concepts, environmental sustainability and TQM have a positive association through a framework known as Total Quality Environmental Management (TQEM) (Curkovic, Melnyk, Hand-field & Calantone, 2000; Curkovic, Sroufe, & Landeros, 2008; Corbett & Klassen, 2006). The same processes that improve quality, reduce waste,

cut costs and improve competitiveness are used to improve environmental outcomes (Curkovic et al., 2000). TQEM efforts start by gathering
easily changed items, such as reducing energy use, and then moves on
to examining more fundamental issues, such as supply chain design
and business models, that require further environmental action with
significant investment, radical changes in operational practices and re-
engineering of existing supply chains (Devinney, 2009).

This discussion has clarified specific frameworks and concepts that
will be used to develop the framework for implementing sustainability in
SCM. It also highlights the integration of key concepts over time. Firms
are increasingly required to offer high quality, innovative products at
competitive prices, and to develop supply chains that are sustainable in the
long run (Gupta & Palsule-Desai, 2011). In order to remain competitive,
today's managers must integrate sustainability efforts with quality,
supply chain and development efforts in order to meet the end customer's
requirements. We continue by discussing the commonalities between
sustainability and SCQM.

SUSTAINABILITY & TQM

Literature contains common themes and concepts between TQM
and sustainability implementation in supply chains. We continue by
discussing the commonalities between sustainability and TQM principles of customer satisfaction, employee involvement and continuous
improvement, consider Cost of Quality and Quality Gurus' philosophies
as they relate to sustainability, and then highlight examples of where
TQM concepts and tools were used to implement sustainability.

Customer focus

In general, the push to incorporate quality into products in the 1980's
in western countries arose as Japan entered the global markets with
products that focused on the end customer's requirements. Governments
responded to encouraging companies to meet the quality requirements
through regulations and programs, such as the Malcolm Baldrige Award

(in the U.S.) and ISO-9000 (quality management system). Good quality has a positive impact upon a company's reputation, while poor quality may increase product liability costs. Quality is a 'global' requirement as products must meet customers' global quality, design and price expectations (Heizer & Render, 2014).

Today, the need to address sustainability arises from several different areas, including: global resource depletion and raw material scarcity, stakeholder demands for information and accountability, consumer's concerns, the deterioration of human rights, and government policies and regulations (Beske et al., 2014; CEOForumGroup, 2009; Seuring, 2004). Similar to quality, sustainability can be positively related to company reputation (Driessen, Hillebrand, Kok, & Verhallen, 2013), and failure to meet sustainability requirements may lead to a company not being selected as a supplier. Today, sustainability is a global requirement. For example, the European Union (EU) current and future legislation focuses on creating regulations requiring sustainability integration - similar to the EU requiring ISO9000 in the past, which increased the global pressure to implement quality (Buyukozkan & Berkol, 2011). ISO14000 (environmental sustainability) and ISO26000 (social sustainability) encourage global sustainability efforts (Gmelin & Seuring, 2014). Many companies require their suppliers to meet these standards in their supplier certification programs. For example, Walmart's supplier sustainability assessment covers 15 questions that include supplier information on energy and climate (reducing energy costs and greenhouse gas emissions), material efficiency (reducing waste and enhancing quality), natural resources (producing high quality, responsibly sourced raw materials) and people and community (ensuring responsible and ethical production) (Walmart Supplier Sustainability Assessment, 2013). With respect to sustainability, customer satisfaction may be assessed through surveys, customer health and safety can be impacted upon through health and safety production standards, quality and safety level control can be through monitoring internal supply chain members, and products, labeling and customer sustainability education (for example, through recycling stations, ecobags and sustainability store communication) can drive sustainability awareness. Hence, we conclude that society – and customers are seeking sustainable products, services and processes.

Cultural Shift (Empowered Employees & Top Management Commitment)

Implementing quality through TQM required a cultural shift that included top management support and value-added, empowered workers and teams. Deming, Juran and Crosby's philosophies require top management commitment to quality, holding top management responsible for the system (Evans & Lindsay, 2002). Similarly, a best practices in implementing sustainability in SCM is top management support and commitment (Delai & Takahashi, 2013; Fish, 2015; Ozcelik & AvciOzturk, 2014). Top management needs to define a sustainability mission, strategy, scope, targets, and processes (Allen, Walker & Brady, 2012; Delai & Takahashi, 2013), so that a culture to foster sustainability develops and supports the strategy, which is linked to relevant performance metrics and reports (Delai & Takahashi, 2013; Fish, 2015; Sroufe & Melnyk, 2013). Top management must strategically align the organization and its associated supply chains toward delivering sustainable products and services. Sustainability is a system opportunity (Sroufe & Melnyk, 2013) as waste is ultimately linked to processes (Sroufe & Melnyk, 2013). The approach a company uses to manage sustainability reflects its priority and the degree that sustainability is embedded in the organizational procedures, and another demonstration of a commitment to sustainability is having a high level position for promoting and guiding sustainability efforts (Delai & Takahashi, 2013). For example, Nike integrated sustainability and innovation initiatives through an organizational structure where the vice president, who reports directly to CEO, is charged with sustainability and innovation efforts (McCarty, Jordan & Probst, 2011). The end-result is that top management is responsible for sustainability efforts.

TQM is founded on a cultural shift within the organization the treats workers as value-added resources through training and an organizational structures that encourage and promote participation in continuous improvement. Similarly, developing a workforce that treats employees as value-added assets is a best practice that can assist in sustainability efforts (Fish, 2015; Ozcelik & AvciOzturk, 2014). A workforce, committed to continuous improvements and innovation, and sustainability can mitigate trade-offs between short term profitability and long term sustainability goals (Wu & Pagell, 2011). Training employees in sustainability provides a competitive advantage over other suppliers (Allen et al., 2012; Delai & Takahashi, 2013). It is essential that the culture of the organization support sustainability efforts.

Continuous Improvement

In TQM, continuous improvement is founded on a philosophy of continually seeking ways to improve processes, typically through Deming's Wheel. The Deming (or Shewhart) circle promotes a process of 'Plan-Do-Check-Act' that identifies problems, plans improvements, tests the plan, studies whether the plan is working, acts to standardize the positive tested plan, and then, returns to plan additional improvements. Using a TQM mentality to implement sustainability allows companies to focus on process-thinking and root causes, correcting the problems, perpetual improvement, problem identification, and then taking action to bring about positive results (Sroufe & Melnyk, 2013). Continuous improvement can be used to drive sustainability efforts.

Cost of Quality

Cost of Quality is a method to categorize the costs of 'doing things incorrectly', and can be grouped into 4 categories: internal failure costs (costs associated with defect prior to delivery to a customer), external failure costs (costs associated with defect once the customer receives the product or service), appraisal costs (costs related to evaluating products, services and processes to ensure quality levels are met) and prevention (costs associated with preventing defective parts or services). While sustainability does not currently have corresponding cost categories,

SSCM focuses on prevention over correction (Sroufe & Melnyk, 2013) – similar to COQ where prevention methods are preferred. People perceive trade-offs between economic, environmental and social sustainability to exist as environmental or social sustainability costs may be significant and potentially negatively impacting upon economic viability (Wu & Pagell, 2011). For example, a retrofitted building may carry positive environmental benefits (smaller footprint and less energy); however, the expense may be unjustifiable (Wu & Pagell, 2011). Other cases demonstrate a positive relationship between sustainability and financial performance in increasing profitability and reducing waste, energy, material and water expenses (Willard, 2012). The SSCM system should encourage innovative cost neutrality or economically viable solutions that are more environmental sustainable in the long term (Wu & Pagell, 2011). Extending the COQ categories to sustainability can assist in reporting and monitoring sustainability efforts.

Quality Gurus
The philosophies of the world-renown quality gurus', W. Edwards Deming, Joseph Juran, Philip Crosby, Armand Feigenbaum, and Genichi Taguchi, can be used to implement sustainability as noted in Table 1. As noted previously, Deming's philosophy formed the basis for TQM, requires top management support and a cultural change towards continuous improvement. Juran defines quality as 'fitness for use' and focused on 'form, fit and function' in product and services. Juran observed that all breakthroughs follow a universal pattern that can be transferred to sustainability implementation (Sroufe & Melnik, 2013). Juran's universal pattern includes proof of need (metrics), project identification (Pareto analysis), an organization to guide the breakthrough (sustainability team lead by upper management), diagnosis (analysis of symptoms) remedial action (take action, measure and deal with resistance to change by using metrics to align business case with sustainability goals), breakthrough cultural resistance and control at the new level. By using the breakthrough approach fostered by Juran, best practices approaches to

sustainability can improve its profitability and revenues, avoid profit erosion, reduce energy, waste, materials and water expenses, increase employee productivity, reduce hiring and attrition expenses and reduce strategic and operational risks (Willard, 2012). Crosby's basic philosophy addressed quality being led by top management; however, he focused on a different culture – that is western (US and European) versus eastern (Japan) and developed a 14-step approach to develop a quality system and culture that fit with the western culture. This brings up a critical point: a system to address sustainability should take into account the culture of the people. Similar to Juran's financial analogy, Crosby's philosophy highlights the need for appropriate measures to promote sustainability. Feigenbaum is best known for his 40 steps to quality improvement, which can be used to implement a quality management system. His work on cross-functional teamwork is related to the need for teams to implement sustainability. Specifically, cross-functional collaboration among departments is a success factor for sustainability (Petala, Weaver, Dutilh & Brezet, 2010), and may include internal organizational integration as well as inter-firm (external) collaboration (Homburg & Kuehnl, 2014). Taguchi's philosophy encourages improved product and process quality through removing adverse conditions. His philosophy of target-oriented quality encourages a philosophy of continuous improvement toward bringing a product exactly on target. Correspondingly, sustainability efforts should be focused on 'thinking outside the box' and 'removing adverse' conditions through carefully defining the system's scope and defining clear sustainability metrics. As the discussion here highlights, quality management philosophies can be used to direct sustainability implementation.

TQM Approaches & Sustainability.
We continue our discussion by reviewing quality approaches that have been applied to sustainability efforts and highlight specific case examples where the approach has been used. Typical TQM approaches include: Continuous Improvement and Employee Empowerment (both discussed

previously), benchmarking, Six Sigma Quality (DMAIC and DMADV), and JIT. Table 2 outlines each TQM approach as it applies to sustainability.

Benchmarking. Benchmarking, or the search for industry best practices that lead to superior performance, promotes a focus on processes and adaptation of other processes that work elsewhere to improve processes. Benchmarking can be used to assess and monitor sustainability performance (Sroufe & Melnyk, 2013), and provides a comparative analysis of the product by taking into account best competitors in the same market share (Fargnoli & DeMinicis, 2014). As an example of incorporating benchmarking into sustainability decision-making, a Medical products manufacture chose DuPont, which uses a 'phased gate approach' to integrate sustainability into NPD (Sroufe & Melny, 2013). DuPont uses a sustainability index that assesses products over 11 different criteria (Sroufe & Melnyk, 2013). SCOR, a SCM performance measurement system, ties emissions to processes that provides a structure for measuring environmental performance and assists in identifying where performance can be improved (Sroufe & Melnyk, 2013). The SCOR model can be used to assess the strategic environmental and through mapping, develop activities to address the gaps (Sroufe & Melnyk, 2013).

Six Sigma Quality. Six Sigma is a comprehensive, flexible system for achieving, sustaining and maximizing business success by minimizing defects and variability in processes (Krajewski et al., 2013). Some researchers view Six Sigma Quality as having a different focus than TQM (Krajewski et al., 2013), while others view Six Sigma Quality as a key concept in a TQM program (Heizer & Render, 2014). We adopt the latter philosophy here, and treat Six Sigma as a value-added approach to addressing quality – and sustainability implementation. Six Sigma Quality is a strategy that focuses on total customer satisfaction, follows the formal six sigma process known as DMAIC and uses seven tools to improve quality (check sheets, scatter diagrams, cause-and-effect diagrams, Pareto charts, flowcharts, histograms and statistical process control). Six Sigma Quality can be used to focus on customer sustainability requirements through data-driven decision-making, risk assessment, critical inputs, processes and outputs (McCarty et al., 2011).

DMAIC. The five-step improvement process, DMAIC (Define, Measure, Analyze, Improve and Control) can be applied to sustainability analysis. In the 'Design' phase, the team identifies the improvement opportunity, understands the task and problem, develops the problem statement, identifies critical customers' requirements, and determines the critical processes. The team is assigned, and develops its team charters, stakeholder analysis, 'Voice of the customer', process maps and barriers through flowchart and value stream analysis. During the 'Measure' phase, relevant sustainability data is collected and provides a product/process baseline. Tools useful during 'measure' include flowcharting, benchmarking, check sheets, and graphing. During the 'Analyze' phase, the true root causes of the sustainability problem that lead to customer dissatisfaction are determined through root cause analysis, statistical analysis, cause-and-effect diagrams, and control charts. In the 'Improve' phase, solutions are identified, evaluated and selected to correct and fix the root cause. Improvement tools include brainstorming, Failure Modes and Effects Analysis, and simulation, as well as a plan to address organizational changes to implement the solution. In the final phase, 'Control', actions and tools are implemented to keep the processes operating appropriately (including process documents and training records), results are disseminated, an ongoing monitoring and reporting plan is implemented, and metrics are gathered to demonstrate improvement.

A variation of DMAIC, DMADV can also be used to implement sustainability. DMADV requires a project champion, a black belt, a project charter and team functional experts. In DMADV, the process begins through 'Defining' project goals and customer (internal and external) deliverables. Then, the process moves on to 'Measuring' and determining customer needs and specifications. Followed by, 'Analyzing' the process options to meet the customer needs, 'Designing' development for the process to meet customer needs, and 'Verifying' design performance and ability to meet customer needs. Apex used the DMADV method to develop a Corporate Sustainability Program and to analyze a paper recycling process (McCarty et al., 2011).

JIT. JIT is a continuous improvement philosophy that is designed to produce products just as they are needed. JIT requires a quality management system to be effective. Specifically in a JIT system, quality must be designed into the products and processes, good quality raw materials must be used, and the employees must be empowered with the proper working equipment, tools, training, support and encouragement. One of JIT's focus is to remove non-value added processes and waste. Similarly, SSCM focuses on products, processes and packaging as sustainability efforts must be addressed in strategic, tactical and operational performance (Sroufe & Melnyk, 2013). SSCM considers waste as a symptom, not the root cause, links waste to processes, and considers waste management and elimination to be economically driven.

TQM TOOLS & SUSTAINABILITY.

Several quality tools were used to implement sustainability in SCM, as shown in Table 3. (Note: Table 3 is an overview and not intended to represent sustainability usage for every TQM tool.) Quality tools include, but are not limited to, affinity analysis, brainstorming, cause-and-effect analysis, check sheets, histograms, House of Quality (HoQ), Plan-Do-Check-Act Wheel, Pareto Analysis, process capability analysis, process control charts, process flow analysis, scatter diagrams, quality at the source, Quality Function Deployment (QFD), Quality and Environment Function Deployment (QEFD), Green Quality Function Deployment (G-QFD), and value stream mapping,

While the intent is not to review each tool in depth, we will review a few to demonstrate the correspondence from quality to sustainability. With Process Flow Analysis, six steps are used to evaluate the effectiveness of a process with respect to quality. To use process flow analysis for sustainability (Sroufe & Melnyk, 2013): (1) Determine desired sustainability outcome for the entire process and the associated sustainability metrics needed to evaluate the process's performance. (2) Identify and bound the critical process to focus efforts. (3) Document the sustainability for the existing process (to determine 'the current state' map). (4) Analyze the process and prioritize opportunities for improvement. (5) Recommend appropriate changes to the process (towards achieving the 'future state' map). (6) Implement the changes and monitor sustainability improvements.

One of the most commonly used TQM tools for sustainability integration is QFD. A literature review demonstrates the evolution of QFD in SSCM, particularly for NPD and process evaluation (Buyukozkan & Berkol, 2011). Green-QFD (that incorporated environmental requirements in NPD) was improved upon through a process noted as Green-QFD II by combining it with Life Cycle Analysis (LCA) and life cycle costing, which provided a mechanism to deploy customer, environmental, and cost requirements throughout the entire product development process (Zhang, Wang & Zhang, 1999). Similarly, researchers incorporated environmental sustainability in a process noted as QFD for Environment (QFDE), which is a four-phase method used in design for the environment in the early stages of NPD (Masui, Sakao, Kobayashi & Inaba, 2003). Later this method was extended further by integrating LCA and the theory of inventive problem-solving into QFD (Sakao, 2007). Other researchers documented a four-phase methodology using QFD that included an eco-profile strategies and analytical hierarchy processes (Reyes & Wright, 2001). Another research team incorporated Taguchi experimental design and the Taguchi loss function into QFD process to assist in NPD (Madu, Kuel &Madu, 2002). Yet another research team introduced an approach for identifying environmental improvement options by taking customer preferences into account and included LCA and a fuzzy approach based on the House of Quality (Bovea & Wang, 2003). Environmental sustainability was considered through a different method that developed an eco-quality function deployment (Eco-QFD) to aid a product design team in considering environmental concerns (Kuo et al., 2009). Several variations of sustainable QFD (sQFD) exist that mainly incorporate environmental factors into the NPD process (e.g. one applies an analytic network process (ANP) combined with fuzzy logic in QFD (Lin, Cheng, Tseng and Tsai, 2010); another used a sustainable concept comparison house (Halog, 2004), and another applied QFD to improving sustainability in Norwegian fishing fleet (Utne, 2009)). Another applied group applied QFD with ANP and zero-one goal programming to determine design requirements to achieve SSCM for a company in the fuel sector of energy (Buyukozkan & Berkol, 2011). In a more recent variation of QFD, researchers redesigned a garden trimmer – but included social and environmental sustainability in their analysis (Fargnoli & DeMinicis, 2014). Obviously, QFD has been used to incorporate sustainability in NPD; but researchers are still developing methods to address all of their needs, particularly social sustainability.

DISCUSSION

We began this paper by reviewing the key concepts of quality, sustainability and supply chains. While we noted much of the integration of key concepts – TQM with SCM yielding SCQM, and sustainability with SCM resulting in the field of SSCM, a framework to integrate sustainability, quality, and global SCM does not exist in literature today. Therefore, we began our discussion by reviewing the similarities between TQM and sustainability in SCM. The literature review of TQM and sustainability demonstrates the strong similarities between implementing quality and sustainability into a supply chain. The three main TQM principles – customer focus, employee involvement (that is, an organizational culture change) and a continuous improvement – are relevant to implementing sustainability as well. There is a call by society and its customers for sustainable products, services and processes to address economic, environmental and social sustainability concerns. The organizational culture must promote sustainability efforts, and employees must be given the knowledge and tools to empower them to make sustainability changes.

The culture must encourage continuous sustainability efforts throughout the organization, so more than 'just the low hanging' easily implemented sustainability efforts are undertaken. Similar to implementing quality over 30 years ago, implementing sustainability requires support and a cultural change.

Regardless of a company's efforts to implement social or environmental sustainability into the supply chain processes, sustainability does not exist if the company is not profitable (Wu & Pagell, 2011). Traditional accounting practices do not facilitate TBL sustainability efforts (Ageron et al., 2012). This paper highlights the similar goals to emphasize prevention costs in both quality and sustainability exists. Researchers can assist practitioners to develop a corresponding 'Cost of Sustainability' framework to assist in reporting and monitoring, as well as encourage sustainability efforts.

A review of the quality gurus' philosophies demonstrates the potential to apply the quality philosophies to sustainability implementation. Regardless of which philosopher's system is used, the underlying principle is to change the culture – from top management through the employees to the supply chain members.

Review of TQM approaches (benchmarking, continuous improvement, employee empowerment, Six Sigma quality, and JIT) indicates that these approaches have been used in sustainability efforts already. A general review of TQM tools indicates that many tools have been used in sustainability efforts as well. In particular, many versions of QFD exist to assist with evaluation and incorporation of sustainability into NPD. The literature review, while not comprehensive, supports the use of TQM – and possibly, the broader SCQM principles – to implement sustainability in SCM.

For the practitioner, this highlights that the framework and techniques to implement sustainability are ones that most already know – that is, quality management approaches and techniques can be applied and assist in sustainability implementation. Managers – particular top management, should develop the strategy, vision, mission, and goals to drive sustainability, provide appropriate resources, and monitor the sustainability efforts through appropriate performance measures (Fish, 2015; Gupta & Palsule-Desai, 2011). Some of the best practices discussed here to support these efforts include an organizational change with a top level manager charged with sustainability efforts, providing sustainability training to employees of the organization – and possibly suppliers' employees, cross-functional teams, enhanced communication, encouraging supply chain partnerships through supplier certification programs that include sustainability, using environmental management systems, and developing visible, transparent and accurate practices and reports on sustainability efforts and disseminating this information to the supply chain and end customers (Fish, 2015; Ozcelik & AvciOzturk, 2014). Much work remains to develop a comprehensive framework to extend these basic principles into the real world. Academics can continue to assist practitioners by fully developing a 'Sustainable Supply Chain Quality Management' (SSCQM) framework.

REFERENCES

Ageron, B., Gunasekaran, A. & Spalanzan, A. (2012). Sustainable supply chain management: An empirical study. *International Journal of Production Economics*, 140(1), 168-182. http://dx.doi.org/10.1016/j.ijpe.2011.04.007

Allen, M.W. Walker, K.L., & Brady, R. (2012). Sustainability Discourse within a Supply Chain Relationship: Mapping Convergence and Divergence. *Journal of Business Communication*. 49(3), pp. 210-236. http://dx.doi.org/10.1177/0021943612446732

APICS Dictionary (2010). APICS Dictionary: Thirteenth Edition. APICS – The Association for Operations Management, Chicago, Illinois. ISBN: 978-0-615-39441-1.

Asby, A., Leat, M. & Hudson-Smith, M. (2012). Making connnections: A review of supply chain management and sustainability literature.

Supply Chain Management: An International Journal, 17(5), 497-516. http://dx.doi.org/10.1108/13598541211258573

Azar, A., Kahnali, R.A., & Taghavi, A. (2010). Relationship between Supply Chain Quality Management Practices and their Effects on Organisational Performance. *Singapore Management Review*, 2010 1st Half, 32(1), 45-68.

Beske, P., Land, A., & Seuring, S. (2014). Sustainable supply chain management practices and dynamic capabilities in the food industry: A critical analysis of the literature. *International Journal of Production Economics*, 152, 131-143. http://dx.doi.org/10.1016/j.ijpe.2013.12.026

Bovea, M.D., & Wang, B. (2007). Green quality function deployment: a methodology for integrating customer, cost and environmental requirements in product design. *International Journal of Environ. Conscious Design Manufacture*, 12(4), 9-19.

Bovea, M.D. & Wang, B. (2003). Identifying environmental improvement options by combining life cycle assessment and fuzzy set theory. *International Journal of Production Research*, 41(3), 595-609. http://dx.doi.org/10.1080/0020754021000033878

Buyukozkan, G. & Berkol, C. (2011). Designing a sustainable supply chain using an integrated analytic network process and goal programming approach in quality function deployment. *Expert Systems with Applications*, 38, 13731-13748.

Campbell, J. L. (2007). Why would corporations behave in socially responsible ways? An institutional theory of corporate social responsibility. *Academic Management Review*, 32(3), 946-967. http://dx.doi.org/10.5465/AMR.2007.25275684

CEOForumGroup (2009). Engaging external stakeholders: Sustainability performance. Retrieved from http://www.ceoforum.com.au/article-detail.cfm?cid=8981&t=/Rob-Hogarth-KPMG/Sustainability-performance/

Corbett, C.J., & Klassen, R. D. (2006). Extending the horizons: environmental excellence as key to improving operations. *Manufacturing & Service Operations Management*, 8(1), 5-22. http://dx.doi.org/10.1287/msom.1060.0095

Crosby, P. (1979). *Quality Is Free.* New York, McGraw-Hill.

Curkovic, S., Melnyk, S.A., Handfield, R.B., & Calantone, R. (2000). Investigating the linkage between total quality management and environmentally responsible manufacturing. IEEE Transactions on Engineering Management, 47(4), 444-464. http://dx.doi.org/10.1109/17.895340

Curkovic, S., Sroufe, R., & Landeros, R. (2008). Measuring TQEM returns for the application of quality frameworks. *Business Strategy and the Environment,* 17(2), 93-106.

Delai, I. & Takahashi, S. (2013). Corporate sustainability in emerging markets: insight from the practices reported by the Brazilian retailers. *Journal of Cleaner Production,* 47, 211-221. http://dx.doi.org/10.1016/j.jclepro.2012.12.029

Deming, W.E. (1986). *Out of the Crisis.* MIT Center for Advanced Engineering Study, Cambridge, MA.

Devinney, T.M. (2009). Is the socially responsible corporation a myth? The good, the bad, and the ugly of the corporate social responsibility. *Academy of Management Perspectives,* 23(2), 44-56. http://dx.doi.org/10.5465/AMP.2009.39985540

Driessen, P.H., Hillebrand, B., Kok, R.A.W. & Verhallen, T.M.M. (2013). Green New Product Development: The Pivotal Role of Product Greenness. *IEEE Transactions on Engineering Management,* 60(2), 315-326. doi:10.1109/TEM.2013.2246792

Ernzer, M. & Birkhofer, H. (2002). Selecting methods for life cycle design based on the needs of a company. *Proceedings of the 7th International Conference on Design,* Zagreb, 1305-1310.

Evans, J., & Lindsay, W. (2002). *The Management and Control of Quality, Fifth Edition.* South-Western College Publishing, Cincinnati, Ohio.

Fargnoli, M. & DeMinicis, M. (2014). Design Management for Sustainability: An integrated approach for the development of sustainable products. *Journal of Engineering and Technology Management,* 34, 29-45. http://dx.doi.org/10.1016/j.jengtecman.2013.09.005

Feigenbaum, A.V. (1956). *Total Quality Control.* Harvard Business Review. Nov/Dec, 34(6), 93-101.

Fish, L.A. (2015). Managerial Best Practices to Promote Sustainable Supply Chain Management and New Product Development. Applications of Contemporary Management Approaches in Supply Chains", ISBN 978-953-51-4197-6, InTech Publisher. http://dx.doi.org/10.5772/59581

Fish, L.A. (2011). Supply Chain Quality Management, Supply Chain Management - Pathways for Research and Practice, Dilek Onkal (Ed.), ISBN: 978-953-307-294-4, InTech Publisher, 25-42. Available from: http://www.intechopen.com/articles/show/title/supply-chain-quality-management.

Foster, S.T. Jr. (2008). Towards an understanding of Supply Chain Quality Management. *Journal of Operations Management,* 26, 461–467. http://dx.doi.org/10.1016/j.jom.2007.06.003

Gmelin, H. & Seuring, S. (2014). Determinants of a sustainable new product development. *Journal of Cleaner Production,* 69, 1-9. doi:10.1016/j.jclepro.2014.01.053

Gupta, S. & Palsule-Desai, O.D. (2011). *Sustainable supply chain management: Review and research opportunities.* Indian Institute of Management Bangalore Management Review, 23, 234-245. http://dx.doi.org/10.1016/j.iimb.2011.09.007

Halog, A. (2004). An approach to selection of sustainable product improvement alternatives with data uncertainty. *Journal of Sustainable Product Design,* 4, 3-19. http://dx.doi.org/10.1007/s10970-006-0002-y

Heizer, J. & Render, B. (2014). *Operations Management, Eleventh Edition,* Prentice Hall, Upper Saddle River, NJ.

Homburg, C., & Kuehnl, C. (2014). Is the more always better? A comparative study of internal and external integration practices in new product and new service development. *Journal of Business Research,* 67, 1360-1367. http://dx.doi.org/10.1016/j.jbusres.2013.08.017.

Krajewski, L.J., Ritzman, L.P., & Malhotra, M.K. (2013). *Operations Management: Processes & Supply Chains.* Pearson Education, Inc., Upper Saddle River, NJ.

Koh, S.C.L., Demirbag, M. & Bayraktar, E. (2007). The Impact of Supply Chain Practices on Performance of SMEs. *Industrial Management & Data Systems*, 107(1), 103-124. http://dx.doi.org/10.1108/0263557071 0719089

Kuo, T.C., Wub, HJ.H. & Shieh, J. I. (2009). Integration of environmental considerations in quality function deployment by using fuzzy logic. *Expert Systems with Applications, 36, 7148-7156.* http://dx.doi.org/10 .1016/j.eswa.2008.08.029

Lin, Y.H., Cheng, H.P., Tseng, M.L., & Tsai, J.C.C. (2010). Using QFD and ANP to analyze the environmental production requirements in linguistic preferences. *Expert Systems with Applications*, 37(3), 2186-2196. http://dx.doi.org/10.1016/j.eswa.2009.07.065

Madu, C.N., Kuel, C.H. & Madu, I.E. (2002). A hierarchic metric approach for integration of green issues in manufacturing: A paper recycling application. *Journal of Environmental Management*, 64, 261-272. http:// dx.doi.org/10.1006/jema.2001.0498

Masui, K., Sakao, T., Kobayashi, M. & Inaba, A. (2003). Applying quality function deployment to environmentally conscious design. *International Journal of Quality and Reliability Management*, 20(1), 90-106. http://dx.doi.org/10.1108/02656710310453836

McCarty, T., Jordan, M. & Probst, D. (2011). *Six Sigma for Sustainability: How Organizations Design and Deploy Winning Environmental Programs.* McGraw-Hill. ISBN 978-0-07-175245-9.

Ozcelik, F. & AvciOzturk, B. (2014). A research on barriers to sustainable supply chain management and sustainable supplier selection criteria. Dokuz Eylul Universitesi Sosyal Bilimeler Enstitusu dergisi, 16(2), 250-277.

Petala, E., Wever, R., Dutilh, C., & Brezet, H.C. (2010). The role of new product development briefs in implementing sustainability: a case study. *Journal of Engineering Technology Management*, 27(3-4), 172-182. http://dx.doi.org/10.1016/j.jengtecman.2010.06.004

Porter, M. & van der Linde, C. (1995). Green and competitive: ending the stalemate. *Harvard Business Review*, 73(5), pp. 120-134.

Reyes, D.E.S. & Wright, T.L. (2001). A design for the environment methodology to support an environmental management system. *Integrated Manufacturing Systems*, 12(5), 323-332. http://dx.doi.org/10.1108/EUM0000000005710

Robinson, C.J. & Malhotra, M. K. (2005). Defining the concept of Supply Chain Quality Management and its relevant to academic and industrial practice. *International Journal of Production Economics*, 96, 315-337. http://dx.doi.org/10.1016/j.ijpe.2004.06.055

Sakao, T. (2007). A QFD-centred design methodology for environmentally conscious product design. *International Journal of Production Research*, 45(18), 4143-4162. http://dx.doi.org/10.1080/00207540701450179

Seuring, D. (2004). Industrial ecology, life cycles, supply chains – differences and interrelations. *Business Strategy and the Environment*, 3(5), 306-319. http://dx.doi.org/10.1002/bse.418

Seuring, D. & Muller, M. (2008). From a literature review to a conceptual framework for sustainable supply chain management. *Journal of Cleaner Production*, 16(15), 1699-1710. http://dx.doi.org/10.1016/j.jclepro.2008.04.020

Simchi-Levi, D. Kaminsky, P. & Simchi-Levi, E. (2008). *Designing & Managing the Supply Chain: Concepts, Strategies & Case Studies, Third Edition*, McGraw-Hill, Irwin, NY, NY.

Sroufe, R.P. & Melnyk, S.A. (2013). Developing Sustainable Supply Chains to Drive Value: Management Issues, Insights, Concepts and Tools. Business Expert Press. ISBN-13:978-1-60649-372-4.

Tague, N.R. (2004). *The Quality Toolbox, Second Edition*, ASQ Quality Press, Milwaukee, WI.

Talib, F., Rahman, Z. & Quereeshi, M.N. (2010). Pareto Analysis of Total Quality Management Factors Critical to Success for Service Industries. International Journal of Quality Research, 4(2), 155-168.

Talib, F. & Rahman, Z. (2010). Critical Success Factors of TQM in Service Organizations: A Proposed Model. *Service Marketing Quarterly*, 31(2), 363-380. http://dx.doi.org/10.1080/15332969.2010.486700

Tan, K.C. (2001). A Framework of Supply Chain Management Literature. *European Journal of Purchasing and Supply Management*, 7(1), 39-48. http://dx.doi.org/10.1016/S0969-7012(00)00020-4

Utne, I.B. (2009). Improving eh environmental performance of the fishing fleet by use of quality function deployment (QFD). *Journal of Cleaner Production*, 17, 724-731. http://dx.doi.org/10.1016/j.jclepro.2008.11.005

Vachon, S. & Mao, Z. (2008). Linking supply chain strength to sustainable development: a country-level analysis. *Journal of Cleaner Production*, 16(15), pp. 1552-1560. doi:10.1016/j.jclepro.2008.04.012

Walmart Supplier Sustainabiltiy Assessment: 15 Questions for Suppliers. Accessed January 27, 2015, http://az204679.vo.msecnd.net/media/documents/r_3863.pdf

Willard, B. (2012). *The new sustainability advantage, 10th Anniversary Edition*. Canada: New Society Publishers.

World Commission on Environment and Development (WCED) (1987). Our Common Future. Oxford University Press. Oxford.

Wu, Z. & Pagell, M. (2011). Balancing priorities: Decision-making in sustainable supply chain management. *Journal of Operations Management*, 29, 577-590. http://dx.doi.org/10.1016/j.jom.2010.10.001

Zhang, Y., Wang, H.-P. & Zhang, C. (1999). Green QFD-II: A life cycle approach for environmentally conscious manufacturing by integrating LCA and LCC into QFD matrices. *International Journal of Production Research*, 37(5), 1075-1091. http://dx.doi.org/10.1080/00207549919141

WEB APPENDIX

A web appendix for this paper is available at:

http://www.businessresearchconsortium.org/pro/brcpro2015p8.pdf

A Literature Review and Directions for Future Research on International Student Perceptions of Online versus Face-to-Face Education: Student-centered Characteristics

Lynn A. Fish and Coral R. Snodgrass

Professors of Management
Richard J. Wehle School of Business
Canisius College
Email: fishl@canisius.edu
Email: snodgras@canisius.edu

Professor Fish is the corresponding author.

Abstract

As higher education institutions continue to integrate online education into their curricula, different cultural perspectives on the value of online versus face-to-face education will undoubtedly impact continued proliferation. Currently, some cultures are more accepting of online (Zhu et al., 2009; Lin et al., 2010), while others believe online education is inferior to traditional education (Asunka, 2008). Research on this topic has accelerated in the last five years and primarily consists of cross-cultural comparisons. While research on student perceptions can be divided into 2 streams: student and program characteristics, the purpose of this study is to review the current literature with respect to student characteristics and offer suggested future directions for research. Perceptions are explored with respect to student characteristics of age, major/level, gender, previous online experience and student perceptions. The current literature has implications for today's administrators and instructors and offers researchers several avenues for continued research.

Keywords: International Student Perceptions, Online, Face-to-face

LITERATURE REVIEW: DIMENSIONS OF DIFFERENCE

The Babson Survey Research Group highlights the increase in online education throughout the higher education system (Allen & Seaman, 2013). Academic administrators believe that learning outcomes through online education are the same or superior to those in traditional FTF class-rooms (Allen & Seaman, 2013); however, critics argue that due to intrinsic differences, online education does not replicate the learning that occurs in the traditional classroom (Bejerano, 2008). As online education continues to expand its horizons and technology continues to evolve, research on student perceptions in the online learning environment continues (e.g. Allen & Seaman, 2013; Fish & Snodgrass, 2014, 2015; Perreault, Waldman, Alexander & Zhao, 2008; Tanner, Noser, and Langford, 2003; Tanner, Noser, Fuselier & Totaro, 2004a; 2004b; Tanner, Noser, Totaro & Birch, 2006; Tanner et al., 2009). Additionally, as online courses reach across borders, and based upon previous literature that suggests that foreign students have different needs than their Western classmates in face-to-face (FTF) classes (Selvarajah, 2006), students' cultural backgrounds affect their perception of the online learning environment (Popov et al., 2012). With this in mind, we present an overview of the literature on student perceptions of online versus FTF education with respect to cultural implications with a focus on the student-centered research.

What do we know about cultural perceptions about online education now? Each culture has its own way of processing information, learning, instructing and solving problems (Lee, Becker & Nobre, 2012). A nation's culture affects students' engagement, relations and perceived benefits from online education (Lee et al., 2012). There are differences in the manner in which people learn and different cultural learning models (Fang, 2007; Brislin et al., 1975; Jin, 2002; Charlesworth, 2008). Cultural backgrounds can differ in terms of cognitive styles, rules of behavior, communication styles, attitudes and belief systems as well as human relations (Hofstede, 1991). Cultural backgrounds present distinct challenges and opportunities to the growth of online education - particularly related differences in academic abilities, gender, perceptions of time, professional status, student expectations and tolerance for criticism (Chase et al., 2002).

Cultural differences impact upon student perceptions between online and FTF education and pose another potential barrier to online education (Grandon et al., 2005; Lin, Liu, Lee & Magjuka, 2010; Olesova et al., 2011). Previous studies examined differences across cultures (Cronje, 2011; Chew & Yee, 2015; Grandon et al., 2005; Li & Kirkup, 2005; Popov et al., 2012, 2014; Zhu et al., 2009) and within cultures (Adler et al., 2001; Chase et al., 2002; Hamdan, 2014; Okwumabua et al., 2010). For example, in a recent cross-cultural comparison, U.S. students tend to work more independently than Chinese (Lin et al., 2010). While a study at a large, southeastern University in the U.S., both African-American and Caucasian American students' perceptions view online learning positively (Ashong & Commander, 2012).

While some countries, such as China and India, appear to be attractive destinations for online education; world-wide acceptance of online learning is not evident. In some countries online education is perceived as second-rate to FTF education or believed to be purchased without assessment (Khoo and Azizan, 2004; Hamdan, 2014), and therefore, these countries enacted policies that do not recognize online degrees (Asunka,

2008; Kathawala et al., 2003; Hamdan, 2014). In many nations where education is different between men and women, such as east African nations, a lack of advancement in online education and a lack of research into how cultural factors may be impacted by online activity (Hamdan, 2014) may impact upon future growth and acceptance in these areas.

A study performed early in the century found that as students experienced more online learning, their attitudes toward online learning and blended approaches may change (Benbunan-Fich & Hiltz, 2003; Karns, 2005). This shift in students' perceptions appears to be continuing. For example, while previous research indicated differences between Australians and Asian students in student perceptions (Ramburuth & McCormick, 2001; Smith & Smith, 1999), a more recent study (as noted previously) found no significant differences existed on many factors for these groups (Chew & Yee, 2015). Another study reported on how Chinese students' motivation and learning strategies changed significantly towards a social-constructivist learning approach after an online collaborative experience (Zhu et al., 2009). Since many studies were performed over a decade ago, what are students' *current* perceptions regarding online versus FTF?

As education methods change to incorporate more online elements, educators and administrators need to understand these perceptual differences to be successful. Recent research noted the importance of instructor skills in teaching and called for instructors to gain a better, stronger understanding of the cultural and technological environment when designing learning activities (particularly discussion forums) (Chew & Yee, 2015). Current research on students' perceptions can be divided into two streams of research: student-centered and program-centered. The amount of research in these areas has increased significantly in recent years, and in this paper we focus on the literature pertinent to student perceptions, specific student-centered characteristics and cultural implications between online and FTF.

In a traditional FTF classroom, instructors recognize and react to student emotional states (facial expressions, gestures, eye contact and speech) and individual student differences (maturity and experience) to modify their lessons toward a positive learning environment (Reilly, Gallager-Lepak & Killion, 2012). However, online instructors cannot perceive these factors in 'real' time and modify their responses instantly. These factors may impact upon students' attitudes and perceptions. Motivation, belief, confidence, computer anxiety, fear, boredom, apprehension, enthusiasm, pride and embarrassment (Konradt & Sulz, 2001) are important antecedents of the student's inclination toward online learning (Chawla & Joshi, 2012). Student-centered studies concentrate on differences between students' perceptions based upon demographic factors, such as age, academic level (undergraduate or graduate), gender, or previous experience (with the online environment), or by student perceptional characteristics, such as student motivation, discipline, self-directed learning, independence, and cost and time investment. Also, relevant to student perceptions are each student's personal preference, happiness, and appropriateness for the learning environment as well as potentially whether the student took an online preparation course. Cultural studies add another dimension. We continue by reviewing some of the literature with respect to culture, student characteristics (divided into demographic and perceptual sections) and online perceptions, and offer recommendations for future research within each subtopic.

Student Characteristics: Demographic

Age. Two streams of research exist with respect to age: one research stream demonstrates that age has a positive impact upon students' perceptions of online learning (Tanner et al., 2004-1; 2004-2), and another research stream that indicates age does not impact student perceptions (Tanner et al., 2003). One study found that adult students (21 and older) perceive online education more favorably than younger students (Tanner et al., 2003). Younger students, regardless of their culture, appear to be more technologically savvy and adaptable to different cultures (Lee et al., 2012). To our knowledge, age and cultural implications have not been fully explored, which leads to Research Questions #1: *Are younger cultures more inclined to accept online courses than older members? As people age, do they accept online courses more readily? Does the Millennial generation accept online education more willingly than Gen-Xers or Gen-Yers?*

Major/ Level. Several studies explored perceptual differences by major and educational level with the majority of online studies since 2004 focusing on undergraduate students (Tsai & Chiang, 2013). For example, cross-cultural researchers compared undergraduate students' perceptions between Dutch and International students (Popov et al., 2012), Malaysian and Australian freshman and sophomores (Chew & Yee, 2015), Korean and American students (Grandon et al., 2005), and Flemish and Chinese students (Zhu et al., 2009). Graduate student perceptual studies explored Australian (Pillay & James, 2014), Asian and European (Selvarajah, 2006), and South African and Sudanese (Cronje, 2011) perspectives. Additionally, one study evaluated the impact of online education on the culture and culture on online education in Saudi Arabia for undergraduate women (Hamdan, 2014). These studies appear to focus on one particular level – undergraduate or graduate, and a comparison between two cultures, which raises Research Question #2a: *Do undergraduates and graduates from different cultures perceive online and FTF learning environments differently?*

Other studies, focused on the U.S., compare undergraduate and graduate perspectives for business versus non-business students (Tanner et al., 2004-1; 2004-2), business graduates and undergraduates (Fish & Snodgrass, 2014), and graduate versus undergraduate nursing student (Billings, Skiba & Connors, 2005). In our previous study, undergraduate and graduate business students did not differ with respect to their perception of online versus FTF environments for students and disliked the instructor interaction (Fish & Snodgrass, 2014). Graduate business students tended to dislike the self-directed online environment slightly more than their undergraduate counterparts, and graduates were slightly more hesitant to accept online as a viable alternative to FTF. Graduate nursing students spent more time on their courses, needed more instructor attention and found faculty availability to be an issue compared to undergraduates. Since the majority of comparative studies focus on American students studying in the U.S., this prompts Research Question #2b: *Within each culture, do undergraduates and graduates perceive online and FTF learning environments differently?*

Gender. With respect to gender differences, results differ with some studies indicating that gender does not play a factor in student perceptions for students (Fish & Snodgrass, 2014; Tanner et al., 2003), while others indicate a difference (Tanner et al., 2004-1; 2004-2). Some research suggests that males are significantly more comfortable with computers (Kay, 2009) and Internet competencies are higher (Tekinarslan, 2011) than females. Other studies indicate that women experience a richer, more valuable presence in online learning and are more satisfied than males (Ashong & Commander, 2012; Johnson, 2011). Regardless of culture, men tend to be more individualistic, while women tend to be collectivistic (Tsaw et al., 2011). (Individualistic people tend to be raised in Western cultures and focus on their own personal goals, while collectivistic people tend to be raised in Eastern cultures and focus on the group goals.) Gender issues can affect online learning as group composition, degree of participation and elaboration may differ by gender (with men using fewer words and less elaboration), and females are more likely to initiate conversation with questions and requests for information while males tend to explain and express disagreement more frequently (Prinsen et al., 2007). In one study of social loafing (whereby one group member does not contribute to group work fully or undermines the group work process), men displayed more social loafing than women (Tsaw et al., 2011). Comparing African-American perceptions to other American perceptions, women's perspectives are significantly different than men's as women view instructor assistance, friendliness, trust and interest in students, student interaction, and collaboration more positively than their male counterparts (Ashong & Commander, 2012). Perhaps, nowhere in the world are gender issues more paramount than in societies that continue to separate men and women in the FTF – and online classroom, such as in Saudi Arabia (Hamdan, 2014). Differences around the world with respect to gender roles in society prompt educational questions as well, specifically Research Question#3: *Do men and women in other cultures (with different gender roles) perceive online education differently? Do women from male dominated cultures experience a cultural shift as in the Saudi Arabian study? Do men from male-dominated cultures differ in their perspective of online education than women?*

Previous Experience. According to learning theory, the more someone is exposed and uses a particular method or technology, the better and more adept they become. Students with prior online experience perceived online courses more favorably than those without prior experience (Tanner et al., 2003). In criminal justice studies, students who have never taken an online course have different perceptions of online learning than those who have (Dobbs et al., 2009). However, in a study of business students – regardless of whether they took or did not take online courses, students favored FTF courses; however, most online respondents only took one course (Fish & Snodgrass, 2014).

As the number of online courses increases, the students' acceptance of online courses increases as well; however, researcher found that at least 5 online courses are necessary for student to perceive that they learn more in the online environment than FTF (Dobbs et al., 2009). Self-efficacy, which is a student's belief in his or her own abilities to perform a given task in the online environment, and ease of use may be significant predictors for online learning (Grandon et al., 2005). Self-efficacy increases as a student's Internet usage frequency increases and is highly related to their prior computer and Internet experiences (Tekinarslan, 2011). Self-efficacy had an indirect impact upon perceived ease of use only for American students but not Koreans (Grandon et al., 2005).

While students without online experience perceive faculty as having low student expectations for students in online classes, students with online experience - especially as the number of online courses increases, perceive faculty as having higher expectations that increases with more experience (Dobbs et al., 2009). Studies evaluating student's perceptions of the continued proliferation of online courses demonstrate an increasing acceptance of online as being equal to or better than FTF (Mortagy & Boghikian-Whitby, 2010; Perreault et al., 2008) particularly as students take more online courses (Dobbs et al., 2009; Mortagy & Boghikian-Whitby, 2010; Perreault et al., 2008). Similarly, our survey instrument indicated that as students take more courses, their perceptions of the online environment improved, and their perception that online courses were more difficult than traditional classes increased (Fish & Snodgrass, 2014). Students modification of their perceptions over time, coupled with culture which lacks studies to test this effect, prompt Research Questions #4: *For different cultures, do students' perceptions change as they take additional online courses? Is '5' the 'magic number' between which students' perceptions between online and FTF shift from FTF to online preference?*

Student Characteristics: Perceptual Characteristics

Student Motivation, Discipline, Self-directed Learning and Independence. With the increase in online courses, understanding the factors that motivate students from different countries and cultures to take online courses is an important factor to consider (Grandon et al., 2005). In general, students are more motivated in courses when course content interests them and they find the material to be relevant (Adler et al., 2001). With regard to student motivation, results are mixed as some studies indicate that the online environment increases student motivation and self-esteem (Kearlsey, 1996) or increases critical thinking and work motivation (Larson & Sung, 2009). Other studies indicate that the online environment offers low motivation for students to learn (Fish & Snodgrass, 2014; Maltby & Whittle, 2000) with retention issues (Abouchedid & Eid, 2004; Carr, 2000) and low student satisfaction (Kenny, 2003; Muilenburg & Berge, 2005). Individualistic students are more motivated to participate in online learning then collectivistic students (Tapanes et al.,

2009); however, in one study, Chinese students' motivation and learning strategies changed significantly towards a social-constructivist learning approach after an online collaborative experience (Zhu et al., 2009).

A more recent study indicates that students view e-learning as a commitment (Chawla & Joshi, 2012). Online students should be motivated and disciplined (Schott et al., 2003) as students that are not self-motivated and committed will not enjoy the online learning environment (Rivera & Rice, 2002). Online learning requires self-directed learning and autonomy, but self-discipline and motivation are also required to complete the course (Gifford, 1998; Kearsley, 2002). One study revealed that the Sudanese exhibited high levels of power distance towards their South African instructors but were reluctant to take responsibility for their own learning (Cronje, 2011). With online learning, students may feel an internal locus of control, which is the ability to exercise a degree of personal, internally-driven control over life decisions (Ohara, 2004). Saudi Arabian women experienced an increase in independence through online education as they had greater control over the learning process and discussed points of view and experienced different ways of thinking, different styles of writing and different approaches to improving their communication skills (Hamdan, 2014). Regardless of the environment, some students regard collaborative learning negatively and always prefer to work independently (Hiltz & Turoff, 2005). Students' desires to work independently versus collectively differ by cultures as shown by a study comparing U.S. students who preferred independent work to Chinese students, who preferred group work (Lin et al., 2010).

The research presented here demonstrates a variety of student perceptions, which leads to the general research question: Research Question #5: *Do business students from different cultural backgrounds perceive motivation, self-directed learning, discipline and independence equally in the online and FTF learning environments?*

Time and Cost Investment. On one hand, while students perceive the time flexibility to take the course (Chawla & Joshi, 2012; Grandon et al., 2005), they perceive online learning to be more time consuming particularly with respect to class activities and homework assignments (Dobbs et al., 2009; Gifford, 1998; Perreault et al., 2008). Good time management skills are critical in online learning (Cheung & Kan, 2002). Saudi Arabian women experienced an increase in time management through online education as they were able to plan their time better (Hamdan, 2014). Student beliefs regarding online include the overall experience, exposure and derived value (Chawla & Joshi, 2012), which may also include the educational benefit and monetary cost associated with a course. Students who had never taken an online course indicated that they felt the value from an online course would be less than FTF (Chawla & Joshi, 2012). In our study, online students were indifferent to time demands (Fish & Snodgrass, 2014). These results prompt Research Question #6: *Do business students from different cultural backgrounds perceive the time and cost investments to online learning and FTF learning equally?*

Preference, Happiness and Appropriateness for Learning Environment. While not intended to be a comprehensive review of literature in this area, clearly ambiguity currently exists in the debate between online and FTF education. Student satisfaction research with online versus FTF formats results are mixed as some studies indicate that the courses are equally effective across formats (Fowler, 2005; Horspool & Lange, 2012; Topper, 2007), while others show a preference to FTF over online environments (Mullen & Tallent-Runnels 2006), and others show a higher satisfaction for online learning (Connolly, MacArthur, Stansfield & McLelan, 2007). One study found that 10-20% of students always prefer FTF (Hiltz & Turoff, 2005). In general, when students perceive e-learning as useful, they are more likely to accept and learn online (Tung & Chang, 2008). In our literature review, a study that compared student perceptions between online and FTF across cultures for appropriateness is lacking. Research Questions #7: *Do students, regardless of their native culture, prefer the online or FTF learning environment? Are students from different cultural backgrounds happy in their learning environment? Do students* *from different cultural backgrounds feel that online learning is appropriate at the University?*

Online Orientation. Online education requires students to believe in their own computer abilities, or self-efficacy. Orientation courses for students new to the online environment should be offered (Perreault Waldman, Alexander & Zhao, 2002) as even students with technical expertise report benefits from an orientation program prior to their online experience (Clerkin, 2004). Initial studies on requirements for students prior to enrollment favored using training or tutorials (Perrault et al., 2002); however, more recent studies indicate that today's online students felt they are adequately prepared for online education without prior training (Perreault et al., 2008; Fish & Snodgrass, 2014). Since student online perceptions are being sought in this study, student's previous background regarding orientations may be an important factor in their perspectives. Research Questions #8: *Regardless of culture, do students take online orientation courses prior to taking an online course? Given different cultures, what is the relationship between an online preparation course and student perceptions?*

Cultural Student Differences. In addition to the demographic and perceptual characteristic differences between students, there are general differences in the way that different cultures address different student learning styles and requirements. For example, Chinese participants feel that they are less opinionated and critical than their U. S. counterparts (Thompson & Ku, 2005). Added to these additional complexities, language competencies magnify cultural issues when completing an online course (Ku & Lohr, 2003). Educational objective differences between cultures may be significantly different. For example, European and students of European backgrounds (such as New Zealanders) have different educational objectives to Chinese students (Selvarajah, 2006). Chinese students took courses to improve their standing with business associates (in support of reducing the power distance through education in a collectivist Confucianist culture (Bond & Hofstede, 1998)), while New

Zealanders took courses to improve individual skills for a potential career challenge and as a personal challenge (in supports of their individualist societies) (Selvarajah, 2006). Another cross-cultural study that compared US and South Korean students intentions to take online courses, American students chose to take online courses due to the perceived convenience, subjective norm ('social pressure to perform') and perceived ease of use, while Korean students chose to take online courses due to perceived quality and subjective norms (Grandon et al., 2005). Online assessment methods as they relate to the learning styles of a changing student population need to be considered (Selvarajah, 2006). In general, other research questions include Research Questions #9: *Does the nationality of a student impact upon his preferred learning environment? Does the nationality of a student impact upon his ability to learn online?*

DISCUSSION

While the above literature review is not comprehensive, it highlights the different and mixed results that exist between and within cultures with respect to student characteristics and preferences for online education. This literature review demonstrates that each individual student with different cultural backgrounds may respond differently based upon their age, academic level, gender, and previous experience in the online environment. Clearly, culture impacts upon each student's perceived motivation, discipline, self-directed learning style, independence, and cost and time investment perspectives. Students' preferences for online and FTF vary as well as their happiness in one environment or the other. Given today's highly technological student body, students accept the online learning community (Fish & Snodgrass, 2014). Several studies note that students' perceptions changed over time (Benbunan-Fich & Hiltz, 203; Karns, 2005; Ramburuth & McCormick, 2001; Smith & Smith, 1999; Zhu et al., 2009), and recent research appears to indicate that the Millennials generation regards online education differently and are more accepting than Gen-Xers or Gen-Yers (Chew & Yee, 2015). As online education continues to be 'borderless', instructors need to incorporate design elements and activities to bridge these cultural gaps. This is a 'moving target' but needs guidance to foster student development – for all cultures. Therefore, as our research questions highlight, much work remains to uncover and guide instructors to address the diverse student body's needs in the online environment in order to meet each individual student's learning requirements.

REFERENCES

Abouchedid, K., & Eid, G.M. (2004). E-learning challenges in the Arab World: Revelations from a case study profile. *Quality Assurance in Education*, 12(1), 15-27. http://dx.doi.org/10.1108/09684880410517405

Adler, R.W., Milne, M.J. & Stablein, R. (2001). Situated motivation: an empirical test in an accounting course. *Canadian Journal of Administrative Sciences*, 18(2), 101-115. http://dx.doi.org/10.1111/j.1 936-4490.2001.tb00248.x

Allen, I., & Seaman, J. (2013). Changing Course: Ten Years of Tracking Online Education in the United States. *The Sloan Consortium (Sloan-C)*, Retrieved on January 11, 2013 from http://sloanconsortium.org/publications/survey/making_the_grade_2006

Ashong, C.Y. & Commander, N.E. (2012). Ethnicity, gender and perceptions of online learning in higher education. *Journal of Online Learning and Teaching*, 8(2), 98-110.

Asunka, S. (2008). Online Learning in Higher Education in Sub-Saharan Africa: Ghanaian University students' experiences and perceptions. *International Review of Research in Open and Distance Learning*, October 2008, 9(3), 1-23.

Benbunan-Fich, R. & Hiltz, S.R. (2003). Mediators of effectiveness of online courses. *IEEE Transactions on Professional Communication*, 46(4), 2980312. http://dx.doi.org/10.1109/TPC.2003.819639

Bejerano, A.R. (2008). Raising the Question #11 The Genesis and Evolution of Online Degree Programs: Who Are They For and What Have We

Lost Along the Way? *Communication Education,* 57(3), 408-414. http://dx.doi.org/10.1080/03634520801993697

Billings, D.M., Skiba, D.J. & Connors, H.R. (2005). Best Practices in Web-based Courses: Generational Differences across Undergraduate and Graduate Nursing Students. *Journal of Professional Nursing,* 21(2), 126-133. http://dx.doi.org/10.1016/j.profnurs.2005.01.002

Bond, M.B. & Hoefstede, G. (1988). Culture-level dimensions of social axioms and their correlates across 41 cultures. *Journal of Cross-Cultural Psychology,* 35(5), 548-570. http://dx.doi.org/10.1177/002022104268388

Brislin, R.W., Bochner, S. & Lonner, W.J. (Eds) (1975). Cross-Cultural Perspectives on Learning, Sage Publications, Beverly Hills, CA.

Carr, S. (2000). As distance education comes of age, the challenge is keeping the students. *Chronicle of Higher Education, 46*(23), A39.

Charlesworth, Z.M. (2008). Learning styles across cultures: suggestion for educators. *Education + Training,* 50(2), 115-127. http://dx.doi.org/10.1108/00400910810862100

Chase, M. Macfayden, L., Reeder, K. & Roche, J. (2002). Intercultural challenges in networked learning: hard technologies meet soft skills. *First Monday,* 7(8), http://dx.doi.org/10.5210/fm.v7i8.975

Chawla, D. & Joshi, H. (2012). E-learning perception and its relationship with demographic variables: a factor analysis approach. *International Journal of Information and Communication Technology Education,* 8(4), 105-118. http://dx.doi.org/10.4018/jicte.2012100109

Chew, R. & Yee, S. (2015). Perceptions of Online Learning in Australian University: Malaysian Students' Perspective – Support for Learning. *International Journal of Information and Education Technology,* 5(8), 587-592. http://dx.doi.org/10.7763/IJIET.2015.V5.573

Cheung, L. L., & Kan, A. C. (2002). Evaluation of factors related to student performance in a distance-learning business communication course. *Journal of Education for Business,* 77(5), 257-263. http://dx.doi.org/10.1080/08832320209599674

Clerkin, T. A. (2005). *An exploratory study of the antecedents and consequences of relationships with executive search firms: Implications for a model of career attainment..* Indiana University, ProQuest, UMI Dissertations Publishing, 2005. 3183914.

Connolly, T.M., MacArthur, E., Stansfield, M. & McLellan, E. (2007). A quasi-experimental study of three online learning courses in computing. *Computers & Education,* 49, 345–59. http://dx.doi.org/10.1016/j.compedu.2005.09.001

Cronje, J. (2011). Using Hofstede's cultural dimensions to interpret cross-cultural blended teaching and learning. *Computers & Education,* 56, 596-603. http://dx.doi.org/10.1016/j.compedu.2010.09.021

Dobbs, R., Waid, C.A., & del Carmen, A. (2009). Students' Perceptions of Online Courses: The Effect of Online Course Experience. *Quarterly Review of Distance Education,* Spring 2009, 10(1), 9-26.

Fang, L. (2007). Perceiving the useful, enjoyable and effective: a case study of the e-learning experience of tertiary students in Singapore. *Educational Media International,* 44(3), 237-253. http://dx.doi.org/10.1080/09523980701491682

Fish, L.A. & Snodgrass, C.R. (2014). A Preliminary Study of Business Student Perceptions of Online versus Face-to-Face Education. *BRC Journal of Advances in Education,* pp. 1-21. DOI: http://dx.doi.org/10.15239/j.brcacadje.2014.04.01.ja01

Fish, L.A. & Snodgrass, C.R. (2015). A preliminary study of international student perceptions of online versus face-to-face education. *BRC Academy Journal of Business, 5, 1, pp. 67-99.* Print ISSN: 2152-8721 Online ISSN: 2152-873X http://dx.doi.org/10.15239/j.brcacadjb.2015.04.01

Fowler, D. (2005). Are on-site courses as effective as online? *Online Cl@ssroom: Ideas for Effective Online Instruction,* March, 1–2.

Gifford, L. (1998). Graduate Students' Perceptions of Time Spent in Taking a Course by Internet versus Take a Course in a Regular Classroom. *Annual Mid-South Educational Research Association Conference,* New Orleans, LA, Nov. 4-6, 1998, 1-10.

Grandon, E.E., Alshare, K. & Kwun, O. (205). Factors Influencing Student Intention to Adopt Online Classes: A Cross-Cultural Study. *Consortium for Computing Sciences in Colleges,* 46-56.

Hamdan, A. (2014). The Reciprocal and Correlative Relationship Between Learning Culture and Online Education: A Case from Saudi Arabia. *The International Review of Research in Open and Distance Learning.* 15(1), 309-336.

Hiltz, S. R., & Turoff, M. (2005). Education goes digital: The evolution of online learning and the revolution in higher education. *Communications of the ACM*, 48(10), 59-64. doi:10.1145/1089107.1089139

Hofstede, G. (1991). *Cultures and organizations: Software of the mind.* London: McGraw-Hill.

Horspool, A. & Lange, C. (2012) Applying the scholarship of teaching and learning: student perceptions, behaviors and success online and face-to-face, *Assessment & Evaluation in Higher Education*, February 2012, 37(1), 73-88. http://dx.doi.org/10.1080/02602938.2010.496532.

Jin, L. (2002). Learning models in different cultures. *New Directions for Child and Adolescent Development*, 2002(96), 45-64. http://dx.doi.org/10.1002/cd.43

Johnson, R.D. (2011). Gender differences in e-learning: Communication, social presence, and learning outcomes. *Journal of Organizational and End User Computing*, 23(1), 79-94. http://dx.doi.org/10.4018/joeuc.2011010105

Karns, G.L. (2005). An Update of Marketing Student Perceptions of Learning Activities: Structure, Preferences, and Effectiveness. *Journal of Marketing Education*, 27(2), 163-171. http://dx.doi.org/10.1177/0273475305276641

Kathawala, Y., Abdou, K., & Elmulti, D. S. (2003). The global MBA: A comparative assessment for its future. *Journal of European Industrial Training*, 26(1), 14-23. http://dx.doi.org/10.1108/03090590210415867

Kay, R.H. (2009). Examining gender differences in attitudes toward interactive classroom communication systems (ICCS). *Computers & Education*, 52(4), 730-740. http://dx.doi.org/10.1016/j.compedu.2008.11.015

Kearsley, G. (2002). Learning and teaching in cyberspace. Belmont, CA: Wadsworth.

Kenny, J. (2003). Student perceptions of the use of online learning technology in their courses. *ultiBASE Articles*. Accessed on January 9, 2013 from http://ultibase.rmit.edu.au/Articles/march03/kenny2.pdf

Khoo, J., &Azizan, H. (2004). Pitfalls of paper chase. *Star Education*, 2-4.

Kim, K., Liu, S., & Bonk, C. (2005). Online MBA students' perceptions of online learning: Benefits, challenges, and suggestions. *Internet and Higher Education*, 8, 33-35. http://dx.doi.org/10.1016/j.iheduc.2005.09.005

Konradt, U., & Sulz, K. (2001). The experience of flow in interacting with a hypermedia learning environment. *Journal of Educational Multimedia and Hypermedia*, 10(1), 69-84.

Ku, H. & Lohr, L. L. (2003). A case study of Chinese students' attitude toward their first online learning experience. *Education Technology Research and Development*,51(3), 94-102. http://dx.doi.org/10.1007/BF02504557

Larson, K., & Sung, C, (2009). Comparing Student Performance: Online Versus Blended Versus Face-To-Face, *Journal of Asynchronous Learning Networks*, 13(1), 31-42.

Lee, J.W., Becker, K. & Nobre, H. (2012). Impact of culture on online management education. *Cross Cultural Management*, 19(3), 399-420. http://dx.doi.org/10.1108/13527601211247116

Li, N. & Kirkup, G. (2005). Gender and cultural differences in internet use: a study of China and the UK. *Computers & Education*, 48, 301-317. http://dx.doi.org/10.1016/j.compedu.2005.01.007

Lin, X,.Liu, S., Lee, S. & Magjuka, R.J. (2010). Cultural Differences in Online Learning: International Student Perceptions. Educational Technology & Society, 13(3), 177-188.

Maltby, J. R., & Whittle, J. (2000). Learning programming online: Student perceptions and performance. *Proceedings of the ASCILITE 2000 Conference*. Accessed on January 9, 2013 from http://www.ascilite.org.au/conferences/coffs00/papers/john_maltby.pdf

Mortagy, Y. & Boghikian-Whitby, S. (2010). A Longitudinal Comparative Study of Student Perceptions in Online Education. *Interdisciplinary Journal of E-Learning and Learning Objects*, 6, 23-46.

Muilenburg, L. Y . & Berge, Z.L. (2005). Student barriers to online learning: A factor analytic study. Distance Education, 26(1), 29-48. http://dx.doi.org/10.1080/01587910500081269

Mullen, G.E., & Tallent-Runnels, M.K. (2006). Student outcomes and perceptions of instructors' demands and support in online and traditional classrooms. *Internet and Higher Education, 9*, 257–66. http://dx.doi.org/10.1016/j.iheduc.2006.08.005

Ohara, M. (2004). Maximizing e-learning ROI: Identifying successful on-line learners. *Allied Academies International Conference*, 8(1), 49-54.

Okwumabua, T. M., Walker, K.M., Hu, X. & Watson, A. (2010). An exploration of African American students' attitudes toward online learning. Urban Education, 46(2), 241-250. http://dx.doi.org/10.1177/0042085910377516

Olesova, L., Yang, D. & Richardson, J.C. (2011). Cross-cultural differences in Undergraduate Students' Perceptions of Online Barriers. *Journal of Asynchronous Learning Networks,* 15(3), 68-80.

Perreault, H., Waldman, L., Alexander, M. & Zhao, J. (2008). Graduate Business Students' Perceptions of Online Learning: A Five Year Comparison. *The Delta Pi Epsilon Journal,*Fall 2008, L(3), 164-179.

Perreault, H., Waldman, L., Alexander, M. & Zhao, J. (2002). Overcoming barriers to successful delivery of distance-learning courses. *Journal of Education for Business*, 77(6), 313-318. http://dx.doi.org/10.1080/0 8832320209599681

Pillay, S. & James, R. (2014). The pains and gains of blended learning – social constructivist perspectives. *Education + Training*, 56(4), 254-270. http://dx.doi.org/10.1108/ET-11-2012-0118

Popov, V., Brinkman, D., Biemans, H.J.A., Mulder, M. Kuznetsov, A. & Noroozi, O. (2012). Multicultural student group work in higher education: a study on challenges as perceived by students. *International Journal of Intercultural Relations*, 36(2), 302-317. http://dx.doi.org/1 0.1016/j.ijintrel.2011.09.004

Popov, V., Noroozi, O., Barrett, J.B., Biemans, H.J.A., Teasley, S.D., Slof, B. & Mulder, M. (2014). Perceptions and experiences of, and outcomes for, university students in culturally diversified dyads in a computer-supported collaborative learning environment. *Computers in Human Behavior*, 32, 186-200. http://dx.doi.org/10.1016/j.chb.2013.12.008

Prinsen, F.R., Volman, M.L.L. & Terwel, J. (2007), Gender-related differences in computer-mediated communication and computer-supported collaborative learning. *Journal of Computer Assisted Learning*, 23(5), 393-409. http://dx.doi.org/10.1111/j.1365-2729.2007.00224.x

Ramburuth, P. & McCormick, J. (2001). Learning diversity in higher education: A comparative study of Asian international and Australian students. *Higher Education*, 42(3), 333-350. http://dx.doi.org/10.1023/A:1017982716482

Reilly, J.R., Gallager-Lepak, S. & Killion, C. (2012). Me and My Computer: Emotional Factors in Online Learning, *Nursing Education Perspectives*, March/April, 33(2), 100 - 105.

Rivera, J. C., & Rice, M. L. (2002). A comparison of student outcomes and satisfaction between traditional and web based course offerings. *Online Journal of Distance Learning Administration*, 5(3).

Schott, M., Chernish, W., Dooley, K. E., & Linder, J. R. (2003). Innovations in distance learning program development and delivery. *Online Journal of Distance Learning Administration*, 6(2).

Selvarajah, C. (2006). Cross-cultural study of Asian and European student perception. *Cross-Cultural Management*, 13(2), 142-155. http://dx.doi.org/10.1108/13527600610662320

Smith, P.J. & Smith, S.N. (1999). *Differences between Chinese and Australian students: Some implications for distance education. Distance Education*, 20(1), 64-75. http://dx.doi.org/10.1080/0158791990200106

Tanner, J.R., Noser, T.C., & Totaro, M.W. (2009). Business Faculty and Undergraduate Students' Perceptions of Online Learning: A Comparative Study. *Journal of Information Systems Education*, Spring 2009, 20(1), 29-40.

Tanner, J., Noser, T., Totaro, M., & Birch, R. (2006). Student Perceptions of The Online 'Classroom': An Update. *International Business & Economics Research Journal*, 5(10), 31-38.

Tanner, J., Noser, T., Fuselier, J., & Totaro, M. (2004-1). 'The Online 'Classroom': Differences in Perception between Business Students and Non-Business Students. *Journal of College Teaching and Learning*, 1(3), 37-44.

Tanner, J., Noser, T., Fuselier, J., & Totaro, M. (2004-2), 'The Online 'Classroom': What Do Students Think? *Journal of Informatics Education Research*, 6 (1), 43-54.

Tanner, J., Noser, T., & Langford, H. (2003). Perceptions of Undergraduate Business Students Toward Online Courses In Higher Education Expanded and Revisited: Do Gender, Age, and/or Past Experiences Make a Difference? *Journal of Business and Economics Research*, 1(2), 13-20.

Tapanes, M.A., Smith, G.G. & White, J.A. (2009). Cultural diversity in online learning: A study of the perceived effects of dissonance in levels of individualism/collectivism and tolerance of ambiguity. *The Internet and Higher Education*, 12, 26-34. http://dx.doi.org/10.1016/j. iheduc.2008.12.001

Tekinarslan, E. (2011). Faculty of Education Students' Self-efficacy Perceptions toward Online Technologies. *Electronic Journal of Social Sciences*, Summer 2011, 10(37), 120-134.

Thompson, L. & Ku, H. (2005). Chinese graduate students' experiences and attitudes toward online learning. *Educational Media International*, 42(1), 33-47. http://dx.doi.org/10.1080/09523980500116878

Topper, A. (2007). Are they the same? Comparing the instructional quality of online and face-to-face graduate education courses. *Assessment & Evaluation in Higher Education*, 32 (6), 681–691. http://dx.doi.org/1 0.1080/02602930601117233

Tsai, C.W. & Chiang, Y.C.(2013). Research trends in problem-based learning (PBL) research in e-learning and online education environments: A review of publications in SSCI0indexed journals from 2004 to 2012. British Journal of Educational Technology, 44(6), E185-E190. http://dx.doi.org/10.1111/bjet.12038

Tsaw, D., Murphy, S., Detgen, J. (2011). Social loafing and culture: Does gender matter? *International Review of Business Research Papers*, 7(3), 1-8.

Tung, F. C., & Chang, S. C. (2008). An empirical investigation of students' behavioral intentions to use the online learning course websites. *British Journal of Educational Technology*, 39(1), 71-83.

Zhu, C. Valcke, M. & Schellens, T. (2009). A cross-cultural study of online collaborative learning. *Multicultural Education and Technology Journal*, 3(1), 33-46. http://dx.doi.org/10.1108/17504970910951138\

A Literature Review and Directions for Future Research on International Student Perceptions of Online versus Face-to-Face Education: Program-centered Characteristics

Lynn A. Fish and Coral R. Snodgrass

Professors of Management,
Richard J. Wehle School of Business
Canisius College

Email: fishl@canisius.edu
Email: snodgras@canisius.edu
Professor Fish is the corresponding author.

Abstract

As higher education institutions continue incorporating online education into their curricula, different cultural perspectives regarding online versus face-to-face education will impact upon its sustained proliferation. Some cultures accept online education (Zhu, Valcke & Schellens, 2009; Lin Liu, Lee, & Magjuka, 2010), while others feel it is inferior (Asunka, 2008) to traditional education. Prior research to study business students' perceptions (Fish & Snodgrass, 2014, 2015) found two research streams: student-centered and program-centered characteristics exist. This study focuses on the current state of literature with respect to program characteristics and culture, and suggests future directions for research in this area. Program characteristics include course organization, academic rigor, program quality, academic integrity, faculty involvement and student-to-instructor interaction, communication mechanisms, student-to-student interaction, and program technologies. Results have implications for instructors and administrators especially as institutions endeavor to attract new international students to their online programs.

Keywords: International Student Perceptions, Online, Face-to-face

LITERATURE REVIEW

The Babson Survey Research Group notes the continued proliferation of online education in higher education (Allen & Seaman, 2013). While academic administrators believe that learning outcomes through online education are the same or superior to those in traditional FTF classrooms (Allen & Seaman, 2013), critics argue that due to intrinsic differences, online education does not replicate the learning that occurs in the traditional classroom (Bejerano, 2008). As technology continues to evolve and online education continues to expand its horizons, researchers continue to study student perceptions in the online learning environment (e.g. Allen & Seaman, 2013; Fish & Snodgrass, 2014, 2015; Perreault, Waldman, Alexander & Zhao, 2008; Tanner, Noser, and Langford, 2003; Tanner, Noser, Fuselier & Totaro, 2004-1; 2004-2; Tanner, Noser, Totaro & Birch, 2006; Tanner Noser & Totaro, 2009). Since online courses may reach across borders, and based upon previous literature that suggests that foreign students have different needs than their Western classmates in face-to-face (FTF) classes (Selvarajah, 2006), students' cultural backgrounds affect their perception of the online learning environment (Popov et al., 2012). Prior research to study business students' perceptions found two research streams exist: student-centered and program-centered characteristics (Fish & Snodgrass, 2014, 2015). With a focus on the program-centered research, we review literature on student perceptions of online versus FTF education with an emphasis on cultural implications.

What do we know about cultural perceptions about online education now? Each culture has its own way of processing information, learning, instructing and solving problems, and a nation's culture affects students' engagement, relations and perceived benefits from online education (Lee, Becker & Nobre, 2012). Differences in the manner in which people learn and different cultural learning models exist (Brislin et al., 1975; Charlesworth, 2008; Fang, 2007; Jin, 2002). Cultural backgrounds differ in terms of cognitive styles, rules of behavior, communication styles, attitudes and belief systems, and human relations (Hofstede, 1991). They present distinct challenges and opportunities to the growth of online education - particularly related to differences in academic abilities, gender, perceptions of time, professional status, student expectations and tolerance for criticism (Chase, Reeder & Roche, 2002).

Cultural differences impact upon student perceptions between online and FTF education (Grandon, Alshare & Kwun, 2005; Lin, Liu, Lee & Magjuka, 2010; Olesova, Yang, & Richardson, 2011). Previous studies examined differences across cultures (Cronje, 2011; Chew & Yee, 2015; Grandon et al., 2005; Li & Kirkup, 2005; Popov et al., 2012; Popov, Noroozi, Barrett, Biemans, Teasley, Slof & Mulder 2014; Zhu, Valcke & Schellens., 2009) and within cultures (Adler et al., 2001; Chase et al., 2002; Hamdan, 2014; Okwumabua, Walker, Hu & Watson, 2010). In a recent cross-cultural comparison between Malaysian and Australian students, no significant differences in students' perceptions existed on computer usage, lecturer support, equity, student interaction and collaboration (Chew & Yee, 2015). In another study at a large, southeastern University in the U.S., both African-American and Caucasian American students' perceptions view online learning positively (Ashong & Commander, 2012).

Some countries, such as China and India, appear to be attractive destinations for online education; however, world-wide acceptance of online learning is not evident. In some countries people perceive online education as second-rate to FTF education or believe the education is purchased and not assessed (Khoo & Azizan, 2004; Hamdan, 2014). As a result, these countries enacted policies that do not recognize online degrees (Asunka, 2008; Kathawala Abdou, & Elmul, 2003; Hamdan, 2014). In nations where gender plays a factor in educational experiences (that is, men and women are separated), such as east African nations, a lack of advancement in online education and a lack of research into how cultural factors may be impacted by online activity (Hamdan, 2014), may impact upon future growth and acceptance in these areas of the world.

Students' perceptions toward online learning and blended approaches may change over time (Benbunan-Fich & Hiltz, 2003). For example, research at the turn of the century indicated differences between Australians and Asian students in student perceptions (Smith & Smith, 1999; Ramburuth & McCormick, 2001); however, a more recent study found no significant differences existed on many factors for these groups (Chew & Yee, 2015). Yet, another study reported on changes in Chinese students' motivation and learning strategies after an online collaborative experience towards a social-constructivist learning approach (Zhu et al., 2009). Since many studies were performed over a decade ago, what are students' *current* perceptions regarding online versus FTF?

As education methods change to incorporate more online elements and technology advances, educators and administrators need to understand these perceptual differences to be successful. Today, instructors skills are critical in online delivery, and as online education crosses global boundaries, instructors need to understand different cultural and technological environments when designing learning activities (particularly discussion forums) (Chew & Yee, 2015). Current research on students' perceptions can be divided into two streams of research - student-centered (concentrating on differences between students' perceptions based upon individual demographic and perceptual characteristics) and program-centered (concentrating on program design issues that may be controlled by the instructor). Since research in each stream has increased significantly in recent years, here we focus on the literature pertinent to student perceptions regarding program-centered characteristics and cultural implications in online education. Program-characteristics addressed here include: a general overview of cultural program issues, course organization, academic rigor, program quality, academic integrity, faculty involvement and student-to-instructor interaction, communication mechanisms, student-to-student interaction, and program technologies. Based upon the literature review, we offer recommendations for future research within each subtopic.

Cultural Program Issues. Hofstede's framework (1986), a seminal article in cross-cultural communications, proposed four dimensions: power distance (social status and its impact upon learning), individualism-collectivism (tendency of individuals to act as individuals or as part of a group), uncertainty avoidance (degree to which individuals accept uncertain situations and results), and masculinity-femininity (masculine cultural values favoring maximization of society outcomes versus female cultural values favoring relationships and quality of life improvements). Several studies explored differences between individualistic and collective societies' perceptions within (Hornik & Tupchiy, 2006; Lin et al., 2010) and across cultures (Selvarajah, 2006; Zhu et al., 2009). Other studies explore dimensions relative to one another and student perceptions. In one study, individualistic students' motives, interaction styles and performance mechanisms are more compatible with distance learning than collectivistic students (Anakwe & Christensen, 1999). And in yet another study, power distance and uncertainty avoidance tend to amplify each other, while together they assist in movement from individualism toward collectivism (Cronje, 2011). In contrast to Hofstede's framework, which critics cite as lacking fluidity, the 'flexible' approach to educational design recommends developing courses that are capable of catering to the diverse cultural perspectives, rather than simply containing 'predetermined content'(Collis, 1999). For example, researchers propose developing the key aspects of the course contingent upon the cultural dimensions but design the course flexible enough to allow students and instructors to choose their own learning and teaching styles as the course progresses (Collis, 1999; Henderson, 1996; McLoughlin & Oliver, 2000).

The ability to transport a course to a different culture may be impacted upon by cultural differences related to course design, delivery and technological medium (Lee et al., 2012). In an online MBA study (Lin et al., 2010), course cultural differences were noted for:

- assessment (exam-oriented (collective; Eastern societies) versus process-oriented (individualistic; Western societies));
- instruction/interaction (lecture versus conversation; structure (Eastern) vs. less structure (Western));
- deductive versus inductive learning;
- asynchronous versus synchronous communication (lack of visual cues causing communication barriers, scheduling issues for cross-cultural collaboration, time zone differences);
- collaboration (collectivism vs. individualism; masculinity versus femininity);
- case learning (lack of global cases, lack of local issues for international students, lack of international experience of online instructors);
- academic conduct (discrepancies between US and other countries' rules of academic conduct), and
- language (barriers in reading, writing and communication).

Several studies explored cultural program differences between two or more cultures. For example, the U.S. instruction style leans toward a learner-centered, process-oriented style with interaction and participation as critical components, while Eastern instruction tends to be lecture-centered with an emphasis on exams (Lin et al., 2010; Zhang, 2007). Appropriate cross-cultural training for instructors is needed so instructors can design appropriate courses (Lin et al., 2010). However, *what advise should instructors be given to address these issues?* Therefore, while we propose other cultural questions below, we pose Research Questions #1: *What cultural issues should be and which should not be addressed in online program design? Do different cultures and their associated relationship to Hofstede's four dimensions differ with respect to students' perceptions regarding online and FTF? Do different cultures regard the 'flexible framework' (Collis, 1999) the same or differently?*

Course Organization. Cultural influences merit consideration in designing and planning an online course that potentially 'has no borders' as the designer needs to understand the various student cultures and provide an equitable and culturally-sensitive platform for knowledge transfer (Chen, Mashhadi, Ang & Harkrider, 1999; Selvarajah, 2006). While flexibility and convenience are the most common reasons American students cite as to why they take online courses (Armstrong, 2011; Horspool & Lange, 2012; Leasure, Davis & Thievon, 2000; Perreault et al., 2008), Americans perceive the course organization – particularly the structure of the learning environment and the nature of online assessment, as key to student learning and success (Armstrong, 2011). Ambiguous instructions increase student distress in online courses (Merisotis & Olsen, 2000; Perreault et al., 2008) as students want concise, specific directions on everything (Armstrong, 2011). Eastern students have an even higher affinity for structured courses than Western students (Lin et al., 2010).

Research-based validated online frameworks and benchmarks to plan, design, deliver and assess online education depend on an effective course design in the West that uses a student-centered model (Mortagy & Boghikian-Whitby, 2010). Eastern educational systems tend to be based upon memorization of material and the instructor as the center of the educational process, while Western education systems tend to focus on the process and discussion between classmates and the instructor (Lin et al., 2010). The traditional Saudi Arabian FTF curriculum requires rote memorization, a single point of view (instructor), passive learning that excludes diversity; however the online environment encourages student-centered learning favoring collaboration, critical thinking and student-to-student interaction (Hamdan, 2014). Russian and U.S. students noticed differences in assessment styles (Lin et al., 2010) as Western assessments tend to be process-oriented, while Eastern assessments tend to be exam-oriented (Lin et al., 2012). As another example of cultural organization differences, Ghana students responded negatively to online constructivist teaching approaches such as asynchronous discussions and ill-structured project-based learning activities (Asunka, 2008). Differences in how instructors organize courses lead to Research Questions #2: *Do different cultures expect and perceive online course structure differently? Do different cultures expect and perceive online assessments differently? Do different cultures need different types of directions regarding how to complete online activities?*

Academic Rigor. With respect to academic rigor, results are mixed as some studies indicate that online is more rigorous than FTF (Dobbs, Waid & del Carmen., 2009), while other studies indicate that FTF is more rigorous than online (Armstrong, 2011). In sub-Sahara Ghana, students perceived collaborative online learning as complex, more demanding and time-consuming than in a FTF environment (Asunka, 2008). In one study of social loafing (whereby one group member does not contribute to group work fully or undermines the group work process), Chinese students displayed less social loafing than American students (Tsaw, Murphy & Detgen., 2011). American online students disliked the academic rigor associated with working independently (Fish & Snodgrass, 2014). Therefore, with respect to academic rigor, we pose Research Questions #3: *Do different cultures perceive differences in the academic rigor associated with online courses? Do different cultures perceive social loafing differently in the online environment?*

Program Quality. While chief academic officers claim that online learning is now of the same quality as traditional courses (Allen & Seaman, 2013), research into student's perceptions of quality are mixed. Some studies indicate students perceive the quality to be better and more fun with a technology-enhanced online learning environment (Fjermestad, Hiltz, & Zhang, 2005; Hannay & Newvine, 2006; Parker, 2003), and other studies indicate the opposite as students held the view that online learning offered no advantage over FTF (Asunka, 2008). Similarly, online experience factors into quality perceptions as students who took an online course disagree with the statement that the quality of online courses was lower than FTF, while those who had not taken an online course felt online quality was lower (Dobbs et al., 2009). Contrastingly, one study noted that in some African countries, people perceive online learning as second-rate to FTF education (Asunka, 2008). Thus, with respect to program quality, we pose Research Question #4: *Do students from different cultures perceive the quality of online programs differently than FTF ones?*

Academic Integrity. Rumors regarding online cheating abound. In general, since the chance of being caught is low, students may be inclined to cheat more online than in the FTF classroom. While most criminal justice students indicated that they never cheated, a comparison of FTF and online student perception indicates that cheating is more common in online courses than FTF (Lanier, 2006). Students with higher grade point averages, females, married and older students are less inclined to cheat (Lanier, 2006). In our previous study, FTF and online students felt cheating is easier online than in the traditional classroom (Fish & Snodgrass, 2014). In FTF classes, different cultures regard different activities as 'cheating'. Different cultures must understand the protocols and guidelines for using online communication prior to joining an online course along with ethical standards (such as privacy, security, plagiarism and academic dishonesty) associated with the online delivery host country (Hamdan, 2014). Therefore, with respect to academic integrity, we pose Research Question #5: *Do different cultures perceive online cheating to be more, the same or less rampant than in the FTF classroom?*

Faculty Involvement and Student-to-Instructor Involvement. Several studies show the positive relationships between the perceived quality of the instructor and perceived student learning (Armstrong,

2011; Richardson & Swan, 2003). In the FTF classroom, results demonstrate that the greater the degree of student involvement, the greater the student learning (Pascarella & Terenzini, 1991). Since it is more difficult for instructors to provide affective support to students in online learning (Mullen & Tallent-Runnels, 2006), Research Question #6a: *do students perceive instructor involvement to be an important factor in online instruction?* Mixed results with respect to student communication with the online instructor exist. Some studies indicate that online interaction with the instructor is equal or even more positive than FTF (Boyd, 2008) as online students perceive faculty as having high expectations and faculty are available to communicate, interact and provide feedback (Mortagy & Boghikian-Whitby, 2010). Yet another study indicates no significant difference between online and FTF interaction with the instructor (Horspool & Lange, 2012). However, other studies indicate FTF student perceive greater interaction than online students (Fish & Snodgrass, 2014; Wang & Morgan, 2008; Wuensch, Aziz, Ozan, Kishore & Tabrizi, 2008). Since traditional Western and East Asian educational systems prepare students differently as Western teaching promotes facilitative, informal relationship between students and the instructor, while East Asian cultures foster more formal relationships in order to show proper respect (Zhu et al., 2009), Research Question #6b: *how do different cultures view the student-to-instructor interaction?* For example, in Saudi Arabia, online education facilitated a cultural shift (for women) from instructor-centered to student-centered learning as student-to-instructor and student-to-student interaction occurred (Hamdan, 2014). Contrastingly, Flemish students disliked the inability to get direct and immediate assistance from their instructors and fellow students as they would in a FTF environment (Zhu et al., 2009). Thus, Research Question #6c: *Do different cultures perceive the student-to- instructor interaction online to be more, the same or less than in the FTF environment?*

Communication Mechanisms. Communication practices are significantly influenced by one's culture (Hall, 1990), and cross cultural communication is about building trust through reduction of communicative uncertainty, constructing shared meaning and optimizing technology use (Cronje, 2011). Online students typically complain about the lack of verbal, visual and social context cues (Popov et al., 2014). Student perceptions are being shaped by communication speed and consistency (Armstrong, 2011). Student satisfaction in online courses improves for students who have immersed themselves in the course through satisfying requirements, and informal and formal chats (Ohara, 2004). Research results are again mixed as some studies indicate online courses enhance learner participation and interactivity (Fredericksen, Pickett, Shea, Pelz, & Swan, 2000; Maeroff, 2004; Wang & Morgan, 2008), and others highlight student distress (Hara & Kling, 2003) or general feelings of 'disconnect' due to the lack of FTF interactions (Stodel, Thompson & MacDonald, 2006). Similarly, the inability to interact through posing questions, sharing opinions, engaging in dialogue, or a sense of belonging to a group influence student perceptions as to how well they perform in an online class (Picciano, 2002; Song, Singleton, Hill & Koh, 2004). Several online studies indicate that students report communication issues with other students (Horspool & Lange, 2012) along with a general unwillingness of other online learners to participate in group activities (Dirkx & Smith, 2004; Maeroff, 2004). Online students report meeting with their peers less often than FTF students and form fewer study groups than FTF students (Horspool & Lange, 2012). In the online environment, a lack of visual cues (which causes communication barriers, scheduling issues for cross-cultural collaboration and time zone differences) adds other barriers to the educational process (Lin et al., 2010).

The design of online courses that potentially 'have no borders' needs to consider the communication, cross-cultural understanding and provide an equitable and culturally-sensitive platform for knowledge transfer (Selvarajah, 2006). Differences exist in the way cultures communicate and control situations (Lin et al., 2010). Eastern students preferred to have more direction from their instructors than Western students who prefer student interaction (Liang & McQueen, 1999). International students being educated through U.S. systems need additional support to reduce cultural language and learning barriers as the international online learners felt 'marginalized' by their American counterparts who essentially 'took over' the learning experience; however, the international students did not feel that this control negatively impacted upon their communication or collaboration in learning (Lin et al., 2010).

Many studies explored the differences between collectivist and individualist cultures. Collectivist (or high context) cultures, such as the Chinese, Korean, Japanese, Vietnamese, Greek and Arabian, use body language and associated gestures along with the immediate physical and social environment in communication (Hamdan, 2014). Collectivistic-oriented are more concerned with social relationships in group projects and work to never offend anyone (Popov et al., 2014). Online education that does not include visual or verbal cues inhibits critical aspects of FTF communication for collectivist societies (Hamdan, 2014), and they respond to the lack of visual cues with respect by using their perceived understanding of the partner's cultural perspective (Popov et al., 2014). Collectivistic-oriented students found the lack of voice tone and facial expression in text-based communication makes it harder for them to interpret and respond in a non-threatening way to a partner, and therefore, they often avoiding expressing differing opinions as they see them as counterproductive (Popov et al. 2014). Low-context (or individualist) cultures, such as U.S. and many northern European countries, tend to be direct and informal communicators (Hamdan, 2014). Individualistic-oriented students seek clarity in conversation, use low-context, direct and explicit messages that focus on the task at hand, and are concerned with verifying the correct information (Popov et al., 2014). Due to a lack of nonverbal, visual and social context cues, individualistic-oriented students often find that it is difficult to get a message across successfully; however, they report that differences in opinions may improve the work quality and the lack of in-depth discussion may hinder successful project performance (Popov et al., 2014). Therefore, instructors should address multicultural differences in collaborative environments to improve the learning experiences and set expectations, such as fostering activities for social interaction early on (particularly for collectivists), and students should have training on how to develop communication skills that may improve coordination between culturally diverse groups (Popov et al., 2014).

Therefore, with respect to communication mechanisms, we pose Research Question #7: *Do students from different cultures perceive online and FTF communication differently?*

Student-to-Student Interaction. Cultural differences within team work between virtual teams and student perceptions exist (Olesova et al., 2011). Cultural background adds an important dimension to collaborative learning as teams are virtual, may be multidisciplinary and potentially multicultural (Popov et al., 2014). Collaborative problem-based learning encourages students to develop teamwork, collaboration, cooperation, critical thinking through analysis, synthesis, evaluation and reflection (Zhu et al., 2009). Cultural background may influence a student's understanding of the required collaborative processes and perceptions, and therefore, the required actions that are likely to be effective (Lans, Oganisjana, Taks & Popov, 2013). Postgraduate management students from different cultural backgrounds, ethnicities and nationalities may respond to educational styles differently (Selvarajah, 2006). A lack of trust in a partner's expertise may seriously inhibit collaboration (Popov et al., 2014). A critical barrier to students learning online may be a lack of social interaction online (Muilenburg & Berge, 2005) as some students are reluctant to participate in interactive learning and others prefer to work individually regardless of cultural background (Pfaff & Huddleston, 2003). Students reported that free-riding, insufficient English skills and students not communicating properly are the most challenging aspects to online performance (Popov, Brinkman, Biemans, Mulder, Kuznetsov & Noroozi, 2012). Cross-cultural learning in blended learning is most effective when personal interaction between the person and the cross-cultural environment occurs (Pillay & James, 2014).

Group work, which includes group membership (members' experiences and skills) and group processes (communication, problem solving and decision making, conflict management and leadership), poses challenges for students regardless of whether national or international members, but multicultural groups increase the complexity (Popov et al., 2012). A key to online success is the student-to-student interaction (especially through asynchronous conferencing), which fosters rich interactions and in-depth thinking as participants can think through responses prior to responding (Kim Liu & Bonk, 2005). In our previous study, online students disliked the student interaction compared to FTF classes (Fish & Snodgrass, 2014). However, when English is the required language, language difficulties may pose challenges for international students and increases the comprehension complexity between group members with different language levels and accents (Popov et al., 2012). Free riding negatively influences group climate, group participation and group performance (Popov et al., 2012).

Group composition variables – homogeneous or heterogeneous groups, are critically important to the functioning and overall success of a collaborative learning environment (Popov et al., 2012) as cultural background differences either benefit or disrupt dynamics (Halverson & Tirmizi, 2008). Coordinating different group perceptions, reasoning and communication styles can pose issues in online collaboration as students with different cultural backgrounds may have different perceptions of collaborative learning, which can lead to conflict (Popov et al., 2014). Culturally diverse groups' expectations and perceptions may be completely different with respect to group learning and moral behavior, possibly leading to misunderstanding and conflict (Popov et al., 2012). The group may approach conflict differently, adding to the online complexity (Popov et al., 2014). Educators should focus on positive experiences while downplaying negative ones to encourage multicultural groups to develop their abilities to be more successful (Popov et al., 2012).

When forming groups, cultural background – as to whether the individual is individualistic or collectivistic, should be taken into account (Popov et al., 2012). Individuals from collectivistic and individualistic cultures differ in their attitudes toward diversity among group members as collectivists dislike diverse groups as they feel they cannot function effectively, while individualistic groups believe group work can be advantageous because of the confrontation and problem solving (Sosik & Jung, 2002). Regardless of the group composition, students from collective cultural backgrounds responded more positively to collaborative work than students from individualistic cultural backgrounds; however, students from individualistic cultural backgrounds performed better on learning outcomes than students with collectivist backgrounds (Popov et al., 2014). Collectivistic-oriented students perceive online collaborative learning more positively than individualist oriented students (Popov et al., 2014), and collectivistic oriented students prefer working in groups and feel that they perform better in groups, share more knowledge and exhibit less conflict-oriented behavior (Phuong-Mai Terlouw & Pilot, 2006). However, collectivistic-oriented students voiced concern regarding learning from a peer (Popov et al., 2014). In general, individualists seek personal goals while collectivists seek group success, individualists prefer working separately from groups which are seen as contrary to individual goals, and individualists are more likely to 'loaf' due to greater need to work alone (Earley, 1989). Students' cultural background (individualistic vs collectivistic) affects their perceptions of the challenges that they must overcome in collaborative projects as students from individualistic cultures consider free riding to be a problem in group work, while students from collectivistic cultures view it as less important (Popov et al., 2012).

In recent years, several researchers began to explore specific cultural differences in group work behavior. In one study, Eastern students tend to exhibit face-saving, modest personalities in group work and prefer group work, while American students appear to be independent, assertive and exhibit a competitive attitude that dominates group work (Lin et al., 2010). Western students are more accustomed to a student-centered class, while Asian students are more teacher-centered (Chin, Chang & Bauer, 2008). Chinese and New Zealanders differed in their educational objectives and preferred different assessment methods (Selvarajah, 2006).

In a comparative study between the Chinese and American culture, Chinese students performed differently than their American classmates in the online environment as they were more passive, diligent, formal and content-oriented, deferent to the teacher, concerned for others and worried about losing face in contrast to their American counterparts (Wang, 2006). In another study, British students were more likely to use computers to study than Chinese students (Li & Kirkup, 2005).

Several researchers noted changes in students' perceptions following collaborative activities. For example, in Saudi Arabia, online education facilitated a cultural shift (for women) from instructor-centered to student-centered learning as more student-to-student and student-to-instructor interaction occurred (Hamdan, 2014). In yet another study, a cultural gap existed between Chinese and Flemish students; however, after a collaborative experience, Chinese students' motivation and learning strategies changed significantly towards a social-constructivist learning approach (Zhu et al., 2009). While Flemish students' perceived the online experience more positively than Chinese students; Flemish students disliked the inability to get direct and immediate assistance from their instructors and fellow students as they would in a FTF environment (Zhu et al., 2009).

Therefore, with respect to Student-to-Student Interaction, we pose the following Research Questions #8: *Do cultural homogenous or heterogeneous online groups perform better? Do students from different cultures perceive homogeneous and heterogeneous online groups differently? Do students from collective societies behave differently than students from individualistic societies in online interactions with other students? Do students from collective societies behave differently than students from individualistic societies in online interactions with instructors? What techniques and methods can online instructors use to facilitate online cultural heterogeneous group work? In gender separated educational systems, do men and women perceive online education the same or differently?*

Technologies. Online education offers greater access to learning resources (Sener & Stover, 2000), and requires skills such as maintaining a stable or wireless Internet connection, Internet navigation, searching for relevant information, using multimedia applications, uploading a file to an asynchronous or synchronous conferencing system, writing and publishing on the Internet, opening a web browser or even publishing on a web-site (Tekinarslan, 2011). With respect to technical issues, students appear technically well-equipped to take online courses as less than 40% reported significant communication issues (Hospool & Lange, 2012). However, many students doubt their abilities and use of the technology, require reassurance before they trust the technology, and some students never trust it (Ohara, 2004). Unfortunately, faculty weak in understanding technology appear to utilize technology in a way that creates confusion (Armstrong, 2011). Students utilize nonacademic resources (e.g. Google) more readily (due to familiarity) than academic resources (cumbersome and difficult to navigate) in completing assignments (Armstrong, 2011). Students reported the most important technology activities include accessing unit information, accessing lecture/lab notes, interacting with unit learning resources, reading online discussions, contacting lecturers/tutors and submitting assignments online (Palmer & Holt, 2010). Students perceived video modules, quizzes and the textbook as valuable to the learning environment regardless of online or FTF (Horspool & Lange, 2012). They indicated receiving feedback on assignments and reviewing unit progress as needing attention by the instructor (Palmer & Holt, 2010). Instant messaging can be a technique to increase dialogue and reduce distance between students in an online course (Wang & Morgan, 2008). In our study, online students perceived homework, discussion and videos as adding the most to their understanding, while instructor lectures and in-class sessions decreased their understanding; however, FTF students perceived instructor lectures, interaction with others and in-class sessions increased their understanding (Fish & Snodgrass, 2014).

Many online courses neglect the relationship between student charac-teristics and instructional methodologies as the important role of culture and its impact on various methods appears to be neglected in online course design (Pillay & James, 2014). Cyberspace has a culture and gaps can exist between individuals as well as between individuals and the dominant cyber-culture, which increases the likelihood of miscommunication (Chase et al., 2002). The lack of elements found in FTF communication acerbates the intercultural communication online by limiting opportunities to give and 'save face' as well as draw meaning from nonverbal cues (Chase et al., 2002). The lack of contextual cues can inhibit students – particularly collectivist students, which may benefit from adding video or voice connection activities to online capabilities (Popov et al., 2014). Through web interface design, websites of high power distance countries may be characterized by high levels of structured information, controlled access to information and several layers to acquire information (Marcus, 2000). One study reports that Yahoo Groups discussions encouraged cultural integration between individualistic instructors and collectivist students (Cronje, 2011). To create and online culture, particular attention should be paid to synchronizing participant and facilitator expectations (Chase et al., 2002). At a large, southeastern University in the U.S., both African-American and Caucasian American students' perceptions view online learning positively; however, African-Americans were significantly less positive toward asynchronous features of online learning (Ashong & Commander, 2012). Common ground versus differences between cultures should be sought through reducing communication uncertainty by shared meaning construction and appropriate use of technology (Cronje, 2011).

With respect to technologies, we pose Research Questions #9: *Do students from different cultures respond differently to the technology? Do students from different cultures require different technological skills in the online environment? What technologies and activities do different cultures prefer in the online and FTF environments?*

DISCUSSION

Obviously our literature review is not a comprehensive review of literature in this area; however, it highlights the ambiguity that exists for student perceptions of online program characteristics and culture. Research shows mixed results for students' perceptions of program characteristics (including course organization, academic rigor, program quality, academic integrity, faculty involvement and student-to-instructor interaction, communication mechanisms, student-to-student, and technologies) between cultures. While many studies demonstrate differences between specific cultures which should be considered in online program design, instructors need tools and methods to address the wide variety of cultures that may be attending each class. Online classes need to be designed for *every culture at the same time*, which is a difficult and complex undertaking. This undertaking is similar to addressing the needs of students with disabilities, and will take research, development and time to properly incorporate into online education.

Mixed results in cross-cultural comparisons exist for many program characteristics; however, recent research appears to indicate that the Millennials generation regard online education differently and are more accepting than Gen-Xers or Gen-Yers (Chew & Yee, 2015). Additionally, several studies note that students' perceptions changed over time (Benbunan-Fich & Hiltz, 203; Karns, 2005; Mortagy & Boghikian-Whitby, 2010; Perreault et al., 2008; Ramburuth & McCormick, 2001; Smith & Smith, 1999; Zhu et al., 2009), which leads to the more general Research Questions #10: *Do today's students perceive cultural differences in the online environment differently than the generations before them? Have student perceptions shifted? Given a shift has occurred, do today's students differ – by culture – in their online perceptions for program characteristics? If yes, for what factors are important for instructors to consider?*

Previous research demonstrates mixed student perceptions of online education that differed in facility size (small, medium, and large universities), audience (e.g. scientific versus social sciences, business versus non-business, and graduate versus undergraduate), method of research (e.g. interview, survey), completion at a large university or in a public forum (Tanner et al., 2003; Tanner et al., 2004-1; 2004-2; Tanner et al, 2006; Tanner et al., 2009), a small environment (e.g. Armstrong, 2011), or in non-business fields (e.g. Dobbs et al., 2009; Lanier, 2006; Leasure et al., 2000; Reilly, Gallager-Lepak & Killion, 2012; Tekinarslan, 2011; Wang & Morgan, 2008). Our previous preliminary results highlighted, the context of the study (a Jesuit, Catholic institution) may be an important factor to consider in interpretation of the student perceptual survey results (Fish & Snodgrass, 2014; 2015), which leads to another set of corresponding research and Research Question #11: *Do students at private institutions perceive online program design cultural issues differently than students at public institutions?*

As online education continues to be 'borderless', instructors need to design courses to bridge cultural gaps; however, this is a moving target as technology and student expectations are changing. Theoretically, instructors should design online education such that students perceive the online and FTF environments equally – regardless of culture. Given the mixed research results as outlined above, we posed several research questions to explore and understand student perceptions of online course design respective of different cultural backgrounds. While cross cultural comparisons offer one point of comparison, the bigger issue is how to address these research questions for *all* of the worlds' various cultures. Obviously, significant work remains!

REFERENCES

Adler, R.W., Milne, M.J. & Stablein, R. (2001). Situated motivation: an empirical test in an accounting course. *Canadian Journal of Administrative Sciences*, 18(2), 101-115. http://dx.doi.org/10.1111/j.1 936-4490.2001.tb00248.x

Allen, I., & Seaman, J. (2013). Changing Course: Ten Years of Tracking Online Education in the United States. *The Sloan Consortium (Sloan-*

C), Retrieved on January 11, 2013 from http://sloanconsortium.org/ publications/survey/making_the_grade_2006

Anakwe, U.P., & Christensen, E.W. (1999). Distance learning and cultural diversity: Potential users' perspective. *The International Journal of Organizational Analysis,* 7(3), 224-243. http://dx.doi.org/10.1108/eb0 28901

Armstrong, D.A. (2011). Students' Perceptions of Online Learning and Instructional Tools: A Qualitative Study of Undergraduate Students Use of Online Tools. *The Turkish Online Journal of Educational Technology* – July 2011, 10(3), 222-226.

Ashong, C.Y. & Commander, N.E. (2012). Ethnicity, gender and perceptions of online learning in higher education. *Journal of Online Learning and Teaching,* 8(2), 98-110.

Asunka, S. (2008). Online Learning in Higher Education in Sub-Saharan Africa: Ghanaian University students' experiences and perceptions. *International Review of Research in Open and Distance Learning,* October 2008, 9(3), 1-23.

Benbunan-Fich, R. & Hiltz, S.R. (2003). Mediators of effectiveness of online courses. *IEEE Transactions on Professional Communication,* 46(4), 2980312. http://dx.doi.org/10.1109/TPC.2003.819639

Bejerano, A.R. (2008). Raising the Question #11 The Genesis and Evolution of Online Degree Programs: Who Are They For and What Have We Lost Along the Way? *Communication Education,* 57(3), 408-414. http://dx.doi.org/10.1080/03634520801993697

Boyd, P.W. (2008). Analyzing students' perceptions of their learning in online and hybrid first year composition courses. *Computers and Composition,* 25, 224–43. http://dx.doi.org/10.1016/j.compcom.2008.01.002

Brislin, R.W., Bochner, S. & Lonner, W.J. (Eds) (1975). Cross-Cultural Perspectives on Learning, Sage Publications, Beverly Hills, CA.

Charlesworth, Z.M. (2008). Learning styles across cultures: suggestion for educators. *Education + Training,* 50(2), 115-127. http://dx.doi.org/10.1108/00400910810862100

Chase, M. Macfayden, L., Reeder, K. & Roche, J. (2002). Intercultural challenges in networked learning: hard technologies meet soft skills. *First Monday*, 7(8), http://dx.doi.org/10.5210/fm.v7i8.975

Chen, A.Y., Mashhadi, A., Ang, D. & Harkrider, N. (1999). Cultural Issues in the Design of Technology Enhanced Learning Systems. *British Journal of Educational Technology*, 30(3), 217-230. http://dx.doi.org/10.1111/1467-8535.00111

Chew, R. & Yee, S. (2015). Perceptions of Online Learning in Australian University: Malaysian Students' Perspective – Support for Learning. *International Journal of Information and Education Technology*, 5(8), 587-592. http://dx.doi.org/10.7763/IJIET.2015.V5.573

Chin, K.L., Chang, V. & Bauer, C. (2008). The use of web-based learning in culturally diverse learning environments. *Proceedings of AusWeb2k, the 6th Australian World Wide Web Conference*, Rihga Colonial Club Resort, Cairns, June 12-17, Norsearch Ltd, Lismore, 12-17.

Collis, B. (1999). Designing for differences: Cultural issues in the design of WWW-based course-support sites. *British Journal of Educational Technology*, 30(3), 201-215. http://dx.doi.org/10.1111/1467-8535.00110

Cronje, J. (2011). Using Hofstede's cultural dimensions to interpret cross-cultural blended teaching and learning. *Computers & Education*, 56, 596-603. http://dx.doi.org/10.1016/j.compedu.2010.09.021

Dirkx, J. M., & Smith, R. O. (2004). Thinking out of a bowl of spaghetti: Learning to learn in online collaborative groups. In T. S. Roberts (Ed.), *Online collaborative learning: Theory and practice*, Hershey, PA: Information Science Publishing, 132-159. http://dx.doi.org/10.4018/978-1-59140-174-2.ch006

Dobbs, R., Waid, C.A., & del Carmen, A. (2009). Students' Perceptions of Online Courses: The Effect of Online Course Experience. *Quarterly Review of Distance Education*, Spring 2009, 10(1), 9-26.

Earley, P.C. (1989). Social loafing and collectivism: A comparison of the United States and the People's Republic of China. Administrative Science Quarterly, 34, 565-581. http://dx.doi.org/10.2307/2393567

Fang, L. (2007). Perceiving the useful, enjoyable and effective: a case study of the e-learning experience of tertiary students in Singapore.

Educational Media International, 44(3), 237-253. http://dx.doi.org/10
.1080/09523980701491682

Fish, L.A. & Snodgrass, C.R. (2014). A Preliminary Study of Business
Student Perceptions of Online versus Face-to-Face Education. *BRC
Journal of Advances in Education,* pp. 1-21. DOI: http://dx.doi.org/1
0.15239/j.brcacadje.2014.04.01.ja01

Fish, L.A. & Snodgrass, C.R. (2015). A preliminary study of international
student perceptions of online versus face-to-face education. *BRC
Academy Journal of Business, 5, 1, pp. 67-99.* Print ISSN: 2152-8721
Online ISSN: 2152-873X http://dx.doi.org/10.15239/j.brcacadjb.2015
.04.01

Fjermestad, J., Hiltz, S. R., & Zhang, Y. (2005). Effectiveness for students:
Comparisons of "inseat" and ALN courses. In S. R. Hiltz & R. Gold-
man (Eds.), *Learning together online: Research on asynchronous learning networks,* Mahwah, NJ: Lawrence Erlbaum, 39-80.

Fowler, D. (2005). Are on-site courses as effective as online? *Online
Cl@ssroom: Ideas for Effective Online Instruction,* March, 1–2.

Fredericksen, E., Pickett, A., Shea, P., Pelz, W., & Swan, K. (2000). Student
satisfaction and perceived learning with online courses: Principles
and examples from the SUNY learning network. *Journal of Asynchronous Learning Networks, 4*(2), 7-41.

Grandon, E.E., Alshare, K. & Kwun, O. (205). Factors Influencing Student
Intention to Adopt Online Classes: A Cross-Cultural Study. *Consortium for Computing Sciences in Colleges,* 46-56.

Hall, E. (1990). Understanding cultural differences. Yarmouth, ME: Intercultural Press.

Halverson, B.C. & Tirmizi, S.A. (2008). *Effective Multicultural Teams:
Theory and Practice.* New York: Springer. http://dx.doi.org/10.1007/
978-1-4020-6957-4

Hamdan, A. (2014). The Reciprocal and Correlative Relationship Be-
tween Learning Culture and Online Education: A Case from Saudi
Arabia. The International Review of Research in Open and Distance
Learning. 15(1), 309-336.

Hannay, M., & Newvine, T. (2006). Perceptions of Distance-Learning: A Comparison of Online and Traditional Learning. *MERLOT Journal of Online Learning and Teaching*, 2(1), 1-11, Accessed on January 11, 2013 from http://jolt.merlot.org/documents/MS05011.pdf

Hara, N., & Kling, R. (2003). Students' distress with a web-based distance education course: An ethnographic study of participants' experiences. *Turkish Online Journal of Distance Education*, 4(2), 557-579.

Henderson, L. (1996). Instructional design of interactive multimedia. *Educational Technology Research and Development*, 44(4), 85-104. http://dx.doi.org/10.1007/BF02299823

Hofstede, G. (1991). *Cultures and organizations: Software of the mind.* London: McGraw-Hill.

Hofstede, G. (1986). Cultural differences in teaching and learning. *International Journal of Intercultural Relations*, 10, 301-320. http://dx.doi.org/10.1016/0147-1767(86)90015-5

Hornik, S., & Tupchiy, A. (2006). Culture's impact on technology mediated learning: The role of horizontal and vertical individualism and collectivism. *Journal of Global Information Management.* 14(4), 31-56. http://dx.doi.org/10.4018/jgim.2006100102

Horspool, A. & Lange, C. (2012) Applying the scholarship of teaching and learning: student perceptions, behaviors and success online and face-to-face, *Assessment & Evaluation in Higher Education*, February 2012, 37(1), 73-88. http://dx.doi.org/10.1080/02602938.2010.496532.

Jin, L. (2002). Learning models in different cultures. New Directions for Child and Adolescent Development, 2002(96), 45-64. http://dx.doi.org/10.1002/cd.43

Kathawala, Y., Abdou, K., & Elmulti, D. S. (2003). The global MBA: A comparative assessment for its future. Journal of European Industrial Training, 26(1), 14-23. http://dx.doi.org/10.1108/03090590210415867

Khoo, J., & Azizan, H. (2004). Pitfalls of paper chase. *Star Education*, 2-4.

Kim, K., Liu, S., & Bonk, C. (2005). Online MBA students' perceptions of online learning: Benefits, challenges, and suggestions. *Internet and Higher Education*, 8, 33-35. http://dx.doi.org/10.1016/j.iheduc.2005.09.005

Lanier, M. (2006). Academic Integrity and Distance Learning. *Journal of Criminal Justice Education*, Sep 2006, 17(2), 244-21. http://dx.doi.org/10.1080/10511250600866166

Lans, T. Oganisjana, K. Taks, M. & Popov, V. (2013). Learning for entrepreneurship in heterogeneous groups: experiences from an international, interdisciplinary higher education student programme. *Trames-Journal of the Humanities and Social Sciences*, 17(67/62)(4), 383-399. http://dx.doi.org/10.3176/tr.2013.4.05

Leasure, A. R., Davis, L., & Thievon, S. L. (2000). Comparison of student outcomes and preferences in a traditional vs. World Wide Web-based baccalaureate nursing research course. *Journal of Nursing Education*, 39(4), 149-154.

Lee, J.W., Becker, K. & Nobre, H. (2012). Impact of culture on online management education. *Cross Cultural Management*, 19(3), 399-420. http://dx.doi.org/10.1108/13527601211247116

Li, N. & Kirkup, G. (2005). Gender and cultural differences in internet use: a study of China and the UK. *Computers & Education*, 48, 301-317. http://dx.doi.org/10.1016/j.compedu.2005.01.007

Liang, A. & McQueen, R.J. (1999). Computer assisted adult interactive learning in a multi-cultural environment. *Adult Learning*, 11(1), 26-29.

Lin, X,.Liu, S., Lee, S. & Magjuka, R.J. (2010). Cultural Differences in On-line Learning: International Student Perceptions. Educational Technology & Society, 13(3), 177-188.

Maeroff, G. I. (2004). *Classroom of one: How online learning is changing our schools and colleges.* Gordonsville, VA: Palgrave Macmillan.

Marcus, A. (2000). International and intercultural user-interface design. In Constantine Stephanidis (Ed.), *User interfaces for all.* New York: Lawrence Erlbaum.

McLoughlin, C. & Oliver, R. (2000). Designing learning environments for cultural inclusivity: A case study of indigenous on-line learning at tertiary level. *Australian Journal of Educational Technology*, 16(1), 58-72.

Merisotis, J. P., & Olsen, J. K. (2000). The 'effectiveness' debate: What we know about the quality of distance learning in the US. *TechKnowlogia*, 2(1), 42-44.

Mortagy, Y. & Boghikian-Whitby, S. (2010). A Longitudinal Comparative Study of Student Perceptions in Online Education. *Interdisciplinary Journal of E-Learning and Learning Objects*, 6, 23-46.

Muilenburg, L. Y . & Berge, Z.L. (2005). Student barriers to online learning: A factor analytic study. Distance Education, 26(1), 29-48. http://dx.doi.org/10.1080/01587910500081269

Mullen, G.E., & Tallent-Runnels, M.K. (2006). Student outcomes and perceptions of instructors' demands and support in online and traditional classrooms. *Internet and Higher Education*, 9, 257–66. http://dx.doi.org/10.1016/j.iheduc.2006.08.005

Ohara, M. (2004). Maximizing e-learning ROI: Identifying successful online learners. *Allied Academies International Conference*, 8(1), 49-54.

Okwumabua, T. M., Walker, K.M., Hu, X. & Watson, A. (2010). An exploration of African American students' attitudes toward online learning. Urban Education, 46(2), 241-250. http://dx.doi.org/10.1177/0042085910377516

Olesova, L., Yang, D. & Richardson, J.C. (2011). Cross-cultural differences in Undergraduate Students' Perceptions of Online Barriers. *Journal of Asynchronous Learning Networks,* 15(3), 68-80.

Palmer, S. & Holt, D. (2010). Students' perceptions of the value of the elements of an online learning environment: looking back in moving forward. *Interactive Learning Environments,* June 2010, 18(2), 135–151. http://dx.doi.org/10.1080/09539960802364592

Parker, M. (2003). Technology-enhanced e-Learning: Perceptions of First Year Information Systems Students at the Cape Technikon. *Proceedings of the South African Institute of Computer Scientists and Information Technologists,* SAICSIT 2003, 316-319.

Pascarella, E.T. & Terenzini, P.T. (1991). *How College Affects Students: Findings and Insights from Twenty Years of Research*, Jossey-Bass, San-Francisco, CA.

Perreault, H., Waldman, L., Alexander, M. & Zhao, J. (2008). Graduate Business Students' Perceptions of Online Learning: A Five Year Comparison. *The Delta Pi Epsilon Journal*,Fall 2008, L(3), 164-179.

Pfaff, E. & Huddleston, P. (2003). Does it matter if I hate teamwork? What impacts student attitudes toward teamwork. *Journal of Marketing Education*, 25(1), 37-45. http://dx.doi.org/10.1177/0273475302250571

Phuong-Mai, N., Terlouw, C. & Pilot, A. (2006). Culturally appropriate pedagogy: The case of group learning in a Confucian heritage culture context. *Intercultural Education*, 17(1), 1-19. http://dx.doi.org/10.108 0/14675980500502172

Picciano, A. (2002). Beyond Student Perceptions: Issues of Interaction, Presence, and & Performance in An Online Course. *Journal of Asynchronous Learning Networks*, 6(1), 21-40.

Pillay, S. & James, R. (2014). The pains and gains of blended learning – social constructivist perspectives. *Education + Training*, 56(4), 254-270. http://dx.doi.org/10.1108/ET-11-2012-0118

Popov, V., Brinkman, D., Biemans, H.J.A., Mulder, M. Kuznetsov, A. & Noroozi, O. (2012). Multicultural student group work in higher education: a study on challenges as perceived by students. *International Journal of Intercultural Relations*, 36(2), 302-317. http://dx.doi.org/1 0.1016/j.ijintrel.2011.09.004

Popov, V., Noroozi, O., Barrett, J.B., Biemans, H.J.A., Teasley, S.D., Slof, B. & Mulder, M. (2014). Perceptions and experiences of, and outcomes for, university students in culturally diversified dyads in a computer-supported collaborative learning environment. *Computers in Human Behavior*, 32, 186-200. http://dx.doi.org/10.1016/j.chb.2013.12.008

Ramburuth, P. & McCormick, J. (2001). Learning diversity in higher education: A comparative study of Asian international and Australian students. *Higher Education*, 42(3), 333-350. http://dx.doi.org/10.1023 /A:1017982716482

Reilly, J.R., Gallager-Lepak, S. & Killion, C. (2012). Me and My Computer: Emotional Factors in Online Learning, *Nursing Education Perspectives*, March/April, 33(2), 100 - 105.

Richardson, J., & Swan, K. (2003). Examining Social Presence In Online Courses In Relation to Students' Perceived Learning and Satisfaction. *Journal of Asynchronous Learning Networks*, 7(1), 68-88.

Selvarajah, C. (2006). Cross-cultural study of Asian and European student perception. *Cross-Cultural Management*, 13(2), 142-155. http://dx.doi.org/10.1108/13527600610662320

Sener, J., & Stover, M. L. (2000). Integrating ALN into an independent study distance education program: NVCC case studies. *Journal of Asynchronous Learning Networks*, 4(2), 126-144.

Smith, P.J. & Smith, S.N. (1999). *Differences between Chinese and Australian students: Some implications for distance education. Distance Education, 20(1), 64-75.* http://dx.doi.org/10.1080/0158791990200106

Song, L., Singleton, E., Hill, J., & Koh, M. (2004). Improving Online Learning: Student Perceptions and Challenging Characteristics. *Internet and Higher Education*, 7, 59-70. http://dx.doi.org/10.1016/j.iheduc.2003.11.003

Sosik, J.J. & Jung, D.I. (2002). Work group characteristics and performance in collectivistic and individualistic cultures. *The Journal of Social Psychology*, 142(1), 5-23. http://dx.doi.org/10.1080/00224540209603881

Stodel, E. J., Thompson, T. L., & MacDonald, C. J. (2006). Learners' perspectives on what is missing from online learning: Interpretations through the community of inquiry framework. *International Review of Research in Open and Distance Learning, 7*(3), 1-24. Accessed on January 9, 2013 from http://www.irrodl.org/index.php/irrodl/article/view/325/743

Tanner, J.R., Noser, T.C., & Totaro, M.W. (2009). Business Faculty and Undergraduate Students' Perceptions of Online Learning: A Comparative Study. *Journal of Information Systems Education*, Spring 2009, 20(1), 29-40.

Tanner, J., Noser, T., Totaro, M., & Birch, R. (2006). Student Perceptions of The Online 'Classroom': An Update. *International Business & Economics Research Journal*, 5(10), 31-38.

Tanner, J., Noser, T., Fuselier, J., & Totaro, M. (2004-1). 'The Online 'Classroom': Differences in Perception between Business Students and Non-Business Students. *Journal of College Teaching and Learning*, 1(3), 37-44.

Tanner, J., Noser, T., Fuselier, J., & Totaro, M. (2004-2), 'The Online 'Classroom': What Do Students Think? *Journal of Informatics Education Research*, 6 (1), 43-54.

Tanner, J., Noser, T., & Langford, H. (2003). Perceptions of Undergraduate Business Students Toward Online Courses In Higher Education Expanded and Revisited: Do Gender, Age, and/or Past Experiences Make a Difference? *Journal of Business and Economics Research*, 1(2), 13-20.

Tekinarslan, E. (2011). Faculty of Education Students' Self-efficacy Perceptions toward Online Technologies. *Electronic Journal of Social Sciences*, Summer 2011, 10(37), 120-134.

Tsaw, D., Murphy, S., & Detgen, J. (2011). Social loafing and culture: Does gender matter? *International Review of Business Research Papers*, 7(3), 1-8.

Wang, H. (2006). *How cultural values shape Chinese students' online learning experience in American Universities*, unpublished PhD dissertation, The University of Georgia, Athens, GA.

Wang, L.C. & Morgan, W.R. (2008). Student Perceptions of Using Instant Messaging Software to Facilitate Synchronous Online Class Interaction in a Graduate Teacher Education Course. *Journal of Computing in Teacher Education*, Fall 2008, 25(1), 15-21.

Wuensch, K.L., Aziz, S., Ozan, E., Kishore, M. & Tabrizi, M.H. (2008). Pedagogical characteristics of online and face-to-face classes. *International Journal on E-Learning*, 7(3), 523–32.

Zhang, J. (2007). A cultural look at information and communication technologies in Eastern education. *Education Technology Research and Development*, 55(3), 301-314. http://dx.doi.org/10.1007/s11423-0 07-9040-y

Zhu, C. Valcke, M. & Schellens, T. (2009). A cross-cultural study of online collaborative learning. *Multicultural Education and Technology Journal*, 3(1), 33-46. http://dx.doi.org/10.1108/17504970910951138

Using Text Analysis to Assess Qualitative Student Works, Deal with Inter-rater Reliability, and Simultaneously Comply with AACSB Standard 8 and Middle States Standard V

Guy H. Gessner* and Karen M. Kutt-Doner

Guy H. Gessner Ph.D.
Associate Professor of Marketing
Department of Marketing and Information Systems
Canisius College
2001 Main St., Buffalo, NY 14208.
Email: Gessner@canisius.edu.
Telephone: (716) 888-2639.

Karen M. Dutt-Doner, Ph.D.
Professor of Teacher Education
Canisius College
2001 Main St., Buffalo, NY 14208.
Email: duttdonk@canisius.edu.
Telephone: 716-888-2596

* Corresponding author

Abstract

The purpose of this research is to determine if the analytical process of text analysis or text mining can be adapted success-fully as a tool to help automate assessment of student works related to ways in which they demonstrate progress in meeting institutional and accreditation standards. Student works in this case are assignments from graduate and undergraduate courses in business. An electronic library with six dictionaries was built containing Jesuit and Catholic keywords, phrases, concepts and synonyms so text analysis has the ability to identify these institutional learning goals within student work products. Conclusions from this study are that text mining can be adapted successfully as an automated solution for assessing large volumes of student works without involvement of large numbers of assessors and therefore without the problem of inter-rater reliability that comes from using multiple human assessors.

Keywords: text mining, text analysis, assessment, faith-based, institutional learning objectives, libraries

INTRODUCTION

Assessing a large number of qualitative student work products for higher-level learning is often a challenge for faculty members. The challenge comes when these student work products are unstructured or open-ended like short answers, essays and papers. When students create original answers they will use different words with similar meanings, different logic to present the knowledge they have acquired, and communicate what they have learned in different sequences. The variation between student work products is what makes assessment of qualitative work difficult, the volume of student work products that needs to be assessed to be representative of the population of students is what makes it laborious, and the use of multiple human assessors can make a manual assessment process unreliable.

It can be difficult for students to communicate their depth of understanding of more complex topics and problems unless they are given the freedom to create their own work products. Structured response formats such as true or false questions, or multiple choice questions, constrain student responses to a process of selecting from among the responses created and communicated by someone else that is assumed to be an expert on the topic. Explicit within these fixed-format response forms is that there is a correct answer, even if it is 'none of the above'. With these assessment instruments students need not think about the knowledge that needs to be communicated nor display the skills necessary to communicate effectively, they only need to focus their attention on how to identify and select among answers that were already composed and communicated by experts.

Unstructured response formats require students to create and communicate a body of organized thought, there are no answers provided by experts to select from in front of them. In unstructured response formats students need to demonstrate they possess the communication skills necessary to convey they have achieved a level of understanding about a topic. More complex topics and challenges often do not have a single correct answer or perhaps is a correct answer even known. For example, an instructor can ask students to construct a response to the question: What is the solution for providing health care to a large population? The correct answer is perhaps unknown, but a credible answer would demonstrate knowledge of the topic, an understanding of the complexities and trade-offs, an analysis and evaluation of other efforts, and skill in creation of communications of a well-reasoned solution. A credible answer would cover much of the range of recognized learning taxonomies such as a revised Bloom's Taxonomy (Center for Excellence in Learning and Teaching).

Even with common rubrics, semantic pattern recognition appears to be at the heart of the challenge. Using a rubric and a manual process of reading and decoding student works, in an effort to recognize key-words and concepts, is extremely laborious and very subjective especially when different semantic structures are presented by different students and assessment is conducted by different assessors. If a manual process using rubrics is applied to large numbers of students, several assessors will be needed creating the conditions for questionable interrater reliability. This paper examines a more automated solution for help with assessing unstructured student work products. The result is a more reliable, transparent, and efficient process for assessment of unstructured student work products.

Automating the process of recognizing semantic patterns in the form of single words or phrases is the reason natural language processors were developed. The use of Natural Language Processors (NLP) on sets of words and phrases is often commonly called 'text-mining' or text analysis. A major advantage of using a NLP as an assessment tool is that it has the ability to recognize different semantic structures that have the same meaning.

TEXT ANALYSIS OF STUDENT WORK PRODUCTS

Text analysis (text mining) is the process of extracting meaning from text. The problem with text is that it is considered unstructured and more ambiguous than numeric data. Different words and sequences of words can have different meanings. The unambiguous properties associated with numeric data are missing from text. Organizing unstructured data is part of the challenge: assigning unambiguous interpretation and meaning is at quite another level of difficulty. The meaning within different blocks of text needs to be determined in advance by analysts preparing to use text analysis software. Users of text analysis software need to first answer the question, what are we searching for? Assessing qualitative student work products is the search for specific content indicative of student possession of specific knowledge or skills as stated in learning goals and objectives. This directed search requires that student work products be compared to a standard or template that determines the extent to which the searched for knowledge or skills are present or absent. In the manual process the template is called a rubric and the rubric requires the support of human intervention to judge if the submitted student work products possess the same content and meaning as the rubric. Text analysis performed in this research paper deployed a computerized natural language processor as the assessor and a library and set of dictionaries as the rubric. (IBM SPSS, 2010)

Text analysis is finding broad commercial applications but is still finding limited use in educational research (Yu, 2009) although it appears that interest in its use is growing (Yu, Jannasch-Pennell, Digangi , 2011). Two recently published papers highlight the use of IBM SPSS Text Analytics for Surveys, the software used in this study, for use in their efforts to assess student written works. Xu and Reynolds (Xu & Reynolds, 2012) applied this software for assessing student written work in their study of teacher leadership. They found significant correlations between assessments conducted manually and by using text analytics. They also discovered that the accuracy of their automated assessments depended upon the natural language libraries that are available. Kaplan, Haudek, Ha, Rogness, and Fisher (Kaplan, Haudek, Ha, Rogness, & Fisher, 2014) compared two different software packages in their ability to help them assess undergraduate written student work. One of the software packages included in their research was IBM SPSS Text Analysis for Surveys, version 4.0. They achieved good results but concluded that both software products required a degree of analyst involvement in the process. For the IBM product involvement was needed in the areas of development of categorization rules and libraries. They also go on to state that one of the benefits of the IBM product is the ability of analysts to create libraries and classification rules. This ability to readily adapt the IBM software product for different applications is one reason the product was selected for use in this study.

A pragmatic reason to look at text mining as a tool to help with assessment of student work products was provided by Kelley, Tong, and

Choi (2010). Their research indicates that the amount of time assessment takes was a major concern of faculty. That finding was not a surprise given that over 90% of their survey respondents indicated that they used written assignments for assessment.

The emerging backbone for text analysis is Natural Language Processing (NLP). NLP is the next step in the evolution from counting words to syntactic representation of text (Cambria and White, 2014). NLP helps to remove some ambiguity in meaning (word-sense disambiguation), multiple meanings of words and phrases that need to be put into context to be understood (textual entailment), and identification of the arguments associated with verbs (shallow semantic parsing). Cambria and White (2014) provide a comprehensive overview of the evolution and future of natural language processing.

This study employs some of the natural language processing capabilities provided by IBM in their software package SPSS Text Analytics for Surveys, version 4.0. An additional library and associated dictionaries are added to the base content to tailor the analysis to this specific application. This research does not evaluate the software; it simply uses it as a platform for assessment of qualitative student responses.

Assessment of Faith-Oriented Institutional Learning Objectives

Of importance to many institutions is the development of assessment tools that help determine if students are meeting institutional learning goals. Assignments that incorporate elements of institutional learning goals and rubrics that systematically evaluate students' work against these goals provide meaningful data. As a Jesuit college, some institutional learning goals focus on knowledge, skills, and connection to Jesuit mission and identity. The assignment utilized and reported in this study, systematically engaged students in considering elements of Catholic and, more specifically, Jesuit ideals in creating their response to the task.

EMBEDDED STUDENT ASSIGNMENT: COMPOSE AN APPEAL

Students in two different online courses in global logistics were given an assignment on providing logistics support for humanitarian relief efforts. This assignment was created by one of the authors. One set of students were enrolled in a graduate business program and the other set of students were enrolled in a senior-level undergraduate course for business majors. As the first part of the assignment students in both courses were asked to compose a message of no more than 250 words to their fictitious global logistics companies asking them to support a request by Catholic Relief Services (CRS) to provide logistics support. Graduate business students were given a choice to provide logistics support to humanitarian relief efforts to the city and region around Akobo in South Sudan or the region and city of Bossangoa in the Central African Republic. Undergraduate students were to provide humanitarian relief to Jimma Ethiopia where a major university is located.

The instructions given to MBA students by the instructor were:

> *"From your reflection you conclude it is important for your company to get involved. As a first step you need to draft a clear and compelling message that appeals to all 1,000 of your employees and your Board of Directors that motivates them to support involvement by your company. This message needs to reinforce the values of your company and their fit with CRS. It needs to be short, 250 words or less."*

Similar instructions were given to the course of undergraduate students:

> *"From your reflection you conclude it is important for your company to get involved. As a first step you need to draft a clear and compelling message that appeals to your fellow employees and the Board of Directors of the company that motivates them to support involvement by your company. This message needs to reinforce the values of your company and their fit with CRS. It needs to be short, 250 words or less."*

In addition to their previous course work which they could reflect on, students were asked to review the following five reference materials to reflect upon when composing their message:

1. A list of 17 quotes on poverty and hunger from Catholic Social Teaching provided found on the web site of Catholic Relief Services(Catholic Relief Services).

2. A video message from Pope Francis announcing the Global Campaign against Hunger (Catholic Relief Services)

3. A video message from Pope Francis regarding hunger (Catholic Relief Services)

4. A video on the Allegory of the Long Spoons (Catholic Relief Services)

5. Catholic Relief Services web site (Catholic Relief Services)

Both graduate and undergraduate students were given the institutional learning goals and objectives associated with this assignment: (Canisius College)

A. Academic Excellence – Knowledge

- Students demonstrate an awareness of the many perspectives that inform human experiences and understand the responsibilities of a global citizen in the modern world.

- Students demonstrate a general knowledge of ethical and moral issues as well as ones specific to their fields of study.

B. Catholic & Jesuit Mission & Identity

- Students demonstrate a familiarity with dimensions of the Catholic and Jesuit intellectual traditions as they occur in literature, art, science and social teaching.

- In the Jesuit tradition, be intentional learners who can adapt to new environments, integrate knowledge, and continue learning throughout their lives.

- Use their gifts for the service of others and the benefit of society.

ASSESSMENT OF INTERRELATED LEARNING GOALS IS REQUIRED

Most schools of business in the U.S. do not stand alone but are part of a larger educational institution. The larger educational institution is usually reviewed for accreditation by a regional accreditor that reports to the U.S. Department of Education. Middle States Commission on Higher Education is the regional accreditor for this academic institution and AACSB has accredited this business school at both undergraduate and graduate levels. It is accreditation by regional accreditors, approved by the U.S. Department of Education such as Middle States that enables students to borrow money from the U.S. Federal Government to pay for tuition so maintaining accreditation from a regional competitor can be critical for the financial stability of any institution of higher education. Accreditation Standard V by the Middle States Commission on Higher education could be interpreted as desiring a connection between the learning goals of the institution at large and each of the programs it offers. Standard V: Educational Effectiveness Assessment (Middle States Commission on Higher Education, 2015) specifically states:

1. "clearly stated educational goals at the institution and degree/ program levels, which are
   a. interrelated with one another..."
2. "organized and systematic assessments, conducted by faculty and/ or appropriate professionals, evaluating the extent of student achievement of institutional and degree/program goals." (p. 10).

Standard V from Middle States Commission on Higher Education appears to require that educational institutions need to be able to demonstrate that institutional educational goals and degree/program learning goals are interrelated. They appear to be requiring linkage between the institution and the each degree or program. This paper selected the institutional learning goals of Academic Excellence – Knowledge and Catholic & Jesuit Mission & Identity to assess to see if students in the business program can demonstrate knowledge and/or skill in the application of these areas of learning. But there is also another reason driven by AACSB accreditation requirements (AACSB, 2015).

One basis used for judging if a business school has met AACSB Standard 8 is if "learning goals derive from and are consonant with the school's mission, expected outcomes, and strategies" (p. 30). The mission statement for this School of Business contains three relevant statements that pertain to the work product students were asked to submit:

1. School develops business professionals to lead within organizations
2. Behave as ethically and socially responsible individuals
3. Needs to accomplish this in the Jesuit tradition.

There are specific learning goals and objectives for both the undergraduate and graduate programs in business pertaining to ethical leadership, social responsibility, and knowledge of ethical frameworks for managerial decision making. The desire for students to be knowledgeable in Jesuit traditions of leadership, and service for others link together the institutional learning goals selected for this research , the mission of this school of business and select learning goals and objectives for the undergraduate and graduate programs of this school of business. The mission of this School of Business and some of the program learning goals and objectives appear to be aligned with some of the Jesuit-oriented institutional learning goals and objectives as desired by both Middle States Commission on Higher Education and AACSB.

SUBSET OF LEARNING OBJECTIVES ANALYZED

Some of the learning objectives as stated contain multiple objectives that needed to be assessed separately. Toward that end the authors selected the following subset of learning objectives to assess in this research study:

1. Students demonstrate knowledge of the human experience. (Academic Excellence – Knowledge)

2. Students demonstrate knowledge of the responsibilities of global citizenship (Academic Excellence – Knowledge)

3. Students demonstrate knowledge of ethical and moral issues (Academic Excellence – Knowledge)

4. Students demonstrate familiarity with dimensions of Catholic Social Teaching (Catholic & Jesuit Mission & Identity)

5. Students advocate using their gifts for the service of others and the benefit society (Catholic & Jesuit Mission & Identity)

SET-UP FOR TEXT ANALYSIS

The major task in preparation for text analysis is constructing the semantic patterns that contain the words and phrases that characterize knowledge of specific learning objectives. These topic-specific libraries and dictionaries can then be used in the analysis of the student works. In data mining what is matched are data patterns, in text mining it is semantic patterns that are matched. Semantic patterns can be thought of as patterns of letters which form words, and patterns of words to form phrases. When the 'jargon' of terms and phrases associated with specific applications are not part of the everyday language used by the majority of the population, special dictionaries need to be built containing these terms. These sets of dictionaries that represent unique applications can be placed into libraries containing the terms grouped into dictionaries by topic or theme. For this research project a new library and set of dictionaries was created to contain terms and phrases that were expected to be found within the student work products that were assessed.

In order to develop a dictionary that can be utilized effectively in the assessment of student work, careful reflection needs to take place. The goals and learning objectives need to be carefully considered and clear terms need to be identified by assessors that would indicate the student's work demonstrates proficiency in meeting them. In order for the text mining process to be effective, dictionaries need to be comprehensive and inclusive of all possible responses that can be identified in student works that would indicate knowledge, skills or dispositions related to the learning goals.

A library called Poverty and Hunger, and six dictionaries were built for this specific application by the authors to provide some of the terms, phrases and semantic meanings needed to determine if students were providing evidence of their level of knowledge of specific learning objectives. The terms, phrases and semantic meanings created in the Poverty and Hunger library are found in references the students were directed to review for the assignment. Semantic meanings are assigned to terms and phrases using the strategy for creating the dictionaries. Different sets of words and phrases that were deemed to have the same meanings were declared as synonyms in the dictionary of synonyms. For example, the authors created a dictionary called Negative Behaviors. The word 'Negative' in the title is the semantic meaning; all terms and phrases in this dictionary are meant to be negative and this must be indicated in the dictionary. The word 'Behaviors' in the title suggests that the terms that will be found in this dictionary represent human behaviors. In our application the human behavior of acquiring superfluous wealth is considered a negative behavior. The phrase superfluous wealth is found within a quote from Pope Paul VI in the set of quotes on Poverty and Hunger from Catholic Social Teaching provided by Catholic Relief Services (Catholic Relief Services). Also created were a number of synonyms to help control for misspellings (poverty and povery are both assigned the correct spelling of poverty) and to limit the number of terms that would have the same meaning for this particular application. For example a term 'Right to Life' was created as a term with the synonyms: right to food, right to clothing, right to shelter, right to medical care and right to rest. When the software finds any of the synonyms in the student work product, it displays 'Right to Life' as the term extracted. Figure 1 displays the library and associated dictionaries created for use in this specific application.

It is through the documented process of library development with its associated dictionaries that the core problem of inter-rater reliability which is a concern with assessment of qualitative work by multiple humans is ameliorated. Yu, Jannasch-Pennell, and DiGangi (2011) discuss how text analysis using natural language processing improves consistency and replicability which help to deal with inter-rater reliability concerns characteristic of evaluations of qualitative works.

TEXT ANALYSIS OF GRADUATE BUSINESS STUDENT WORK PRODUCTS

Data for this study included eighteen assignments turned in by graduate students and twenty assignments turned in by undergraduate students. The input files created for analysis are MS Excel files. The authors had to cut each answer from MS Word files submitted by students and paste it into a row in a MS Excel file, a format used by this text analysis software product. This provided ample opportunity to read the communications provided by each student. Based upon this initial reading it appeared these graduate students created work products that contained more recognizable content from the reference materials provided than did the work products from the undergraduate students. Based upon this reading it was decided to analyze the graduate student work products first anticipating there would be a better match rate with the terms in the dictionaries and that new synonyms, in the words commonly used by graduate students, might be identified and added to the dictionary of synonyms. Why the graduate work products contained more relevant content than the undergraduate students is unknown and was unanticipated in advance. It could simply be a result of the self-selection process as to which subset of undergraduate students decides to go on to graduate school or perhaps because of the differences in the curricula between these particular graduate and undergraduate programs.

In the process of text analysis student works are taken as verbatims and matched against the terms and phrases in the library. Terms and phrases that match are 'extracted' for further processing. In this first step of the process 472 concepts were extracted from the 18 graduate student works. Extraction is the identification of concepts for which matches were found in one or more libraries and dictionaries used in the analysis.

In the second step, the concepts that pertain to the same topic are grouped together into categories. This study examined four categories; one for each of the institutional learning objectives. Table 1 exhibits each of the four institutional learning objectives assessed in this study and the set of extracted concepts that were assigned to this objective. The process of assigning concepts to categories is shared between the software that automatically assigns some, and the analyst that assigns some. The software only has the ability to associate extracted concepts to categories if the association was built into the libraries and the natural language processor. The more application specific are the concepts, the more the analyst needs to be involved in the assignment process for the early iterations of analysis. Once the associations have been programmed then the assignment will become more automated. The student work in which each extracted concept appears is retained by the software package and displayed for the analyst so there is a clear, visible mapping between student works, extracted concepts, and assigned categories. A clear, visible mapping adds transparency to assessment processes. This iterative process of engaging a human assessor who then adds content and associations to the dictionaries is how the library improves its ability to identify relevant content. It is in spirit a similar process as to how manual rubrics are improved over time.

In this study only 46 of the 472 concepts extracted from the works provided by graduate business students are directly related to the institutional learning goals. Most of the other concepts that were extracted were matches with other libraries already built into the software and were not relevant for this study. Some of the built-in libraries that are included in the software package are large and some matches are likely in almost any text that is analyzed.

ASSESSMENT RESULTS FOR GRADUATE BUSINESS STUDENTS

Data were analyzed across the four institutional learning objectives and results are organized within these themes. Table 2 exhibits results for the four institutional learning objectives using work products from eighteen graduate students. The table indicates that 13 of 18 (72%) students employed concepts from the references associated with 'Dimensions of Catholic Social Teaching' and 'Use of Their Gifts for the Service of Others and Benefit of Society'. The focus on the humanitarian relief exercise given to students was more strongly placed on these institutional learning objectives and correspondingly more terms and phrases from these references were built into the dictionaries which led to this result. The assessment conclusions of meeting, exceeding or not meeting expectations are completely arbitrary by the authors and used to provide an example.

Table 3 exhibits the breadth of coverage of the set of learning objectives in the graduate student work products. Four institutional learning objectives were assessed and this table indicates how many of the 18 students covered from none (0) up to four (4) of these learning objectives in their work product. It was very encouraging to see that 16 of 18 (89%) of the student work products covered two or more institutional learning objectives.

ASSESSMENT RESULTS FOR UNDERGRADUATE BUSINESS STUDENTS

The same libraries, categories, extracted concepts assigned categories, and institutional learning objectives were used to analyze the undergraduate work products. There was no apparent reason to modify in advance what was done for analyzing the graduate level student work products. Graduate and undergraduate students were all given the same basic instructions and references.

Table 4 exhibits results for the four institutional learning objectives using work products from 20 undergraduate students. The table indicates that eight students (40%) students employed concepts related to 'Dimensions of Catholic Social Teaching' and five students (5%) incorporated concepts related to 'Use of Their Gifts for the Service of Others and Benefit of Society'. A comparison of the results presented in Tables 2 and 4 indicate that undergraduate students did not incorporate concepts from any of the institutional learning objectives at the same rate as did the graduate students. Why there was such a difference is unknown because this difference was not apparent or anticipated before the student works were assigned.

Table 5 exhibits the breadth of coverage of the set of learning objectives in the undergraduate student work products. Four institutional learning objectives were assessed and this table indicates how many of the 20 students covered 0-4 of the learning objectives. Thirteen of 20 (65%) of the undergraduate student work products covered less than two institutional learning objectives. Only 7 of 20 undergraduate students (35%) provided evidence of incorporating content on two or more of the institutional learning objectives in their work products. A comparison with graduate student results presented in Table 3 indicates that undergraduate students did not communicate as much coverage of institutional learning objectives as did the graduate students.

EVIDENCE OF COVERAGE OF MULTIPLE INSTITUTIONAL LEARNING OBJECTIVES

The IBM software product produces webmaps to graphically display the degree of coverage of pairs of categories which have been defined as institutional learning objectives for the purposes of this study. Coverage is defined as the number of student work products that were assessed to contain evidence of both learning objectives in a pair. Figure 2 displays the webmap for the graduate business students. The webmap displays four nodes as circles with labels; each node representing one of the four institutional learning objectives. The nodes are connected as pairs by lines that vary in their thickness. The thickness of each line represents the number of student works that were assessed and found to contain both learning objectives that are connected in the webmap. A legend is provided that indicates how the number of student works is represented by different line thicknesses.

For example in Figure 2 the learning objectives of 'Demonstrating Familiarity with Dimensions of Catholic Social Teaching' and 'Use Their Gifts for the Service of Others and Benefit Society' are connected with the thickest line. Both nodes are characterized with the largest circle corresponding to the most students (n=13), displayed in the upper legend in Figure 2 and previously exhibited in Table 2. The number of student work products that the thickest line represents is displayed in the lower legend, 9. Nine student work products were assessed to possess evidence of coverage of both of these institutional learning objectives. Nine students represent 50% of the 18 student works that were assessed and 69% (9 of 13) of the students that covered either of these learning objectives. In this exercise graduate business students made a strong connection between these two learning objectives.

Figure 3 displays the webmap for undergraduate business students. The label on each node has been shortened. As expected given the results exhibited in Table 4, this webmap exhibits smaller counts at each node and fewer student works that covered each pair of learning objectives. The most frequent pairs that were covered were ILG-Catholic Social Teaching and IL-KHE (Knowledge of the Human Experience), and IL-KHE (Knowledge of the Human Experience) and ILG-Gifts for Service of Others. The undergraduate student works tended to put emphasis in their work products on the number of people suffering from hunger as evidence of their knowledge of the human experience.

Webmaps help to identify some of the instructional challenges. The challenge is to increase the number of student work products that cover multiple learning objectives. In the case of this study with four learning objectives, there are six binary pairs as represented in Figure 2. A comparison of webmaps over time can be used as a measure of how well a curriculum is helping student acquire the desired knowledge and skills.

Conclusions

The data from this study provides evidence that text analytics can be used for assessment of qualitative student works. Using the same assignment and 'rubric' comprised of terms, phrases, sematic meanings and synonyms, applied by an unbiased rater - the computer software, these results indicate that undergraduate work products did not provide as much content as graduate work products about specific institutional learning objectives. For reasons unknown at this time graduate students provided coverage of more learning objectives and a higher percentage of students covered provided content on each individual learning objective.

A possible conclusion is that separate libraries and dictionaries need to be created for use in assessing graduate and undergraduate work products. The alternative is to use the graduate results and libraries as a benchmark to work against for improving performance of undergraduate curricula.

Implications

The purpose of assessing academic programs is to measure if students are graduating with the knowledge and skills the programs were designed to deliver. Results in this study suggest that perhaps the graduate business curriculum be reviewed to try and identify if there are some things that could be adopted by the undergraduate program to improve student performance.

Decisions need to be made as to the specific evidence students need to include in their work product to demonstrate they have achieved a certain level of learning regarding the learning objectives. Builders of text analysis packages need to decide which terms, phrases, and sematic meanings need to be matched to conclude a student work product provides evidence of having a grasp of the content they were asked to study. These terms, phrases and meaning do not need to be verbatim from reference materials but can be created by the instructors of the courses in which the content is studied. This is a process of continuous improvement that will improve the ability of a text analysis package to identify semantics that provide evidence of student learning on specific learning objectives. Each time an assessment is administered there will probably be some additions to custom-built dictionaries and libraries for different learning goals and objectives.

This process is the same with a manual rubric, but the difference is transparency and an ability to eliminate interrater reliability. When assessors use a manual rubric they can draw mental conclusions as to if the words and phrases in the student work products captured the concepts the students were asked to learn. Unfortunately, their conclusion can vary from student work product to student work product. Reliability is an issue when human judgement is involved. The automated process does not have the same intuition and ability, it only matches linguistic patterns. In this regard outside reviewers can look at the libraries, dictionaries, terms, semantic meanings, and synonyms to review and improve the process. Problems of inter-rater reliability regarding assessment of a student work are no longer an issue. An analogous problem emerges though when building the dictionaries and deciding on the most important terms, phrases and synonyms as well as assignment of extracted concepts to categories.

REFERENCES

AACSB International - The Association to Advance Collegiate Schools of Business. (2015). Eligibility procedures and accreditation standards for business accreditation. *Tampa: AACSB International.* Retrieved from www.aacsb.edu

Cambria, E., & White, B. (2014, April 11). Jumping NLP curves: A review of natural language processing research. *IEEE Computational Intelligence Magazine*. doi:10.1109/MCI.2014.2307227

Canisius College. (n.d.). Goals and objectives. Retrieved from Canisius College: http://www.canisius.edu/about-canisius/mission/goals-objectives/

Catholic Relief Services. (n.d.). *Catholic Relief Services*. Retrieved from CRS.org: http://www.crs.org/

Catholic Relief Services. (n.d.). One human family, food for all. Retrieved from CRS.org: https://www.youtube.com/watch?feature=player_embedded&v=qhU5JEd-XRo

Catholic Relief Services. (n.d.). Pope Francis announces global campaign against hunger. Retrieved from CRS.org: https://www.youtube.com/watch?feature=player_embedded&v=A-sY_Olwkio

Catholic Relief Services. (n.d.). Pope Francis on caritas food for all week of action. Retrieved from CRS.org: https://www.youtube.com/watch?feature=player_embedded&v=5W5pYudNeQY

Catholic Relief Services. (n.d.). Quotes on poverty and hunger. Retrieved from CRS.org: http://resources.crs.org/wp-content/uploads/2015/01/Quotes-on-Poverty-and-Hunger.pdf

Center for Excellence in Learning and Teaching. (n.d.). Revised bloom's taxonomy. Retrieved from http://www.celt.iastate.edu/teaching-resources/effective-practice/revised-blooms-taxonomy/

IBM SPSS. (2010). Text analytics for surveys 4.0. *SPSS Inc., an IBM Company*.

Kaplan, J. J., Haudek, K. C., Ha, M., Rogness, N., & Fisher, D. G. (2014). Using lexical analysis software to assess student writing in statistics. *Technology Innovations in Statistics Education, 8*(1). Retrieved from https://escholarship.org/uc/item/57r90703

Kelley, C., Tong, P., & Choi, B.-J. (2010). A review of assessment of student learning programs at AACSB schools: A dean's perspective. *Journal of Education for Business, 85*, 299-306. doi:10.1080/08832320903449519

Middle States Commission on Higher Education. (2015). Standards for accreditation and requirements of affiliation, thirteenth edition. *Philadelphia: Middle States Commission on Higher Education.*

Xu, Y., & Reynolds, N. (2012, August). Using text mining techniques to analyze students' written responses to a teacher leadership dilemma. *International Journal of Computer Theory and Engineering, 4*(4), pp. 575-578.

Yu, C. H. (2009). Merits and characteristics of text mining. Retrieved from Creative Widom: http://creative-wisdom.com/computer/sas/text_mining.pdf

Yu, C. H., Jannasch-Pennell, A., & DiGangi, S. (2011, May). Compatibility between text mining and qualitative research in the perspectives of grounded theory, content analysis, and reliability. *The Qualitative Report, 16*(3), 730-744. Retrieved from http://www.nova.edu/ssss/QR/QR16-3/yu.pdf

WEB APPENDIX

A web appendix for this paper is available at:

http://www.businessresearchconsortium.org/pro/brcpro2015p11.pdf

A Suggested New Approach to Management Science Topic Coverage

William Leslie Langdon

SUNY Polytechnic Institute
Department of Business Management
fwll@sunyit.edu

BACKGROUND OF MANAGEMENT SCIENCE AS A DISCIPLINE

It is the opinion of some that the origins of Management Science can be traced to Operations Research. During World War II the Allied forces made use of specialists in a number of fields to help with the operations of the military. These specialists made use of mathematical models to maximize the use of existing resources. The application of these models within the corporate world became known as Management Science (1). Stafford Beer termed the field of management science as "the business use of Operations research."(2)

The initial development of scientific management is often credited to Frederick Winslow Taylor in work carried out in the early 1900's, although as noted above, some consider the World War II period as the origin of management science. George Dantzig developed the simplex method in 1947 making linear programming applications feasible (3). The first operations research textbook was published in 1957 by C. West Churchman, Russell Ackoff and Leonard Arnoff (1)

Techniques typically subsumed within Management Science typically included:

- Mathematical programming
- Linear programming
- Simplex method
- Dynamic programming
- Goal programming
- Integer programming
- Stochastic programming
- Markov processes
- Queuing theory/waiting line theory
- Transportation method
- Simulation

Several other techniques were typically added to this list in recent years, these are:

- Decision Analysis
- Computer simulation
- Inventory models
- Project scheduling: PERT/CPM
- Network models
- Forecasting
- Calculus-Based solution procedures

THE AACSB'S SHIFTING VIEWPOINT WITH RESPECT TO MANAGEMENT SCIENCE

During the year 1991 the AACSB eliminated the Management Science course requirement. These courses were viewed as irrelevant because they were being taught primarily as math courses (4). The management science course requirement has been eliminated from many MBA programs. Programs such as Harvard, Stanford, Chicago and Tuck reduced or eliminated management science from the required core courses. (5).A task force created by INFORMS surveyed the top 20 MBA programs. This report (Jordan et al, (5)) indicated that business school management science courses were failing to "serve the needs of the business school programs of the 1990's" (6). The report, known as the Magnanti report, described the irrelevancy of the algorithm and model-focused courses. The report noted (Jordan et al. 1997) that: "There is little support for the role of the solo OR/MS faculty member providing advanced, specialized education in the framework of an MBA program. There is clear evidence that there must be a major change in the character of the OR/MS course in this environment. There is little patience with courses centered on algorithms. Instead, the demand is for courses that focus on business situations, include prominent non-mathematical issues, use spreadsheets, and involve model formulation and assessment more that model structuring." This decline in the prominence of management science in the MBA curriculum has also been attributed to the weak connection between management practice and the practice of general management. (Grossman).Russell Ackoff attributed the problem to be that of "professional introversion." Ackoff observed that the MS profession has generally been unwilling to learn what business students need on in their professional life. Grossman has noted the" near total absence from the literature of how managers apply management science of those occasions when they do use it."

Grossman's study noted that teaching a mathematically-oriented management science course to students with little skill in mathematics resulted in "frustrated instructors, frustrated students and poor teaching ratings. (4).

Palmer (6) observed that" Instructors who agonize about students' poor preparation sounded like doctors in a hospital saying 'Don't send us any more sick people—we don't know what to do with them. Send us healthy patients so we can look like good doctors.'.... (this) helped me understand something critical about teaching: The way we diagnose our students' condition will determine the kind of remedy we offer. You think your students are brain dead? Then you're likely to drip data bits into their veins, wheeling their comatose forms from one information source to the next.., hoping they will absorb enough intellectual nutrients to maintain their vital signs until they have graduated and paid their tuition in full. The problem, of course, is that when the living and breathing arrive in our classroom, this kind of treatment kills them. But the power of this self-fulfilling prophecy seems to elude us: we rarely consider that our students may die in the classroom because we use methods that assume they are dead."

Grossman summed up the lesson of Palmer's words by noting that "trying to teach mathematical material to the unprepared-no matter how well-intentioned-will serve to destroy interest in mathematics and in the valuable tools of management science." (4) He observed that "an instructor needs to act based on what students actually know, rather than what he wishes they knew."

SUGGESTED TOPIC STRUCTURE FOR A BASIC UNDERGRAUDATE OR GRADUATE MANAGEMENT SCIENCE COURSE.

The AACSB reintroduced Management Science as an "expected learning experience" in 2003. The problems that were present with the management science courses resulting in their elimination from AACSB requirements were still present but a need was perceived for some sort of management science course content in the curriculum.

It is suggested hereinafter that a movement away from the traditional business school management science course focus on an algorithm and model-based body of knowledge be taken. Such a course should also take into explicit consideration of the goals of the business program to which the management course is attached. This approach has been suggested by Jordan et al. (5) and Bell (2). A reasonable approach to a general course of study in Management Science is the provision of a succinct definition of the topic. This can be stated as:

THE MEANING OF MANAGEMENT SCIENCE

A clarification of the terminology should be made at the outset of the course these to include:

- Management Science implies: The Science of Management.
- A Science implies: (1) A collection of Proven Propositions and (2) A Methodology, i.e. the scientific method.
- Management Implies:
- General Management implies "Doing things right"
- Strategic Management implies "Doing the right things"

It is likely that professors of Management Science may have many objectives in mind for a course of study , those provide below are, in the opinion, of this author, congruent with those of the AACSB as well as most schools of business.

COURSE OBJECTIVES IN A MANAGEMENT SCIENCE COURSE

- To prepare for life-long learning in the Management Science Area
- To improve Decision Making Skills
- To increase knowledge level of Management Science.

- To increase skill level in selected topics in Management Science.

Given that preparation for life-long learning , and life-long learning in Management Science in particular, is a worthwhile objective, the inclusion of some rudimentary concepts in learning theory appear an appropriate inclusion in a Management Science course of study. This inclusion is summarized below:

THE LAWS OF LEARNING AS THEY RELATE TO MANAGEMENT SCIENCE

- Intensity
- Organization
- Contiguity
- Exercise
- Effect
- Whole Learning is better than part learning
- Distributed Practice is better than massed practice
- Search for meaning
- Interference

It is intended that these laws be demonstrated for most of the topics included in the Management Science course of study.

The lack of integration of the topic of Management Science into the other study areas in the business school curriculum has been noted as a weakness in the teaching of Management Science (6). One way of mitigating this problem is the review/introduction of the traditional steps in strategic management into the Management Science course itself. The reinforcement of the idea that all decisions developed should be congruent with the overall corporate mission, and methods of attainment, are suggested herein as a legitimate part of the course of study in Management Science.

A summary of the usual steps in strategic management can be summarized as:

THE STEPS IN STRATEGIC MANAGEMENT
- Development of a Mission
- Development of Measurable Objectives
- Development of a Strategy
- Implementation
- Evaluation and Corrective Measures

Given the introduction to the topic of Management Science has progressed from (1) A general definition of the topic, to (2) A statement of the overall objectives of the course of study (3) Included some basic theoretical principles with respect to learning the topics included in the proposed course of study , addressed the overall potentially unifying concept of a (4) corporate mission and related strategic management, the next topic appropriate topic is suggested to be the general concept of and steps included in Decision Making. The introduction to decision theory is to exclude any specific mathematical applications at this point. The idea is to introduce the notion that decision making is not inexorably connected with the application of mathematics. A suggested non quantitative introduction to Decision Theory is presented below as:

OVERVIEW OF DECISION MAKING
- Decision Making Environments (1) Certainty, (2) Uncertainty and (3) Risk
- Steps in Decision Making (1) Problem recognition, (2) Diagnosis of the problem (a) Examining the structure, (b) Determining the Objective/Objectives
- Hypothesis Generation i.e. the development of alternative solutions to the problem.
- Deduction ,i.e. trying out the alternative solutions symbolically

- Solution selection and implementation of the solution.

Given the preliminary steps stated above, the introduction of basic statistics has the potential of providing more precision in the decision making process. Problem recognition can be accomplished with efficiency with the use of statistical measures, e.g. exception reports. The idea that the use of Descriptive Statistics makes it possible to recognize subtle problems before they become unmanageable is a useful concept to be introduced at this point in the Management Science course of study. Students are able to discern why each of the basic components of Descriptive Statistics in an important topic in the development of decision making skills. It is suggested herein that the topic of Statistics be introduced in the outline form below.

OVERVIEW OF BASIC STATISTICS
- Levels of Measurement (1) Nominal, (2) Ordinal, (3) Interval Scale and (4) Ratio Scale
- Definition of Statistics: The (1) Collection, (2) Organization, (3) Presentation, (4) Analysis and (5) Interpretation of numerical data.
- Descriptive Statistics: The (1) Collection, (2) Organization and (3) Presentation of numerical data.
- Inferential Statistics: The (1) Analysis and (2) Interpretation of numerical data.
- The Development of A Complete Numeric Descriptive Statement to include (1)Central Tendency,(a) Mean, (b)Median and (c) Mode (2) Absolute Dispersion (a)Range (b)Standard Deviation, (3) Relative Dispersion i.e. the Coefficient of Variation and (4) Skewness.

Subsequent to the completion of the basics of Descriptive Statistics, and before the introduction of Inferential Statistics, the student should be introduced to the overall concept of Probability Distributions. This, even if done at a cursory level, introduces the concept of scholasticism which is necessary for the decision making techniques applied under conditions of risk, e.g. Expected Value of the Net Present Value in the area of Finance.

OVERVIEW OF PROBABILITY RULES AND PROBABILITY DISTRIBUTIONS

Given the basics of probability rules it is suggested herein that a brief, as little as one two hour class, be devoted to demonstrating how probability rules can be utilized to develop various probability distributions. Introducing the topics of the mean and standard deviation of a discrete random variable provides a basis for the introduction of the Binomial Distribution. Since both the Student's t and Normal can be approximated by the Binomial distribution, it appears logical to introduce students to each of this distribution subsequent to discussing the Binomial Distribution.

It is hypothesized that business students would develop an appreciation of the potential for using probability as part of the decision making process.

OVERVIEW OF LINEAR PROGRAMMING

A unique feature of the approach suggested in this paper with respect to the delivery of a Management Science course, is the introduction of Linear Programming subsequent to the introduction of the rudiments of Management Theory, Statistics (both deterministic and stochastic) and decision theory.

Linear Programming topic coverage should be a logical extension of the Linear Regression area. Emphasis upon the concept of stating an objective in algebraic form in a first order form, i.e. highest exponent a 1 depicting a straight line, and recognition of activity constraints in the same general form should also be stated. It is suggested that the Simplex Algorithm be mentioned, and perhaps briefly explained, but not included as part of the course requirement. The use of the graphic method is demonstrated only as a way to understand the LP concept. The use of Microsoft Excel Is suggested a solution methodology to be demonstrated and practiced by students. The development of the topic of Linear Regression as a precursor to Linear Regression provides the opportunity to maximize the benefits for time spent learning Linear Regression as well as illustrating how an iterative methodology such as Linear Programming can be combined with a deterministic methodology such as Linear Regression.

CONCLUDING COMMENT

The central theme in the suggested approach to Management Science coverage is the careful building of knowledge and skill with an emphasis upon concepts rather than specific techniques. It is an integral part of the suggested approach that each part of the course be focused on the concept of management with the use of science with a heavy emphasis on decision making. Methods suggested hereinbefore are not intended to be collectively exhaustive, but rather a demonstration of the uniqueness of the suggested approach as it differs from current teaching practice. This report is intended as a succinct statement of unique approach to the teaching of Management Science.This uniqueness if believed to be the emphasis on the integrative build up of prerequisite knowledge as it contributes to the students' decision making skill in the area of general management.

PARTIAL BIBLIOGRAPHY

1. C.W.R., R.L. Ackoff, and E.L. Arnoff, Introduction to Operations Research, Wiley, 1957.

2. Bell,P. (1998) "Teachers Aid from INFORMS," OR/MS Today, Vol. 24., No 3,pp8-10.

3. Stafford Beer (1967), Management Science: The Business use of Operations Research

4. Danzig, G.B. Linear Programming and Extensions. Princeton University Press, 1963

5. Grossman, Thomas A. Jr. Causes of the Decline of the Business School Management Science Course. INFORMS Transactions on Education , March 2015

6. Jordan, E., L. Lason, M. Lenard., J. Moore, S. Powell, and T. Willemain (1977), "OR/MS and MBAs" OR/MS Today, Vol 24, No 1, pp.36-41.

7. Palmer, P.J. (1998) *The Courage to Teach,* Jossey-Bass, San Francisco, C.A.

8. Powell, S.G. (1998), "Requiem for the Management Science Course?" Intervaces, Vol. 28, No 2, pp 11-117.

How to Build It So They Come: Using the Interrelationship Quality Function Deployment Matrix to Design a Professional Business Student Club

*Nate Luciano, Mary Bolo-Blum,
Tyler Lokietek, and Lisa M. Walters*

Nate Luciano
Senior Management Major

Mary Bolo-Burr
Master's Program, Interdisciplinary Studies

Tyler Lokietek
Senior Management Major

Lisa M. Walters
Assistant Professor, Operations Management
The State University of New York-Fredonia
Fredonia, NY

Correspondence concerning this article should be sent to:

Lisa M. Walters
The State University of New York-Fredonia

350 East Thompson Hall
Fredonia, NY 14063
716-673-3504

Abstract

This case study focuses on how the operational tool of interrelationship matrix of Quality Function Deployment (QFD) tool was used by a group of operations management students to design an on-campus branch of a national professional organization, specifically the American Society for Quality (ASQ). To develop the QFD interrelationship matrix, secondary research was conducted to establish the Voice of the Customer (VoC) requirements in terms of potential future employers of business students. Because these requirements were derived from secondary sources, the weights of the importance of the requirements were considered uniform, as the research sources did not identify emphasis of any one requirement in preference of another. Primary research was also conducted by use of a business student focus group to identify the types of activities students would find desirable, thereby encouraging their alignment with the ASQ student group. Such activities constituted the design requirements of the group. These requirements were further weighted by the focus group and correlated to the VoC requirements to determine the specific student group activities that would be most advantageous to facilitate future employment opportunities for business students. The two key pursuits identified through the QFD process were live consulting projects and technical workshops. The results are useful for advisors and leaders of professionally-linked student groups in any profession as well as university career development offices.

Keywords: operations management, quality function deployment, student groups, employability, critical thinking, retention, ASQ, interrelationship matrix

INTRODUCTION

Student activities and groups are a part of collegiate life. Students are able to establish relationships and engage in activities that make their lives richer and their collegiate experience that much more memorable with varied group goals. Groups differ in their goals and activities, providing a virtual banquet to students interested in participating. At The State University of New York-Fredonia, 172 student groups are currently formally recognized, representing the spectrum of intents, from athletics to academics.

However, do these student groups provide any tangible benefit to the student while in school? And does membership provide further benefit to the student in terms of employability? This study seeks to determine how to design a student group that facilitates such benefits.

LITERATURE REVIEW

The role of student groups in a student's educational life has not been the subject of significant research on the whole. In past few years there has been some research on dynamics of small group impact on student development (Gellin, 2003); fewer studies have focused on retention and marketability (Astin, 1984) (Lotkowski et al., 2004). However, some work is available on the subject, and this body of work, as discussed below, suggests that student groups indeed offer positive outcomes to students. The focus of this research is on the role of student groups in facilitating student success beyond a student's academic career.

The work of Lotkowski et al. (2004) focuses on methods to facilitate student retention. The study assessed various aspects of student life, both academic and non-academic, in an effort to understand the factors that influence student retention. The study suggests academic self-confidence and achievement-orientation have the strongest relationship to college grade point average (GPA). In addition, the study indicates even students who perform well academically may still be at risk of dropping out of college, suggesting that a focus on academic performance as a means to retention is inherently flawed. As a result, the role of non-academic issues, such as confidence and motivation, play a key role in retention. Such aspects may be bolstered by student groups if the student groups are designed to provide opportunities to develop confidence and secure achievements.

Two works, by Peter D. Hart Research, Inc. (2006) and Tugend (2013), suggest an on-going gap between employer needs and the skillset of business graduates. Peter D. Hart Research, Inc. (2006) study found that 63% of business executives believed a majority of college graduates were not equipped with the skills necessary to be successful in the global economy, particularly in terms of teamwork and problem-solving. Tugend (2013) indicates employers felt skills involving writing, speaking, adaptability, prioritizing, decision-making, and problem-solving are lacking. Tugend (2013) further indicates that although new graduates are skilled technically, they lack the ability to put those skills into practice in the real-world business environment. Germane to this skill set is the ability to think critically.

A meta-analysis by Gellin (2003) looked at the previous decade's studies to determine the effect of various aspects of life, including student groups, on the development of critical thinking within students. Critical thinking is imperative to the problem-solving and decision-making skills necessary to be successful in the modern business environment. Gellin (2003) establishes that clubs and groups, including overall campus life, have a significant positive effect on the development of critical thinking, highlighting the work of Tsui (1998) that provided the most significant insight into the positive effects of clubs and societies in terms of critical thinking. Gellin's conclusions suggest that students who live on campus and participate in clubs and societies that involve significant social interaction show increased levels of critical thinking over their peers. The club or society activities that result in the largest benefit remain unidentified within the study, suggesting that critical thinking improvements from involvement with clubs and societies stems from the increased social interaction which facilitates stronger commitment to the organization (Astin, 1984). This notion of increased social interaction implies a larger exposure by the student to varying opinions and perspectives from within the group. Thus, a student group that engages its members will enhance a student's social interactions which can improve his or her marketability and career success.

While the literature available on the benefits of student groups is minimal, the research available suggests that not only does a group membership foster positive outcome for students, but it may also fill the gaps the employers find lacking in graduates (Gellin, 2003) (Tsui, 1998). To accomplish this goal, it makes sense that the activities of such a club must not only address the needs of potential employers (Peter D. Hart Research, Inc., 2006) (Tugend, 2013), but also the interests of the students, facilitating the social interaction necessary to benefit student retention (Lotkowski et al., 2004) and critical thinking development (Tsui, 1998). An industry tool that relates the needs of the customer to the design of a process, product, or service is Quality Function Deployment (QFD). This tool has also been applied in academic settings in a variety of applications, including the design of kindergartens (Moura e Sa and Saraiva, 2001), the improvement of secondary education academic experiences (Bedi and Sharma, 2006a), the development of business case studies (Bedi and Sharma 2006b), and the establishment of a governance system within a higher education system (Hafeez and Mazour, 2011). These applications are further discussed below.

QFD was developed by Yoji Akao (1972). Its essential purpose is to provide a tool to ensure the critical requirements of the customer, known as the Voice of the Customer (VoC) requirements, are effectively addressed by a product or service design (Akao, 1994). Essentially, it is a tool for listening to the VoC. QFD requires four pieces of information (Ross, 1988). First, it is essential to know what is important to the customer (the "what's"). Second, how those important requirements can be met in the product or process must be established (the "how's"). Third, the relationship between the "what's" and the "how's" must be determined. Lastly, the emphasis of the "how's" is identified; that is, how much of the "how's" must be provided by a product or service to address the "what's;" this emphasis is known as the "how much."

QFD is associated with a variety of techniques. One such technique predominantly used in QFD is the House of Quality (HoQ), a matrix which not only utilizes the four pieces of information described in the preceding paragraph, but also seeks to understand the inter-relationships of the technical specifications as well as the benchmarks and targets for the technical specifications (Akao, 1972). However, the practice of QFD should not be associated solely with the HoQ, and practitioners are cautioned to use the techniques which will assist them in achieving their goals (http://www.qfdi.org/what_is_qfd/qfd_approaches.html). For example, Danilo Sirias (2012) developed an experiential learning activity to teach operations students QFD using only the interrelationship matrix of the HoQ in an effort to improve a business course. Thus, depending on the practitioner's needs, the approach to QFD may be diverse.

QFD has been used successfully in academic settings. Moura e Sa and Saraiva (2001) used QFD to determine what would be an ideal kindergarten from the stakeholders' view. This study was inspired by a need to become more responsive to educational expectations in the academic and socialization arenas. Researchers determined that a study for kindergartens was appropriate because attitudes toward education in general are largely determined by the kindergarten experience, and kindergartens tend to have more control over their policies, procedures, staff, and the physical environment. Moura e Sa and Saraiva (2001) collected opinions (voices) of the customers (parents, children, and teachers) from diverse circumstances. Specifically, these included personal experiences, feelings, and expectations of the customers which were then transformed into customer requirements. The researchers converted the requirements into characteristics of the target product, thereby designing a kindergarten curriculum which ensured all stakeholder voices were heard.

Bedi and Sharma (2006a) applied the QFD concept to secondary education. They interviewed randomly selected students regarding their preferences in affecting better academic procedures at the school. The study focused entirely on curriculum, teachers, and examinations and asked how the school experience could be improved. Two schools supplied a random sample of students and rated the performance of the school on its ability to prepare them for standardized testing. The researchers hold that Quality Function Deployment (QFD) was effective in discerning which policies should be implemented to provide more satisfaction of students studying at the secondary level. Further, Bedi and Sharma (2006a) held a view of informing schools about the use of QFD is a matter of urgency to improve secondary education.

Bedi and Sharma (2006b) also applied QFD at the collegiate level to the development of business case studies. The study identifies student expectations and looks at the differences between cases that are available and student expectations. Further, the study wanted to find a way to develop case studies that would eliminate the difference between what the students wanted and the case studies that were already available. In essence, students wanted "hot" subjects in real life businesses. The researchers concluded that QFD is useful in finding the voice of students regarding what they prefer in case studies. In fact, they believe QFD should be used with every new class of students because each classes' expectations are unique and case studies should be designed that will capture and hold their interest.

QFD can also benefit in higher education administration. Hafeez and Mazour (2011) defined QFD as "a comprehensive quality governance system" which in this case links customer (student) demands with program and course outcomes, course assessments, and student and faculty course evaluations; the purpose of QFD was to ensure alignment between the various factions to accomplish set program goals as well as university goals and missions. The emphasis of the study was in terms of program cycle. The researchers argued their results identified strengths and weaknesses within programming in terms of meeting program goals, program outcomes, and course outcomes.

In summary, QFD has been exercised in a variety of industries, including academic settings. These academic settings range from the elemental setting, that of kindergarten, to the higher education setting. Additionally, in terms of higher education, it has demonstrated use in terms of administration. Its use in terms of designing activities to support the non-academic aspects of a student's life has not been evaluated.

INTRODUCING THE AMERICAN SOCIETY FOR QUALITY

The American Society for Quality (ASQ) considers itself to be the "Global Voice for Quality"^{TM} (American Society for Quality [ASQ], 2014), advancing the use of quality methodologies, tools, and concepts to enhance the world's businesses and communities. The organization provides its 76,000 domestic and international individual and organizational members with resources, professional certifications, and training to enhance their ability to meet today's societal and business challenges (ASQ, 2014). It has been in existence for 65 years, with its beginning roots planted just after World War II, with such distinguished members as quality giant Dr. Joseph Juran (ASQ, 2014). ASQ has its roots in engineering, and as such, it advances quality as a notion centered on quantitative decision-making, systematic problem-solving, and standardization. For example, its many certifications include those in terms of Lean manufacturing and Six Sigma, among others.

It is a certified standards developer, providing significant input on the global standards of quality management, environmental management, dependability and reliability, statistics, and social responsibility. It additionally supports the volunteer organizations that develop and approve the well-known ISO standards, which promote consistency and harmony in international business (ASQ, 2014).

One aspect embraced by ASQ is its support of collegiate student sections. Students, with a faculty advisor, at an Institute of Higher Learning (IHL) can make application to become a student section, with that student section supported not only by its IHL, but also by a local section of ASQ. By working with a local ASQ section, the student section has the opportunity to network with those already practicing in various careers as well as benefit from those individuals' experiences and perspectives. Student sections of ASQ include such institutions as the Ohio State University, University of North Carolina at Charlotte, and the University of Southern California, among others (ASQ, 2014).

With its emphasis on problem-solving, quantitative decision-making, organizational efficiency and effectiveness, and management, an ASQ student section appears to be a worthy endeavor for an IHL. Indeed, as a result of the ASQ foci, the management students at The State University of New York-Fredonia began the formation of its own student section, sponsored by the Erie, Pennsylvania ASQ 0809 Section. The vision of this student section is "Grow Quality, Improve the World." Its mission is "by bridging the gap between academics and workplace, we will model, practice, and explore the Quality Body of Knowledge, thereby improving our club, our communities, and our world, one student at a time." The issue in terms of developing this section to achieve its mission is to determine how it should be structured to meet the needs of its student members so that membership is sustainable, facilitating interaction, while also addressing the needs of potential employers, thereby providing increased marketability and career-growth to those students who participate.

PURPOSE AND RESEARCH QUESTIONS

The purpose of this study is to determine if Quality Function Deployment is a credible tool to design a student section of ASQ that will meet not only the desires of the students to facilitate their engagement with the section, but also meet the needs of the potential employers, thereby improving the marketability of the student members. The study is important as it seeks to determine the credibility of an established industry tool to foster positive student outcomes, both as a current student and beyond a student's academic career. The following research questions guided the study:

Research Question 1: What student section activities would the prospective ASQ student section members find advantageous and in what priority? These activities constitute the service design aspects of the student section, also known as "the how's" of the design.

Research Question 2: What specific skills are sought by prospective employers of business program graduates? These skills represent the Voice of Customer (VoC) requirements of potential employers, also known as "the what's" in terms of employer needs.

Research Question 3: What are the most advantageous student section activities that will meet the needs of the prospective student members as well as those of future employers? These activities represent the "how much" of an activity is necessary to meet the VoC requirements.

METHODOLOGY

This case study employed a mixed-methods approach. Quantitative data consisted of responses to Likert-scaled items and the numeric outcomes from the Quality Function Deployment tool, while qualitative data comprised focus group and interview responses.

To answer Research Question 1, "What student section activities would the prospective ASQ student section members find advantageous and in what priority?", a review of the activities conducted by current business school student groups on the campus of The State University of New York-Fredonia was conducted by the research team. The list of those groups is identified in Appendix A: School of Business Student Groups Evaluated for Activities. Those identified activities were collated. A focus group comprised of six senior level business students was presented with this slate of activities, and asked to identify other activities they felt might be valuable but not identified as part of the initial review. The activities noted by the focus group were added to the slate of activities. This final menu of activities were then formatted into a Likert-style survey to be administered to a sampling of upper-level business students who might be prospective ASQ student section members to evaluate if the noted activities were indeed considered desirable. The survey is found as Appendix B: Proposed Desired Student Group Activities Survey and Results. The survey was administered via the online survey tool Survey Monkey^{TM}, providing for confidentiality in the survey response process. Here the administrator was the research team and also responsible for the data analysis. The link to the survey was emailed to the students via the college's email system. The link was accompanied by an email that included the purpose of the survey and offered the option for a student not to participate.

Activities would be considered desirable if the survey results demonstrated a preponderance of responses for each positively worded activity statement as "agree" or "strongly agree." If the preponderance of responses reflected ambivalence, "disagree" or "strongly disagree" to the positively worded activity statements, those activities would be removed from the list.

Those activities identified as desirable through the survey to prospective ASQ student section members would be subjected to a weighting process where each activity was assigned a weight value (W) reflective of the importance of the activity on a scale of 1–5 (1 = least important; 5 = most important). The weighting process was performed by the six member focus group that constructed the menu of desirable activities. The weights (W) were determined by asking each focus group member to weigh the importance of the activity using the 1–5 scale. The resulting measure of central tendency (mean or median) would be calculated for each activity using statistical software to determine the weight used in the analysis. The higher the weight, the more important the focus group found that activity to be. The resulting weighted list of activities constitutes "the how's" of the student section design.

By employing the weighting process on design characteristics, this Quality Function Deployment could be considered "reverse," in that typically, the weighting is done on the VoC components. However, by using the weighting process on the design, the student voice is also heard, thereby facilitating the ability to identify activities that would lead to greater participation among the students in the student section.

To answer Research Questions 2, "What specific skills are sought by prospective employers of business program graduates?", available literature was reviewed to determine the top skills desired by prospective employers in terms of graduating business students. The resulting attributes were provided to several management members of local businesses to validate the attributes and provide additional attributes if necessary. The resulting characteristics consistitue "the what's" of the VoC, specifically potential employers. Because these requirements are derived from secondary sources which did not prioritize the characteristics, the weights of the importance of the requirements would be considered uniform.

To answer Research Question 3, "What are the most advantageous student section activities that will meet the needs of the prospective student members as well as those of future employers?", a Quality Function Deployment interrelationship matrix was constructed to understand the relationship between the "what's" and the "how's." This relationship was represented as a Relationship Rating (RR). To determine the RR, the project team used the Delphi technique to provide a value which represented the strength of the relationship between each "what" (each need of the employers) with each "how" (each activity proposed by the ASQ student section). The strength of the relationship was scaled as 1–9 (1 = no relationship; 9 = strongest relationship). Specifically, each project team member anonymously provided a RR for each item; the results were shared among the project team, and this relationship rating assignment process was repeated until consensus was reached.

The RR value was multiplied by the W value of each proposed activity to facilitate the identification of priority activities in terms of potential employer needs. Lastly, a weighted average was calculated for each proposed activity, with the highest weighted averages representing those activities which would address most potential employer needs. For example, referring to Appendix C, Table 1, *Quality Function Deployment Interrelationship Matrix for Building a Strong ASQ Student Section*, the proposed activity of consulting projects with local businesses was weighted (W) as 5, which is most important. When evaluating that activity (the how) against team-building (the what), the relationship rating (RR) was determined as the strongest, represented by a value of 9. Thus, the weighted relationship between team-building and consulting projects is 40, calculated as the product of the weight and the relationship rating (RR). This calculation process is repeated for the entire column, providing a final weighted average for the proposed activity, calculated as ΣW^*RR for each column/ΣW.

RESULTS

The results of the study are noted below. These results are considered in terms of each individual research question.

Research Question 1: What student section activities would the prospective ASQ student section members find advantageous and in what priority? These activities and priority represent the design aspects of the ASQ student section; that is, these activities represent "the how's." The student groups associated with the School of Business (Appendix A) were evaluated by the research team with regard to their specific activities. Both consistencies and non-consistencies in activities existed among the groups. In terms of consistent activities, all groups held periodic meetings and sponsored speakers. These consistent activities were added to a menu of activities to be considered by prospective ASQ student section members. A focus group of six senior level business school students considered and determined other possible activities to be evaluated as desirable by prospective ASQ student section members. These included plant tours, consulting projects, and technical workshops. All these identified activities were combined into a final menu organized in terms of an on-line survey, found as Appendix B. The survey was administered using Survey Monkey™ to 80 business students. The students selected were those in the capstone strategic management courses, as these soon-to-be graduating students would have had the most opportunity to explore the available academic student groups within the school of business. The number of responses was n = 37.

In terms of the survey, results indicated that consulting projects with local businesses, plant tours, guest speakers, and technical workshops are perceived as highly beneficial to potential student group members. Further, the frequency of general membership meetings should be every other week, as specified by over half of respondents.

Those activities perceived as highly beneficial to potential ASQ student group members were subjected to a weighting process where each activity was assigned a value by the six member focus group that contributed to the menu of desirable activities. The weights (W) were determined by asking each focus group member to weigh the importance of the attribute on a scale of 1–5 (1 = least important; 5 = most important). The measure of central tendency for each for each activity was determined using statistical software to establish the weight used in the analysis. The median was the measure of central tendency chosen to accommodate any non-normality in the data. The higher the weight, the more important the focus group found that activity to be. The focus group determined consulting projects with local businesses, technical workshops, and plant tours to be the most heavily weighted, with each median value as 5.

Guest speakers and bi-weekly meetings were weighted less important, with median values of 2 and 3, respectively.

To answer Research Questions 2, What specific skills are sought by prospective employers of business program graduates? The literature review was re-visited, and the key characteristics noted as lacking but desired by potential employers were distilled from those studies. The two works, by Peter D. Hart Research, Inc. (2006) and Tugend (2013), suggest that a need exists to develop student skills and abilities in terms of teamwork, problem-solving, prioritization, decision-making, adaptability, and communication (both written and speaking). Further, the ability to apply technical skills is suggested by Tugend (2013). These characteristics were provided to the management members of several local businesses for validation and elaboration.

As a result of this management review function, the notion of technical application was further defined as meaning data analysis, computer software proficiency, and practical applications related to a job. They additionally suggested that prioritization encompass planning and organizational functions as well. Lastly, these individuals also recommended the ability to influence be added. Thus, the VoC skill and ability requirements were determined to be: teamwork, problem-solving, prioritizing/planning/organizing, communication, decision-making, data analysis, computer software proficiency, practical application, adaptability, and influence. These VoC requirements represent "the what's."

To answer Research Question 3, What are the most advantageous student section activities that will meet the needs of the prospective student members as well as those of future employers? A Quality Function Deployment matrix was constructed using the information from Research Questions 1 and 2. This matrix is found as Appendix C.

The first column of the QFD matrix provides the specific skills identified by potential employers, as derived from the results of Research Question 2. The top two rows of the matrix identifies the student section activities prospective ASQ student section members would find advantageous, along with their weights of importance, as identified in the results of Research Question 1.

A relationship column is provided for each student section activity as it relates to the skills identified by potential employers, represented by the RR value, with the scale of 1–9 (1 = no relationship; 9 = strongest relationship). The relationship value was determined by the project team, using the Delphi technique. Specifically, each project team member anonymously provided a RR for each item; the results were shared among the project team, and this relationship rating assignment process was repeated until consensus was reached, for a total of four reiterations. The RR value was multiplied by the W value of each proposed activity to facilitate the identification of priority activities in terms of potential employer needs; these weighted RR values are represented within each relationship column. Lastly, a weighted average is presented for each proposed activity, with the highest weighted averages representing those activities which would address most potential employer needs.

Consulting projects with local businesses is a clear priority for this student section, with a weighted average of 17.0. This activity is followed by technical workshops, which provided a weighted average of 10.5. Plant tours and guest speakers resulted in similar weighted averages, with values of 4.5 and 4.2, respectively. The least beneficial activity as provided by the QFD matrix is bi-weekly meetings, with a weighted average of 2.1.

DISCUSSION

From this study, it appears that Quality Function Deployment is a tool that has utility in identifying key activities a student section of ASQ should pursue that will meet not only the desires of the students to facilitate their engagement with the section, but also meet the needs of the potential employers, thereby improving the marketability of the student members. Specifically, by emphasizing consulting projects and technical workshops, the student section has the greatest opportunity to enhance the skill set desired by potential employers.

In terms of the applicability of the tool itself, the findings are consistent with Moura e Sa and Saraiva (2001), in that the collection of differing perspectives, experiences, and expectations of students in terms of student group activities allowed the research team to develop a menu of design characteristics that could be used to answer the future potential employer voices. Further, consistent with Bedi and Sharma (2006b), QFD was useful in discerning which design characteristics should be implemented to better facilitate interaction and market preparedness in terms of student members, allowing for a more efficient use of resources. Moreover, Bedi and Sharma (2006b) also identified that students wanted "hot" subjects in real-life businesses as case studies; overwhelmingly, consulting for local businesses was the most desirable design characteristic in terms of what student members wanted, a consistent desire with that found by Bedi and Sharma (2006b).

The work of Lotkowski et al. (2004) suggests that confidence and motivation play a key role in retention. In terms of the design aspects advanced through the Quality Function Deployment construction, the use of consulting projects and technical workshops are activities that require a great deal of engagement and application; indeed, successful completion of such activities may bolster confidence and achievement motivation within the participating student.

Considering this study in terms of those of Peter D. Hard Research, Inc. study (2006) and Tugend (2013), the use of QFD provided activities that can be clearly linked to achieving or at least enhancing the skill set desired by employers. Indeed, the consulting projects alone were determined to have a positive relationship with all the skills identified. Further, with respect to critical thinking enhancement as advanced by Gellin's (2003) meta-analysis, the implementation of the activities denoted as priority as part of the QFD are those that would require the most interaction among the students, specifically consulting projects and workshops.

CONCLUSION

Student groups are certainly a fact of collegiate life, and if these student groups are properly designed, it is likely that they may provide tangible benefits to the student while in his or her academic career and further into his or her future careers. An important tool to facilitate such a proper design is Quality Function Deployment, a tool used not only within the manufacturing industry, but also within other fields, including academics.

As noted in the literature review, student groups may enhance retention, specifically in terms of provisions of confidence and achievement motivation. Additionally, increased student interaction has been determined to facilitate critical-thinking skills. Critical-thinking skills are foundation to the skill set desired by potential employers of business school graduates. By using QFD to identify student group activities that facilitate student interaction within an established student group, and relating those activities to skills required of potential employees, the likelihood of establishing a beneficial student group is enhanced.

LIMITATIONS AND FURTHER STUDY

This study was limited by several factors. The first factor was the construct of the initial survey to determine the slate of activities to be evaluated. Because the slate was devised by a review of activities which already existed, the survey had limited the ability of the respondent to provide insight into activities that might be desirable but not noted on the survey. A better construct of the survey might be to ask a student what activities they would like a student section to pursue, and then allow the respondents to also determine how important those activities are to them, using a Likert-scale. In this way, a larger, more diverse slate may result, coupled with more insight into what the appropriate importance rating should be. Indeed, it may also be beneficial to ask employers what activities might be helpful in skill development, as these employers have broad experiences which might be useful to develop specific skill sets.

In terms of the skills desired, it would be beneficial to do a broad survey of local employers instead of reliance on secondary research. In this way, a more geographically relevant understanding of desired skills might result.

Moreover, an inquiry could be made in terms of the importance of these skills from the employers' perspectives, resulting in the ability to do a traditional QFD, as opposed to one which weighted the design aspects. In this case, the study would be repeated; however, no weighting of the design aspects would occur.

Additionally, in terms of limitations, using both a student panel as well as an employer panel to determine the relationship ratings may provide a more accurate representation of the relationship between skill sets and design attributes. For example, because of their unique perspective, employers might be aware of a relationship that is not readily apparent.

The construction of this interrelationship matrix was constrained by time, as the ASQ student branch was recently chartered, and it was imperative to design and implement the branch in a timely fashion. To that end, as the student branch has been implemented, a full HoQ matrix could be constructed, to better understand the relationships among the technical specifications and to determine targets for these specifications.

Lastly, an analysis could be performed to evaluate the career success of ASQ student members who participated in the resulting student group model as compared with students from other student groups which were not designed using QFD. This evaluation could consider such factors as job title, salary, and job performance. The analysis could be conducted from the perspectives of both the students as well as employers, with the results used to evaluate the effectiveness of the QFD process in this application.

REFERENCES

Akao, Y. (1972). New product development and quality assurance – quality deployment

System (in Japanese). *Standardization and Quality Control, 25*(4), 7-14.

Akao, Y. (1994). Development history of quality function deployment. *The Customer Driven Approach to Quality Planning and Deployment.* Minato, Tokyo 107 Japan: Asian Productivity Organization. p. 339.

American Society for Quality. (2014). *We are the global voice of quality.* Retrieved from http://asq.org/about-asq/brochure/

Astin, A. W. (1984). Student involvement: A developmental theory for higher education. *Journal of College Student Personnel, 25,* 297-308.

Bedi, K. & Sharma, J. (2006a). Benchmarking the quality of secondary education at the micro level and policy imperatives. *Social Science Research Network* (1-16. U21 Global Working Paper No. 013/2006). Retrieved from http://ssrn.com/abstract = 1606182.

Bedi, K. & Sharma, J. (2006b). Quality function deployment in business case studies. *Social Science Research Network* (1-16. U21 Global Working Paper No. 015/2006). Retrieved from http://ssrn.com/abstract = 1606302.

Gellin, A. (2003). The effect of undergraduate student involvement on critical thinking: A Meta-analysis of the literature 1992-2000. *Journal of College Student Development, 44*(6), 746-762. doi.org/10.1353/csd.2003.0066

Hafeez, K. & Mazour, A. (2001). Using quality function deployment as a higher education management and governance tool. *Business and Law, 6*(1), 31-52. doi:10.5200/1822-9530.2011.02

Lotkowski, V. A., Robbins, S. B., & Noeth, R. J. (2004). *The role of academic and non-academic factors in imporving college retention* (ACT Policy Report). ACT Publication. Retrieved from http://files.eric.ed.gov/fulltext/ED485476.pdf

Moura e Sa, P., & Saraiva, P. (2001). The development of an ideal kindergarten through concept engineering/quality function deployment. *Total Quality Management, 12*(3), 365-372. doi.org/10.1080/09544120120034500

Peter D. Hart Research Associates, Inc. (2006). *How should colleges prepare students to succeed in today's global economy?* Washington: Peter D. Hart Research Associates, Inc.

QFD Approaches and Techniques. (n.d.). Retrieved January 5, 2016, from http://www.qfdi.org/what_is_qfd/qfd_approaches.html

Ross, P.J. (1998, June). The role of Taguchi methods and design of experiments in QFD. *Quality Progress,* 41–47.

Siria, D. (2012). An Experiential Learning Activity to Teach the Main Quality Function Deployment Matrix. *International Journal of Business, Humanities and Technology,* 76-81.

Tsui, L. (1998). Fostering critical thinking in college students: A mixed-method study of influences inside and outside the classroom. *Dissertation Abstracts International, 60*(1), p. 1081A.

Tugend, A. (2013). *What it takes to make new college graduates employable.* Retrieved from http://www.nytimes.com/2013/06/29/your-money/a-quest-to-make-college-graduates-employable.html?pagewanted=all&_r=0

WEB APPENDIX

A web appendix for this paper is available at:

http://www.businessresearchconsortium.org/pro/brcpro2015p13.pdf

The Financial Statements Articulation Fence: An Expanded and Refined Visual Model of Financial Statement Articulation

John Olsavsky

Assistant Professor of Accounting
Department of Business Administration
School of Business
State University of New York at Fredonia
W311 Thompson Hall
Fredonia, NY 14063
716-673-4601 (Office)
Email: olsavsky@fredonia.edu

Abstract

This paper presents the introduction of a visual aid for use in teaching the interrelationship of financial statements and the effect of transactions on the elements of the financial statements. The Financial Statements Articulation Fence is a merging of Mobley's Matrix, Ittelson's Structural Connections Model and Sellman's Financial Fence®. The Financial Statements Articulation Fence provides students with a visual aid to improve understanding of the financial statement articulation of the four basic financial statements. The model uses the figure of a post and rail fence where posts represent the Statements of Financial Position and the rails represent the changes between two posts with three specific rails - the Statement of Cash Flows, Statement of Income and Statement of Statement of Changes in Equity.

INTRODUCTION

Students come to us in the intermediate accounting courses with different levels of knowledge of the accounting process learned in the introductory accounting courses. Their knowledge of the financial statements and how they are connected to one another may vary widely. The purpose of the Financial Statements Articulation Fence is to provide a big picture, one-page summary of the four basic financial statements and their interrelationships.

LITERATURE REVIEW

Ever since Mann (1984) proposed a worksheet for demonstrating the articulation of financial statements several authors have proposed their version of a rows and column model to help students see how financial statements are interrelated. The Financial Statements Articulation Fence is a merging of Mobley's Matrix, Ittelson's Structural Connections Model and Sellman's Financial Fence®.

Accounting students come to us with all combinations of the four sensory modalities - Visual, Aural/Auditory, Read/write, and Kinesthetic (VARK). This model is aimed at those students whose stand out mode is visual.

Mobley's Matrix Model

An engineer by training, Mobley (1989) describes how he developed the "Mobley Matrix" over a twenty-seven year period starting in 1956 to train executives at the IBM Executive School at Sand's Point, NY. This model is a one-page worksheet with five columns used to classify the changes in the balance sheet accounts from the beginning to the end of the accounting period (Figure 1).

The beginning and ending balance sheets are located in the first and fifth column, respectively. They are footed to prove the balancing of each balance sheet. For each row on the balance sheet the middle three columns in between are used to explain the change in that account's balance across the matrix and which periodic financial statement is affected, if any.

The second column is entitled Balance Sheet Transfer & Adjustment and is used to enter non-cash balance sheet only transactions and the adjusting entries. The amounts in each element on the balance sheet - assets, liabilities and equity - are footed and verified that the element totals balance.

In the third column are the amounts from the Income Statement which when combined at the bottom of the column equal the net income on the retained earnings row. The Mobley Matrix Income Statement Vertical Math is calculated top to bottom with the sales minus cost of goods sold minus depreciation/amortization minus intangible amortization minus MSG&A expense minus/plus interest and other expense/income minus income tax expense to equal net profit.

The Cash Statement in the fourth column uses the direct method to explain how each balance sheet account row is affected by the cash flows. The account amounts are combined at the top of the column to explain the change in cash on the cash row. The cash flow statement vertical math is calculated bottom to top where the change in cash equals collections (OCF) minus inventory paid (OCF) minus prepayments (OCF) minus fixed asset investments (ICF) minus other investments (ICF) minus expenses paid (OCF) plus/minus borrowings/paybacks (FCF) minus interest and others paid (OCF) minus income tax paid (OCF) plus capital paid in (FCF) minus dividends declared and paid (FCF).

The beauty of this model is that it must account for every change in the balance sheet accounts (i.e., extensions and footings must crossfoot) and every change in the income statement accounts and statement of cash flow activities (i.e., each column must foot). Keep in mind that this was a time when GAAP did not require a statement of cash flows. It tied together these three basic financial statements in a one-page summary.

Ittelson's Structural Connections Model

Ittelson (2009), trained as bio-chemist, not an accountant, developed his model during his business development consulting in order to teach entrepreneurs how to us financial statements in their businesses. The model (Figure 2) uses a three column design to explain the effect of individual transactions or events on the accounts and activities of one, two or three financial statements. The columns are labeled prior, transaction and sum, where balances in the prior column plus transactions equal the balances in the sum column. These columns demonstrate the amounts of the items included in each row before, during and after a transaction.

Ittelson's matrix model uses simplistic accounting terminology to label the rows which represent the accounts, groups of accounts or activities in three of the four basic financial statements. This terminology used to label these rows is sometimes inconsistent with current accounting terminology, but is still understandable and useful to the non-accountant. The financial statements are stacked vertically with the Income Statement at the top, the Cash Flow Statement in the middle and the Balance Sheet at the bottom.

The beauty of Ittelson's model is that any change in an income statement account must also reflect a change in net income on the income statement equal to the change in the retained earnings account on the balance sheet and any change on the cash flow statement must reflect a change in the cash account on the balance sheet.

Sellman's Financial Fence® Model

Sellman's Financial Fence® Model (Figure 3), as stated in his slides entitled "A Systematic Framework for the Creation of Wealth" on his web site purports to combat the lack of financial literacy and to help you achieve financial freedom, step by step (Sellman, n.d.). Sellman proposes in a screencast entitled "The Financial Fence Way of Thinking" (Sellman, n.d.) using a post and rail fence model whereby the left post represents "Where I am", the rails represent "A plan to get there" and the right post represents "Where I want to be". He describes the fences as made of two parts - posts that anchor the fence into the ground at a point and rails that carry the fence over a distance. Fences incorporate milestones (i.e., posts) and activity (i.e., rails) in the same analogy. Milestones represent the balance sheet and activity represents the "Profit and Loss Account & Cash Flow Statement."

This model also utilizes a color-coding scheme where sky blue represents Income (i.e., "The Sky is the limit"), orange represents Expenses (i.e., "Proceed with caution"), green represents Capital (i.e., "The Garden where I grow things"), red represents Debt (i.e., "Danger, use with extreme caution") and dark blue represents Equity (i.e., "Accumulated wealth").

Sellman states that the Financial Fence® helps you to make decisions in context, make better decisions which leads to better financial results, see how all the pieces of your financial world fit together, see that not all payments are equal and see how you can use leverage to work for you rather than against you.

Sellman proposes a different way of thinking about the accounting information generated by one's business as "fund a business versus measure its performance", that is to say, focus on building wealth rather than income.

Sellman explains how the Financial Fence® works. Net working capital is the accruals and deferrals. The balance sheet post is composed of working capital and fixed capital equaling assets on the top half and debt and equity equaling liabilities and equity on the bottom half. The income statement rail, also referred to as the "Top Financial Rail" or "Consumption Rail", consists of separate sections for sales, cost of interaction (i.e., cost of goods sold and operating expenses), contribution margin (i.e., gross profit), infrastructure expenses (i.e., all other cost items) and net profit. The statement of cash flows rail, also referred to as the "Bottom Financial" or the "Accumulation Rail", contains separate sections for net profit, movement of (change in) working capital, operating cash flow, movement of (change in) fixed capital and net cash flow.

The beauty of Sellman's model is its simplicity of structure and terminology. He uses labels that are understandable by the average layman.

MODEL DESIGN

Overview

The Financial Statements Articulation Fence is a merging of Mobley's Matrix, Ittelson's Structural Connections Model and Sellman's Financial Fence®. The Financial Statements Articulation Fence provides students with a visual aid to improve understanding of the financial statement articulation of the four basic financial statements. The model uses the figure of a post and rail fence where posts represent the Statements of Financial Position and the rails represent the changes between two posts with three specific rails - the Statement of Cash Flows, Statement of Income and Statement of Statement of Changes in Equity. The model incorporates the indirect method for determining operating cash flows unlike Mobley's direct method.

Structure

The Financial Statements Articulation Fence model (Figure 4) consists of two posts and three rails. The two posts represent the beginning and ending statements of financial position (i.e., balance sheets). The three rails represent the statement of cash flows, the statement of stockholders' equity and the statement of income (which eventually becomes part of the statement of comprehensive income). Each is appropriately dated for an accounting period from 1/1/x2 to 12/31/x2.

The statements of financial position "posts" at the beginning and end of the accounting period contain the three financial statement point in time elements of assets, liabilities and equity. Within those elements accounts are grouped according to how they are classified on the statement of cash flows. Assets are comprised of cash, accrued revenues, deferred expenses and all other assets. Liabilities contain the groups of accrued expenses, deferred revenues and all other liabilities. Equity is broken down into contributed capital, dividends, retained earnings and accumulated other comprehensive income. Table 6 provides a listing of the typical accounts included in each of these classifications.

Across the statement of cash flows "rail" are the three types of cash flow activities that appear on this statement - operating cash flows, investing cash flows and financing cash flows. Table 6 provides a listing of the typical activities included in each of these types.

The statement of stockholders' equity "rail" encompasses the changes in all of the equity accounts, including changes in the other equity accounts (owners investments and distributions), the change in retained earnings (net income) and the changes in accumulated other comprehensive income (other comprehensive income gains or losses). The other equity cell is positioned in the right column between the two statements of financial position under the financing cash flows section of the statement of cash flows. The statement of comprehensive income is positioned in the left column between the two statements of financial position under the operating cash flows section of the statement of cash flows.

The statement of comprehensive income "rail" includes the statement of income and other comprehensive income. The statement of comprehensive income is positioned in the left column between the two statements of financial position under the operating cash flows section of the statement of cash flows. In between the statement of cash flows and the statement of comprehensive income "rails" and in the left column are the adjustments that reconcile net income on the statement of income with the operating cash flows section of the statement of cash flows. This includes the removal of non-operating items contained in net income, such as, gain or loss on disposition of other assets or other liabilities, and adjustments for changes in the accrual and deferral accounts on the statement of financial position.

The other changes in the statement of financial position that need to be accounted for on the statement of cash flows are the investing cash flows in the center column that come from changes in other assets and the financing cash flows in the right column that come from changes in other liabilities.

Teaching Method

The Financial Statements Articulation Fence model is introduced to students via a handout with a blank worksheet (Figure 5) on the front and the label key (Figure 6) on the back and a 45-page PDF file of slides that steps through the completion of the worksheet in the following sequence.

First, I state that to prepare the statement of cash flows we explain the *change in the cash balance* from the beginning to ending statement of financial position by examining the *changes in all of the balance sheet accounts other than cash*. Then, the building of the model begins by introducing the beginning and ending statements of financial position as the "posts" in a post and rail fence. Then, the point in time elements of assets, liabilities and equity and their definitions from Statement of Financial Accounting Concepts #6 are presented. Next, each of the classifications within each element, along with account listings for each listed in the label key, are presented. In this model assets are classified as Cash... (Cash and cash equivalents), Accrued Revenues, Deferred eXpenses and Other Assets. Liabilities are classified as Accrued eXpenses, Deferred Revenues and Other Liabilities. The equity accounts are classified as Contributed Capital, Dividends, Retained Earnings and Accumulated Other Comprehensive Income.

Second, the first "rail" is introduced. The major classifications of the statement of income are progressively entered into the cell between the two statements of financial position on the retained earnings line in the operating cash flows column of the statement of cash flows (to be introduced as the second rail later). An acronym for each classification is added to the cell in the following order - SR (Sales Revenues), CGS (Cost of Goods Sold), OX (Operating eXpenses), OIG (Other Income & Gains), OXL (Other eXpenses & Losses) and IT (Income Tax) after which they are replaced with the label of Net Income (Loss).

Third, the "rail" for the statement of cash flows is entered between the two statements of financial position on the cash line. The Operating Cash Flows (i.e., Net cash provided by/(used in) operating activities) cell is placed in the first of three columns of the statement of cash flows each representing one of the three activities. Before covering the two remaining activities, net income (loss) on the statement of income is reconciled to operating cash flows on the statement of cash flows by entering adjustments for changes in certain balance sheet account classifications. The adjustments for changes in the four accrual and deferral account classifications (Accrued Revenues, Deferred eXpenses, Accrued eXpenses and Deferred Revenues) are reviewed and introduce the "add credit change, deduct debit change" rule. The changes in the other assets on the statement of financial position are located in the investing cash flows column and the changes in the other liabilities are located in the financing cash flows column. Before moving on the intersection of each change in the statement of financial position row and the statement of cash flows column is discussed.

Finally, the area covered by the statement of shareholders' equity is shown. The changes in other equity accounts and the statement of income already appear. The final step is to add other comprehensive income and expand the statement of income to a statement of comprehensive income.

Now, the model can be used to practice classifying transactions on the statement of cash flows and determining the direction of the cash flows.

USES

The Financial Statements Articulation Fence model can be used in the early chapters of an intermediate accounting course to:

1) illustrate how the financial statements interrelate,

2) provide a framework and a process for classifying changes in the accounts of the statement of financial position other than cash as operating, investing or financing activities in order to prepare the statement of cash flows,

3) reinforce the time labeling of each of the financial statements as either for a point in time or period of time and

4) identify the adjustments needed to reconcile net income on the statement of income with operating cash flows on the statement of cash flows,

LIMITATIONS AND CONCLUSIONS

Limitations

Like any model, the Financial Statements Articulation Fence model has its limitations. The statement of financial position portion of the model does not use the typical classifications found statements used for financial reporting, such as, current assets, investments, property plant and equipment, intangible assets and other assets in the asset element and current liabilities and long-term liabilities in the liabilities element.

The classification of accounts on the statement of income portion is simplistic. Even though the calculation of net income makes the distinction between operating and non-operating items, it does not include intermediate components, such as, discontinued operations and extraordinary items (which are still required as of this writing).

The statement of cash flows area of the model explains the indirect method of preparing the operating activities section of the statement of cash flows, but not the direct method. The model also does not demonstrate how to handle the reclassification of cash flows among the activities.

CONCLUSIONS

Even with its limitations, the Financial Statements Articulation Fence model presented here can be useful in teaching intermediate accounting students several concepts used in the construction of a set of financial statements.

REFERENCES

Ittleson, Thomas R. (2009) . Financial Statements: A Step-by-Step Guide to Understanding and Creating Financial Reports, Revised and Expanded Edition. Franklin Lakes, NJ: The Career Press, Inc.

Mann, Harvey (1984). A Worksheet for Demonstrating the Articulation of Financial Statements, The Accounting Review, LIX(4), 669-673..

Mobley, Lou & McKeown (1989), Kate. Beyond IBM, New York, NY: Mc-Graw-Hill.

Sellman, Andee & Galt, Lindsay. (n.d.). The Financial Fence®. Retrieved from http://www.thefinancialfence.com/

Sellman, Andee & Galt, Lindsay Galt. (n.d.). How The Financial Fence Works. Retrieved from http://www.thefinancialfence.com/bFence_works.php

The VARK Modalities (2015). Retrieved from http://vark-learn.com/introduction-to-vark/the-vark-modalities/

APPENDIX

The appendix for this paper is available from the author. Please email olsavsky@fredonia.edu.

Application of Marketing to an Evolutionary Business Framework

Mark Parker and Paul Richardson

Mark Parker (mparker@niagara.edu) is Adjunct Professor, Marketing, College of Business, Niagara University, 5795 Lewiston Road, NY, 14109. Paul Richardson (psr@niagara.edu) is Associate Professor, Marketing, College of Business, Niagara University.

Abstract

The traditional perspective on evolution, which describes the continuous change and survival of biological species under specific notions, has been applied to better understand foundational concepts in marketing. Specifically, prior research has suggested that the Resource Advantage Theory, which is an evolutionary process that determines a firm's competitive advantage performance through competition for a comparative advantage in resources, may be adapted to marketing strategy. This paper attempts to illustrate how marketing's role within the Resource Advantage framework, through the accumulation and dissemination of knowledge and intelligence, can potentially underpin firm value by establishing a common awareness and understanding among the firm's stakeholders. It will propose that an emerging role for marketing is to foster a "unity of consciousness" which, as inferred from more contemporary evolutionary theory, is the ultimate objective of firms that have evolved into greater complexity. Further research is essential to validate this concept and concomitant operational measures.

Application of evolutionary theory, especially as it pertains to the role of marketing and competitive intelligence in the growth and development of a business, has gained increasing recognition in the field of business research. Evolution, from a biological perspective, is a construct that outlines the continuous change and survival of biological species under the following four notions. First, it is cumulative, which suggests that change occurs as an extension from previous alterations. Second, it is motivated, inferring that defined forces affect change. Specific forces that are in place include a) *intrinsic generative*, referring to the genetic system enabling the promise of species variation underpinning natural selection b) *external selective,* that influence origin and survival of the species, or c) *interventionist mediative*, referring to human intervention that has altered natural selection. Third, it is directional, which defines the linear sequence of changes. And fourth, it is patterned. This characteristic refers to the four distinct patterns that illustrate evolution as the environmental stimulus behind new species development, including adaptation to the environment, increasing variation among the species, stagnation of species development, and extinction. All four notions suggest that evolution is a complex process of diversity, is in a continuous state of disequilibrium, and occurs according to well-defined stages.

Within the field of marketing, Tellis and Crawford have applied the evolutionary framework to the Product Growth Theory and the Product Life Cycle (PLC). They argue that the classical curve is inappropriate, and that while the PLC is time dependent, the evolutionary approach suggests that the defined forces that affect change are greater factors beyond a predictable progression over time. As well, creative efforts by management to mediate forces (i.e. interventionist mediative forces) that define continuous change are particularly relevant. Saad and Gill have utilized the increasing interest in evolutionary psychology as a means of explaining gender related consumer behaviour, in contrast to socialization models that suggest consumer behaviour is derived from traditional social roles. Their study suggests gender related consumer behaviour is a consequence of learned behaviour that has evolved under external conditions to which the human species has adapted – in other words, cumulative.

A more generic evolutionary framework that may be adapted to marketing strategy is the Resource Advantage (R-A) Theory, as proposed by Hunt and Morgan. This framework is regarded as an evolutionary process theory of competition, and fulfills the characteristics of such a process. It states that competition is in a state of disequilibrium, whereby firms compete for a comparative advantage for resources. This ongoing directional and patterned process results in a marketplace competitive advantage, which in turn results in superior financial performance. This signals market position, which then signals relative resources. Important in this framework are the existence of heterogenous resources, market segments, comparative advantages in resources, and marketplace positions.

The development of competitive advantage in resources refers to the *intrinsic generative* forces that enable species variation, influencing natural selection. This parallels a diversity of firms within an industry, each with a unique competitive position, as measured by relative resource costs and the resource-produced value matrix of the R-A framework. Each firm will have unique resources not easily copied, offering a long-term competitive advantage in the marketplace for certain market segments. In an effort to be competitive with advantaged firms, firms may imitate resources, find an equivalent resource, or create a new resource. Furthermore, the framework defines *external selective* forces that influence the competition for competitive advantage – public policy, consumers, and competitive suppliers.

Innovation and learning is a critical facet for creating a new resource and establishing a new competitive advantage, and is achieved through knowledge accumulation and transfer. The R-A framework, according to Hunt and Morgan, is an important model around which marketing strategy, and its role in facilitating knowledge accumulation and transfer, can be understood. In particular, four normative theories of marketing strategy contribute to resource development and ultimately to meaningful competitive advantage - brand-equity, market orientation, relationship marketing, and segmentation strategy. Each of these contributes resources to the firm that supports the development of meaningful competitive advantage. However, the interaction between all four can contribute to knowledge accumulation, and ultimately a common understanding among firm's internal and external stakeholders. The alignment of resources alongside targeted market segments should establish the foundation for relationship marketing strategies. Relationship marketing establishes an intangible resource of co-operation that can contribute to strong market position, and also the firm's knowledge base. Once these relationships have been established, firm credibility and ultimately brand equity building is established. Brand equity is a resource that acts as a heuristic and signals the meaning and value of a brand, and establishes a relationship with customers through favourable associations and understanding of the firm and its objectives. Marketing therefore plays an important role in the evolution of the firm, by facilitating knowledge accumulation, storage and dissemination through pertinent functional activities, resulting in an enhanced consciousness of the firm within itself and amongst its customers.

This adaptation of the R-A framework is interesting, as contemporary theories on evolution, as postulated by Pierre Teilhard de Chardin, suggest evolution expands beyond simply physical evolution, but also an evolution of consciousness. By this it is meant knowledge, awareness and understanding. Consciousness may also be regarded as merely an elaboration of perception, which is the organization of complex sensory experiences that contributes to understanding. Regardless of the semantics, it is argued that as species become more physically complex, they also become more consciously complex as part of a co-ordinated information system between its components that results in physical and mental sensory activities. According to Chardin, evolution's ultimate goal is a "unity of consciousness" established through a global network of information and knowledge, achieved through the voluntary interaction of people's worldwide. In effect, mankind emerges as one species into what Chardin refers to as the "noosphere" – the culmination and systematic co-ordination of recorded social knowledge, or "know-how". Evidence that mankind, regarded as the most complex of all species, is moving towards a unity of consciousness, may be observed through the rise of information technology that transmits and records social knowledge, and the establishment of multilateral institutions that is unifying the thoughts and common understanding of all peoples.

If we integrate this perspective on evolution and the transactional link between all four normative theories of marketing, several facets of a firm can be observed. First, as a firm evolves, there is a complexity of organizational structure and the interaction of the functional components of the firm, especially through knowledge dissemination. This is consistent with Chardin's perspective of increasing consciousness associated with physical complexity. Second, the dissemination of knowledge and complementary understanding of the firm and industry amongst itself, customers, and other industry stakeholders alludes to a unity of consciousness suggested above. Thirdly, this unity of consciousness may contribute to a more advanced and sustainable position with a superior competitive advantage. This is on the premise that common knowledge exchange is critical in the competition for resources and comprehension of the firm's best competitive strategic position it should develop. As a consequence, the four normative theories of marketing strategy underpin a unique perspective on this dynamic evolutionary model of the firm. It may further suggest that an emerging role for marketing is to foster that "unity of consciousness".

The question becomes "What constitutes a unity of consciousness?" Psychological research, as conducted by Bayne and Chalmers, identifies different varieties of consciousness and unity. The most significant is the notion of "subsumptive unity", which states individual experiences, or states of consciousness, are integrated into to single state of consciousness, regardless of whether these states are somehow related or not. Furthermore, they specify "phenomenally unified consciousness" as two conscious states being jointly experienced – i.e. experiencing a red square completely, but aware of the two states of the presence of a square, and the presence of red. These concepts are integrated into a notion of "subsumptive phenomenal unity", which is defined as a unique state of experiencing two conscious states simultaneously. For example, I can experience pain or no pain, and I can read literature on pain relief simultaneously. The state of experience is different or unique, when I am reading the literature while in pain or not in pain. Applying this to business and marketing may suggest "unity of consciousness" among the firm and customers is a unitary state of understanding or perception, driven by multiple experiences in the implementation of marketing strategy, reflecting the context of the specific market segment in which both participate.

It is clearly a challenge attempting to make this concept relevant to industry and marketing. Nevertheless, it may be a concept worth considering, given the evolving role of marketing today. According to V. Kumar, he envisages marketing practice as evolving from a resource and investment based activity, to one that is an integral part of the organization that must integrate with other business functions. Several developments allude to a changing role. First, the rise of social media and concomitant social networks enables the engagement of many to influence purchase decisions and build experiences. Second, marketing must illustrate how its investments underpin firm profitability and value, and demonstrate its effectiveness and efficiency, especially through customer engagement and retention, valued added, and long-term relationships. Thirdly, the rise of social media encourages customer interaction and information exchange that, if properly tracked, can result in increased profitability. Specifically, firms must influence attitudes and not simply behaviour. Kumar further postulates that a firm's value is generated through engaging all stakeholders in an integrated manner.

The simultaneous engagement of all stakeholders and the influence over attitude, or perception even, really amounts to a "unity of consciousness". Referring to the prior discussion, this suggests unity of consciousness must reflect a unique state of experience among all stakeholders collectively, in response to a diversity of stimuli. Measures of "unity of consciousness" may infer the success of stakeholder engagement in aligning marketing and firm strategy, and define an emerging role for marketing beyond the traditional notions of sales, target marketing, customer relationship management, and more recently the "experience economy". More specifically, a well-defined measure of unity of consciousness may prove a complement to, or a determinant of, existing measures of marketing performance, including marketing profitability, customer retention, market share, and brand equity that underpin firm value.

Several questions necessitate an enquiry to best define unity of consciousness within business and marketing. For example, does this measure offer an additional determinant of brand equity in creating customer and ultimately firm value? Or is it a necessary condition for maintaining value in a highly competitive landscape with an ever more demanding customer base? What specifically are the operational drivers of unity of consciousness? Does unity of consciousness correlate well with market measures that align with corporate strategy and value creation?

Further investigation is required to undertake a comparison of firms and establish viable measures measure of "unity of consciousness" among the internal and external stakeholders of a firm. Specifically an attempt to measure to what extent the various industry participants have a common understanding of the firm, its role and advantage, and the understanding of the competitive nature of the industry. It would then be critical to determine if these measures then correlate with competitive performance and value added. This would attempt to prove if a common understanding, or "unity of consciousness" does in fact enhance the competitive position and value of the firm. Further to that, a qualitative assessment of the processes in place that establish an effective and efficient transfer of knowledge through transacting the four normative marketing strategies is required. Specifically it would map out the systems and processes within the firm, along the framework outlined that incorporates the four normative theories.

Potential research into this concept is important for several reasons. With the prominence of big data, the "internet of everything", and digitization strategies, knowledge management has become a complex task, and there is uncertainty as to its benefit. This research will offer a pragmatic understanding of knowledge management, and may offer a data analytics model that illustrates an emerging influence of marketing on firm value. The rising influence of social media and the consequent knowledge base it develops certainly augurs well for an advancement of "unity of consciousness", and possibly an ability to quantify it. Equally, social media poses a challenge for the firm in establishing a stable and co-ordinated system of information and knowledge, given the greater participation of external players in a "many-to-many" form of communication, and the temporal popularity of certain social media vehicles. Overall, any study will attempt to highlight the importance and underpinnings of marketing in the advancement of broader strategy and value creation. It will attempt to illustrate marketing's holistic role in firm success and need to establish proper guidance for marketing investments, especially those related to knowledge accumulation. The ability to validate this concept and its practical application will enable marketing to define itself not simply as a transactional activity within the firm, but as a more transcendent role that becomes integral in firm decision making.

REFERENCES

Aaker, D. A., (1996). Measuring Brand Equity Across Products and Markets. California Management Review, Vol. 38, No. 3, 102-120.

http://dx.doi.org/10.2307/41165845

Achrol, R.S., (1991). Evolution of the Marketing Organization: New Forms for Turbulent Environment. Journal of Marketing, Vol. 55, 77-93.

http://dx.doi.org/10.2307/1251958

Bayne, T., Chalmers, D., (2003). What is the Unity of Consciousness? The Unity of Consciousness: Binding, Integration, Dissociation. Oxford.

de Chardin, P.T. (1959). The Phenomenon of Man. Harper and Row.

Gowan, J.A., (2014) Teilhard de Chardin – Prophet of the Information Age. http://johnagowan.org/chardin.html.

Hunt, S.D., Morgan R.M. (1997). Resource Advantage Theory: A Snake Swallowing Its Tail or a General Theory of Competition. Journal of Marketing, Vol. 61, 74-82.

http://dx.doi.org/10.2307/1252088

Kumar, V., (2015) Evolution of Marketing as a Discipline: What Has Happened and What to Look Out For. Journal of Marketing, Vol. 79, 1-9.

http://dx.doi.org/10.1509/jm.79.1.1

Sad, G., Gill, T. (2000). Applications of Evolutionary Psychology in Marketing. Psychology and Marketing, Vol. 17(12), 1005-1034.

http://dx.doi.org/10.1002/1520-6793(200012)17:12<1005::AID-MAR1>3.0.CO;2-H

Tellis, G.J., Crawford C.M. (1981). An Evolutionary Approach to Product Growth Theory. . Journal of Marketing, Vol. 45, No. 4, 125-132.

http://dx.doi.org/10.2307/1251480

Resources and Speed: Entrepreneurial Strategies of US Biomedical Firms

Ronald M. Riva

Ronald M. Rivas, PhD
Associate Professor
Canisius College
Department of Management
2001 Main Street
Buffalo, NY 14208
Tel: 716-888-2603
Fax: 716-888-3215
Email: rivasr@canisius.edu

Abstract

This study compares two entrepreneurial strategies: speed of entry and speed of accumulation of resources after entry. It tests whether the speed of accumulation of resources after entrance overcomes the advantage gained by early entrance into bio-medical and genetics. The findings show that the effect of speed of accumulation of resources is larger than the effect of early entrance, which suggests that first mover advantages are temporary and dependent on speed of accumulation of resources. These propositions are tested on a sample of firms from North America. Strategic implications are discussed.

Keywords: First-Mover Advantage, Late-Mover Advantages, Resources, Bio-medical and genetics, Entrepreneurial strategies

INTRODUCTION

How different are the effects of early entrance and of rapid accumulation of resources on firm performance? Understanding the impact of timing of entry and the impact of speed of accumulation of resources is crucial for corporate managers facing high velocity environments (Christensen, 1997; Eisenhardt, 1989; Eisenhardt and Tabrizi, 1995; Lieberman and Montgomery, 1998). The case of the biomedical and genetics industry offers a particular opportunity for studying these issues from the perspective of practitioners and academics. Bio-medical and genetics technologies are transforming the life sciences throughout all discovery and development processes. This emerging multidisciplinary field brings professionals from biotechnology, pharmaceutical, healthcare, academic and government decision makers to learn how the latest tools, services and best management practices will help revolutionize our health, our environment and our society.

This paper contributes to a body of work addressing the impact of timing, and resources on competitive advantage (Lieberman and Montgomery, 1998; Cockburn, Henderson, and Stern, 2000) by exploring whether first mover advantages- the advantage of early entrance into a market via a creative process – are moderated by accumulation of resources after entrance. The study contributes to the strategic management literature by providing evidence on how firms combine two entrepreneurial strategies: speed of entry and speed of accumulation of resources.

THEORY AND HYPOTHESES

Entrepreneurial strategies that accelerate entry and resource accumulation are essential for firm growth (Lieberman and Montgomery, 1988, 1998). The resource-based view of the firm (RBV) portrays the company as a bundle of interrelated resources, capabilities and competences. These have been labeled as resources, assets, routines, and compound resources by many authors. Such unique resources yield competitive advantage because better resources lead to better products that give companies an edge over competitors (Penrose, 1959; Wernerfelt, 1984; Barney, 1986, 1991, 1996).

Early entrance is essential to achieve competitive advantage (Lieberman, 1988; 1998). Early entrants have a favorable position to acquire scarce resources from the environment faster and cheaper than competitors do. If early entrants exploit the resource opportunity then they achieve superior performance (Teece, 1987; Dierickx and Cool, 1989; Prahalad and Hamel, 1990). Thus, companies that manage to reach favorable initial conditions and race to overcome their lack of resources achieve superior performance (Nelson and Winter, 1982; Teece, 1988).

Early entrance facilitates the appropriation of scarce resources, and creates opportunities for new organizational learning which enhance competitive advantage. However, the achievement of superior performance depends ultimately on the ability that firms have to accumulate critical resources. Thus, firm performance depends on both, speed of entry and speed of accumulation of resources after entry. A two by two matrix describes the impact of speed of entry and speed of accumulation of resources on competitive advantage as follows.

Technological leadership is one of the main first mover advantages Lieberman and Montgomery, 1988, 1998). Technological leadership can only be sustained with a continuous process of accumulation of resources. A firm that fails to do so is at risk of loosing the early entrance advantage to late entrants that have a superior speed of accumulation of resources.

Thus, speed of accumulation of resources produces larger competitive advantage than speed of entry. Combining this logic into the two by two matrix of Figure 1, we have the following hypotheses:

Hypothesis 1: Firms achieve superior performance by early entry into an industry.

Hypothesis 2: Firms achieve superior performance by rapid accumulation of resources.

Hypothesis 3: Accumulation of resources moderates first mover's advantage.

METHODS

Sample and Data

The sample comprises 112 firms from the Bio-Medical and Genetics industry from North America. The main reference for the data is Bloomberg. The sample is obtained by cross-referencing Bloomberg data with a variety of sources, including, MarketGuide, Hoovers, Research Insight, and SEC filings. The biomedical and genetics industry offers and ideal testing ground because it's quickly evolving technological and competitive environment makes this a high-velocity industry. Speed is critical in high velocity environments (Bourgeois and Eisenhardt, 1988; Eisenhardt and Tabrizi, 1995). This industry is entrepreneurial per excellence providing the ideal ground to test two essential entrepreneurial strategies. The technology bubble–bust happened in the first quarter of 2000. Entering into the market via an IPO became extremely difficult right after that date. In 2002, this industry presented a two year window suitable for research because companies that entered before 2000 would have evidence of first mover advantages, whereas firms entering after 2000 would be clearly at a disadvantage.

Variables

Independent Variable
Firm Performance: measured as Enterprise Value in the last reported quarter of 2002. Enterprise Value is the Market Value plus Total Debt and Current Preferred Stock minus Cash and Equivalents.

Table 1 shows the regression results. Figure 2 shows the relative proportion of the regression coefficients within the speed of entry versus speed of accumulation of resources matrix. The numbers on each the matrix cell represent the size of enterprise value relative to the late/slow cell. The late/slow level of enterprise value is set to one.

These findings support hypotheses 1, namely, that first movers have superior performance. Early entrants have higher enterprise value than late entrants, namely, with rapid accumulation of resources, first movers are valued [2.4/1.9] -1 = 30% more than late movers; with slow accumulation of resources, first movers are valued [1.4/1.0] -1 = 40% more than late movers. Findings also show that early entrance followed by rapid accumulation of resources yields higher performance than late entrance and slow accumulation. Entrepreneurial firms have 140% higher enterprise value than non-entrepreneurial firms, as calculated as follows, [2.4/1.0] – 1 = 140%.

These findings support hypothesis 2, namely, that the speed of resource accumulation after entrance is significant, regardless of order of entry. These findings show that among first movers enterprise give an advantage of 71% higher enterprise value when there is rapid accumulation of resources ([2.4/1.4] -1= 71%); Whereas, among late movers the advantage given by rapid accumulation of resources is 90% higher enterprise value, ([1.9/1.0] – 1 = 90%).

CONCLUSIONS

This study had two main purposes. First, it intended to assess the magnitude of the competitive advantage created by two entrepreneurial strategies: speed of entry and speed of accumulation of resources after entry. Second, it set out to evaluate whether late entrants with superior speed of accumulation of resources could challenge first mover advantages. Third, it theorized that resource based advantage is desirable after entry whether the entry was early or late. The study anticipated that early entrants that accumulated resources rapidly would have the best competitive advantage over the other alternatives. This study introduced a two by two matrix stylizing the competitive advantage of speed of entry versus speed of accumulation of resources. The findings provide strong support for the argument that the competitive advantage gained from speed of accumulation of resources after entrance overcomes the advantage gained by early entrance into the bio-medical and genetics industry. In sum, first mover advantages are ephemeral when taking into account advantages accrued by rapid accumulation of resources achieved by later entrants.

REFERENCES

Barney, J. (1986) "Strategic Factor Markets: Expectations, Luck and Business Strategy," Management Science, 32:1512-1514.

Barney, J. (1991) "Firm resources and sustained competitive advantage," Journal of Management, 17, pp. 99-120.

Barney (1996) "The resource-based theory of the firm, Organizational Science, 7:469.

Barney, J. (2001) "Is The Resource-Based "View" a Useful Perspective for Strategic Management Research? Yes," The Academy of Management Review, v26, 1:41-56.

Christensen, C. (1997) "The Innovator's Dilemma: When New Technologies Cause Great Firms to Fail," Cambridge, Mass.: Harvard Business School Press.

Resources and Speed   313

Cockburn, I. R. Henderson, and S. Stern (2000) "Untangling the Origins of Competitive Advantage," Strategic Management Journal, 21, 10-11:1123-1145.

Dierickx, I. and K. Cool, (1989) "Asset Stock Accumulation and Sustainability of Competitive Advantage," Management Science, v35, n12, (December), pp:1504-1511.

Greene, W. (1993) Econometric Analysis, 2nd. edition, New York, NY: Macmillan.

Gulati, R. (1999) "Network location and learning: the influence of network resources and firm capabilities on alliance formation." Strategic Management Journal, 20, 5:397-420.

Gulati, R., N. Nohria, and A. Zaheer (2000) "Strategic Networks," Strategic Management Journal, 21, 3:203-215.

Hamel, G. and C. Prahalad (1994) "Competing for the Future," Cambridge, Mass.: Harvard Business School Press.

Helfat, C. (2000) "Guest editor's introduction to the special issue: The Evolution of Firm Capabilities," Strategic Management Journal, 21, 10-11:1061-1081.

Helfat, C. and R. Raubitschek (2000) "Product Sequencing: Co-evolution of Knowledge, Capabilities and Products," Strategic Management Journal, 21, 10-11:961-979.

Hsiao, C. (1986) Analysis of Panel Data, New York: Cambridge University Press.

Kogut, B. (1991) "Country Capabilities and the Permeability of Borders", Strategic Management Journal, Vol. 12., Summer 1991.

Lieberman, M., L. Deemester, and R. Rivas (1995) "Inventory Reduction in the Japanese Automotive Sector," Working paper, MIT International Motor Vehicle Program, Cambridge: Mass.

Lieberman, M. and D. Montgomery, (1988) "First-Mover Advantages," Strategic Management Journal, Summer Special Issue, 9:41-58.

Lieberman, M. and D. Montgomery, (1998) "First-Mover (DIS)Advantages: Retrospective and Link with the Resource-Based View," Strategic Management Journal, 19:1111-1125.

Little, R., and D. Rubin (1987) Statistical analysis with missing data, New York : Wiley.

Makadok, R. (1999) "Interfirm Differences in Scale Economies and the Evolution of Market Shares," Strategic Management Journal, 20:935-952.

Miller, D. and J. Shamsie (1996) "The Resource Based View in Two Environments: The Hollywood Film Studios from 1936 -1965. Academy of Management Journal, 39:519-543.

Nelson R. and S. Winter, (1982) An Evolutionary Theory of Economic Change, Cambridge: Mass.: Beljnap Press of Harvard University.

Penrose, E. (1959) The Theory of the Growth of the Firm, London: Basil Blackwell.

Porter, M.(1990) The Competitive Advantage of Nations, New York: Free Press.

Porter, M.(1991) "Towards a Dynamic Theory of Strategy," Strategic Management Journal, n12, pp 95-117.

Prahalad C.K. and G. Hamel, (1990) "The Core Competence of the Corporation," Harvard Business Review, (May-June), v68, n3, pp:79-91

Priem, R and J. Butler (2001) ""Is The Resource-Based "View" a Useful Perspective for Strategic Management Research?" The Academy of Management Review, v26, 1:22-40.

Rumelt, R. (1987) "Theory, Strategy, and Entrepreneurship," chapter 7 in The Competitive Challenge edited by D. Teece, Cambridge: Mass., Ballinguer.Sollow, R. (1957) "Technical Change and the Aggregate Production Function," Review of Economics and Statistics, v39, pp.312-320.

Teece, D. (1987) "Profiting from Technological Innovation: Implications for Integration, Collaboration, and Public Policy," Chapter 9 in The Competitive Challenge, edited by D. Teece. Cambridge Mass: Ballinguer.

Teece, D. (1988) "Technological Change and the Nature of the Firm." in G. Dosei, et al. (eds.) Technical Change in Economic Theory

Teece, D.; G. Pisano, and A. Shuen, "Dynamic capabilities and strategic management." Strategic Management Journal v18, n7 (Aug 1997):509-533.

Wernerfelt, B. (1984) "A Resource-Based View of the Firm," Strategic Management Journal, n5. pp. 171-180.

White, (1980) "A Heteroskedasticity-consistency Covariance Matrix Estimator and a Direct Test for Heteroskedasticity," Econometrica, vol. 48, 817-838.

WEB APPENDIX

A web appendix for this paper is available at:

http://www.businessresearchconsortium.org/pro/brcpro2015p16.pdf

CROSS-DISCIPLINE COLLABORATION IN BUSINESS RESEARCH: FILLING A GAP IN BUSINESS EDUCATION

Mary Tone Rodgers and Lisa Dethridge

Dr. Mary Tone Rodgers, CFA
Marcia Belmar Willock Professor of Finance
State University of New York at Oswego
United States

Dr. Lisa Dethridge
Senior Lecturer in Media and Communications
Royal Melbourne Institute of Technology
Australia

Acknowledgments

The authors would like to thank Sarfraz Mian, Hema Rao and other attendees at the January 2015 SUNY-Oswego faculty meeting for helpful comments. Insights from participants at the April 2015 Business Research Consortium of Western New York at St. Bonaventure University were also greatly appreciated. Generous technical support for the international collaboration was made possible by the State University of New York's Collaborative Online International Learning program.

Abstract

We accessed best practices from the collaboration and consultancy literatures to design a learning exercise that fills a gap in the most popular financial statement analysis textbooks: how to conduct industry analysis. Rather than relying on legacy pedagogy to teach industry analysis, we undertook a collaborative online international learning exercise between American business students and Australian communication students to analyze the digital communications industry. By using a consultancy model, students achieved a thorough understanding of the industry's profit drivers, subsequently imbuing meaning to the analysis of target companies' financial statements, and ultimately yielding meaningful valuation models. Suggestions are provided for generalizing the consultancy model as an innovation in business education. The model can be used wherever industry analysis is a curriculum component including management and marketing courses as well as accounting and finance courses.

SECTION ONE. INTRODUCTION

Broadening the learning process to include a global context has been considered a useful enhancement to curricula. In this article, a business professor from the United States and a communications professor from Australia collaborate to create a learning exercise to enhance their respective curricula. The article is organized in three sections. Following this brief introduction, Section Two identifies a gap in the pedagogy surrounding industry analysis. Section Three describes the process of how the professors designed a learning experience to fill the gap. Section Four generalizes the process, suggesting other applications for the pedagogy innovation.

SECTION TWO. IDENTIFYING A GAP IN LEGACY PEDAGOGY: INDUSTRY ANALYSIS

In general, financial statement analysis text books devote a few pages in an early chapter to a discussion of how important it is to understand the profit drivers in an industry before trying to decipher the financial statements. Textbooks agree that a rich narrative of strategy and competitive advantage must accompany accounting data in order to make sense of the data. "To effectively analyze and use accounting information, we must consider the business context in which the information is created."Textbooks agree that only after that is accomplished can useful valuation models of companies' equity be constructed. "Financial statements often present a blurred picture. Where the picture in financial statements is incomplete, the analyst supplements with other information."Yet we find none of the textbooks provides students a detailed roadmap for how to accomplish the necessary task. Wahlen, Baginski and Bradshaw's text addresses the issue most comprehensively. They go so far as to suggest three tools for studying the economic characteristics of an industry. First, they explore industry analysis as a value chain issue, next within Porter's Five Forces classification framework, and finally as an economic attribute framework, noting that microeconomic analysis can be a source for additional frameworks. Nonetheless, that text only devoted 12 pages out of a total of 1,100 pages to the topic. Other texts allot 4 pages out of 720, 3 pages out of 500 and 2 pages out of 300 to what each deems to be a critical step in the analysis of financial statements.

The traditional way that industry analysis is taught in textbooks is to construct common-sized financial statements that allow for quick comparisons among companies to identify typical industry patterns in asset and liability configuration and patterns in revenue and expense recognition. Outlying companies are flagged for scrutiny. However, accountants and financial analysts that rely solely upon common-sized financial statement analysis cannot readily discern whether non-conforming companies may generate better value for shareholders or whether they may be cooking their books or losing competitive ground in the industry. Again, textbooks point the student back to the centrality of understanding industry context in order to deliver worthwhile analysis of the outliers, but still fall short of providing a way to construct industry context: "A review of financial statements cannot be undertaken in a vacuum. It is contextual and can only be effectively undertaken …in the broader forces that impact company performance."

A recent financial statement analysis class elected to study four segments of the digital communications industry, social networking, browsers, advertising and entertainment. Companies in the segments include Facebook, Twitter, LinkedIn, Pandora, Time Warner Cable, Dish Network, WPP Group, Yahoo! and Google. Students found the common-sized financial statement segment analysis particularly mystifying, revealing irregular patterns for net fixed assets, inventory, research and development expense patterns, and volatile selling and administrative expenses. In short, students were unable to form a meaningful narrative of the profit drivers in either of the industry segments by using traditional methods of industry analysis, common-sized statements.

To overcome the deficiency of legacy pedagogy, we first tried accessing resources about communications stocks on the Bloomberg Information System. We found industry reports compiled by other Wall Street analysts helpful but still dissatisfying. They did not get down to the brass tacks of what makes one communication platform more attractive to a human being than another platform. We recognized that the metrics were clearly different than those used by other industries: frequency of visits to the platform measured by clicking, frequency of communicating from a platform measured by posts and numbers of subscription services sold. Equity analysts' reports were deficient in helping us understand how and why the activity of communication translated into a sustainable business.

SECTION THREE. FILLING THE GAP WITH A COLLABORATIVE CONSULTANCY LEARNING EXERCISE

Firms such as Wall Street banks that specialize in developing equity valuation models use a consultancy model in the early stages of forming an industry narrative to explain profit drivers. Consultants typically provide an interface between academic expertise and commercial research, often within an international environment. Consultants are typically used in situations like what we faced in a fifteen week semester: we had no expertise in the area of need and the time of need is only fourteen weeks, insufficient to develop the industry knowledge ourselves.Consultants can function as bridges for information and knowledge and they can provide these services more economically than client firms themselves. They take on tasks that would involve high internal coordination costs for clients. Their specialization renders their information search less costly than if clients performed the information search themselves. Very importantly, consultants can provide new viewpoints from which to understand complex issues, exactly what our business students needed.

Typically, in commercial research, after industry experts are consulted and competitive advantages are identified, ratio analyses make sense and valuation modeling proceeds. That consultancy model is rarely explored in standard textbooks, however, and for understandable reason. It is expensive to consult with experts and it is hard to know a priori whether the experts will be able to translate exceedingly technical jargon into language and concepts that are accessible to business analysts. It is hard to find a consultant whose knowledge domain encompasses the unknown information yet overlaps enough with the client's domain so that meaningful translation of concepts can occur.

If a communications industry consultant could be found, the intent of the business students was to conduct an industry analysis grounded in the literature about competitive advantage. We expected that our consultants would provide input to models such as Porter's Five Forces or the Critical Success Factors model of Holms (University of California at

Santa Barbara) and Abraham (Cal State Poly Tech at Pomona). Each model seeks similar learning outcomes in the form of answers to questions such as how does the company stack up to competitors, does it have a competitive edge, and where might it be vulnerable. Does the industry have desirable characteristics with sustainable growth opportunities? Following Holms and Abraham, we defined our industry as a collection of competitors that produce similar or substitute products or services to a defined market. We defined industry segments as those competitors that cluster to target a subset of the general market.

We used the learning platform provided by the State University of New York called Collaboration for Online International Learning to proxy for the consultancy model. Within the system, we searched for a knowledge partner with academic credentials and a specialization in communication. We reached out to a master's level class of communications students at the Royal Melbourne Institute of Technology as our consultants. This group had the advantages of being relatively inexpensive to access and the advantage of being able to translate specialized language into conversational language accessible to undergraduate students. They also had the unique advantage of being able to provide an international perspective to the process. The RMIT students had a disadvantage of not yet having reached leadership positions in the industry the way that consultants hired by Wall Street analysts typically have. We concluded the advantages outweighed the disadvantages and proceeded with the collaboration. Our central goal was to understand whether any of the target companies could sustain a competitive advantage.

Substantial time was spent by the two professors in establishing whether the knowledge domain of the communications students would be adequate to answer the business students' questions. We decided to provide about two dozen articles about the art and science of the communication process to the business students and about a dozen Wall Street analysts' reports about stock valuations to the communication students. We hoped a cross-fertilization of ideas would develop as each learned about the other discipline. We organized one group-to-group Skype session to meet each other, centered on a light-hearted, trust-building ice-breaker in which we discussed each other's preconceived notions of Australians and Americans.

Cognizant of the boundaries of each group's knowledge domain, and anticipating where the domains might overlap, the professors developed a common website called the Canvas Learning Management System which housed articles, assignments and questions. The professors' choices of dozens of open-ended questions were meant to prompt the students to discover profit drivers, strategic competencies and competitive advantages of each target company within each industry segment. We posted questions such as "What makes for a good digital communication platform? What might be differences among international users of digital communications platforms? Where is the frontier of digital communications?"

The students communicated various answers to those and thought of other questions to ask each other in Facebook groups that corresponded to the four industry segments. Following Abraham's (2003) model of using conversation as a learning process, we rewarded students for participating in the digital chats. "*Real strategic thinking often occurs in the conversations that take place, sometimes entirely informally and sometimes more formally.. during those conversations, real decisions are made, real issues are confronted, real knowledge is developed. This conversational mode is key to the process of learning. Whether formal or informal, a conversation is the learning vehicle whereby the group adjusts to a new worldview. The sequence is: shared conversations and shared learning become the vehicles for changing one's mental maps.*"

The Facebook posts amounted to an asynchronous conversation, a tool for shared learning, between the communications experts and the business analysts. Each group came to understand the viewpoint of the other. Posts began to fall into patterns about the ease of use of each of the target company's digital platform. Posts began to center around how the target companies matched the analytical framework in a report posted by Professor Dethridge, authored by the advertising firm, Universal McCann, in which humans' fundamental needs for communication were dissected.

Through a combination of the Facebook conversations and the communications report from Universal McCann professors were able to format a matrix that described the dimensions along which the target companies met the fundamental needs of humans to communicate. We were able to distinguish between which companies succeeded across the factors and which companies faltered. Thus, through collaborating within a consultancy model, we achieved our goal of understanding the profit drivers and sources of competitive advantage for our industry segments.

We faced challenges in the consultancy process that routinely emerge in the field, specifically the transfer of knowledge between the consultant and client. Twelve hour time zone differences between locations impeded the free flow of ideas. Responses to questions took longer than expected. Insights and breakthroughs in understanding are never possible to schedule; the business analysts were anxious that the "a-ha moment" would not materialize. Hurdles we met that were different than field consultancy models were because of our academic institutional settings. The courses had different grading systems that generated different expectations of each of the groups. While the exercise was optional for the Australian group, it was mandatory for the American group. Without the input from the RMIT consultants, SUNY-Oswego students would not be able to progress to the end-of-course assignment to build a valuation model. Therefore, our students struggled with the irregular pace of insight formation inherent in cross-discipline, cross-cultural collaboration.

Fortunately, students from both universitites persevered and final results were extremely useful. The communications students, guided by professors' trouble-shooting and engagement in the process, produced a report that broke down the process of communication to elements around which the business students came to learn how the target companies had designed their competitive strategies.

SECTION FOUR: GENERALIZING OUR MODEL

This consultancy model can be adapted to all kinds of industry analysis. Business students studying the defense contracting or automotive industry for example can consult with engineering students. Business students studying the health care industry can consult with health sciences students. Industry analysis, in turn, is not confined to classes in financial statement analysis; it is integral to most accounting, finance, management and marketing courses.

Reaching out to international students added an element of understanding to our project that would not have been obtained had we collaborated with domestic students. Australian students live in a different legal environment in which some of the companies under study were prevented from operating in. The Aussies shared with us how they worked around those institutional constraints to use Netflix for example. They also knew about Korean and Japanese competitors that we would not have known about otherwise. We reached a richer understanding of industry context by engaging with an international knowledge partner.

That said, domestic collaboration could still be very useful. The cross-fertilization of the two groups of students would still take place across disciplines even if not across cultural boundaries. The process of finding common language between technical languages unique to disciplines would still be a powerful learning outcome. The goal of developing a narrative about profit-drivers to make sense of financial statements could still be achieved.

In conclusion, this global collaboration represents a fresh, collaborative, multidisciplinary industry model for the enhancement of financial analysis. The American finance students engaged in an international collaboration that allowed them to source significant information and insights from their Australian "consultants." The learning experience filled the gap in finance pedagogy by providing the finance analysts with first-hand knowledge of how and where to identify and locate the kind of "inside" industry knowledge that supplements the analysis of raw financial statements. The keys to a successful learning outcome seemed to be the willingness of the two professors to find the knowledge domain overlaps between the groups and to find a way to stimulate conversations between the consultants and the business researchers.

REFERENCES

Abraham, Stan. "Experiencing strategic conversations about the central forces of our time." Strategy & Leadership 31.2 (2003).

Abraham, Stan. "Will business model innovation replace strategic analysis?." Strategy & Leadership 41.2 (2013): 31-38.

Canback, S. Transaction Cost Theory and Management consulting: Why do Management Consultants Exist?" working paper 981002, 1998a, Henly Management College Henley on Thames

Easton, Peter; McAnally, Mary Lea; Sommers, Greg and Zhang, Xiao-Jun. Financial Statement Analysis and Valuation, third edition, Cambridge, 2015

Fincham, Robin. The Agent's Agent: Power, Knowledge and the Uncertainty in Management consultancy, International Studies of Management & Organization, (32)4, 2002, pp. 67-86, published online Dec 23, 2014.

Lundberg, Craig C. and Finney, Michael, Emerging models of consultancy, Consultation: An International Journal Vol (6)1m 1987; 32-42.

Palepu, Krishna G., and Healy, Paul. Business Analysis and Valuation Using Financial Statements, fifth edition, Cengage Learning, 2013

Penman, Stephen H. Financial Statement Analysis and Security Valuation, fifth edition, McGraw-Hill, 2013

Steptoe-Warren, Gail; Howat, Douglas; Hume, Ian. (2011) "Strategic thinking and decision making: literature review," Journal of Strategy and Management, (4) 3, pp. 238-250.

Tseganoff, Laith, "Benefits and Best Practices of Management Consulting," Institute of Management Consultants and Trainers, March 31, 2011.

Universal McCann report, Wave 7 Cracking the Social Code by Glen Parker, September 24, 2013.

Wahlen, Baginski and Bradshaw, Financial Reporting Financial Statement Analysis and Valuation, A Strategic Perspective, Cengage Learning

WEB APPENDIX

A web appendix for this paper is available at:

http://www.businessresearchconsortium.org/pro/brcpro2015p17.pdf

THE END BEFORE THE MEANS: A CRITIQUE OF MUHAMMAD YUNUS' CONCEPT OF SOCIAL BUSINESS

Zachary Rodriguez and Jim Mahar

Zachary Rodriguez, M.B.A
St. Bonaventure Universit
P.O. Box 25, Saint Bonaventure, NY 1477
Rodrigzt14@bonaventure.edu

Dr. Jim Mahar
Department of Finance
Saint Bonaventure University
P.O. Box BY, St. Bonaventure, NY 14778
Jim.mahar@gmail.com

Abstract

If we accept the conceptual premise of Muhammad Yunus' social business, then we are advocates for a world without poverty, unemployment, or hunger. Though beautiful, such teleological worldviews often presume humanity moving toward an end, one that can only be realized through the manipulation and governance of a larger, more developed outside body. Drawing on the work of economist, Dr. William Easterly and historian, Dr. Joyce Appleby, this paper will offer a critique of Muhammad Yunus' concept of social business, as rooted in a particular ideological trajectory, thus making it subject to a fundamental bias in its prediction of the conclusion of human endeavor. In conclusion, the paper will offer several, more humble possibilities for how to address issues of poverty and disparity in quality of life that allow for humanity to shape its own future, given its cultural histories and communal desires.

INTRODUCTION

With increased globalization The Arab Spring and The Occupy Movement are two recent examples of this distrust. For this, Muhammad Yunus must be commended. Adding to his Nobel Prize-winning work in Development Economics, and particularly through the microfinance activities of the Grameen Bank in Bangladesh, Yunus' offers another mechanism through which we can further solve the social problems that affect humanity and its future. He calls this mechanism Social Business (SB).

SB can be defined in accordance with the principles of a traditional profit-generating business. The difference between a profit-generating business and a social business is the intention behind the products or services they offer. SBs offer products and services that provide a social benefit, for which it charges a price or fee, while profit-generating businesses have no bias in what they produce.

Yunus goes on to differentiate this entity from a non-profit organization (NPO), as SBs do focus on generating profits, but those profits, or capital surplus, are reinvested in the activities of the business, with no money being earned by stock holders. Thus, SB is a non-loss, non-dividend business. The non-loss identifier is seemly innocuous, since all businesses, for-profit or non-profit, aim to be non-loss. So, it may be more accurate to describe SBs as *non-gain* corporate entities. SB also differs from Corporate Social Responsibility (CSR) in that its focus is more like a charity fund that works in tandem with profit-maximizing companies, whereas SBs completely focus on addressing and changing social problems.

Furthermore, SB adheres to several basic principles of responsibility, that, according to Yunus, even some profit-maximizing companies could benefit from implementing into their organizational strategy. These principles include a responsibility to not imperil anybody's life on this planet; a responsibility to contribute to making the planet safer than it would have been without the business; and a responsibility to conduct its activities within a framework of social and political responsibilities established by the state and global authorities.

As we position SB among other business entities, the latent ideology out of which SB operates becomes increasingly apparent. Yunus' writings and activities, like the Grameen Bank and SB, seem to imagine a world where we can influence people to be more altruistic, guiding them accept their duty to humanity, and thus encouraging unity toward the growth of honest, generous human communities.

This is an example of a teleological argument. Teleology is a doctrine explaining phenomena by final causes. It assumes a particular design to reality and acts to push us along that design. For Yunus, this design begins with the essential goodness of humanity and leads to the creation of a more selfless, generous, multi-dimensional human society. This type of argument is similar to the reasoning of large international development entities, like Partners In Health and The Bill and Melinda Gates Foundation.

It is out of this design that Yunus develops the SB framework as a way for businesses to operate within a free market, while limiting its internal interests, in order to suppress any selfish or exploitative human impulses. By doing this, Yunus explains that we can learn to understand the deeper aspects of human nature and "the contributions one [can] make to the well-being of the world."

The intention of this paper is to parse out and expose the ideology that underlies Yunus' entire SB framework. I will then argue that Yunus' ideological position could isolate, rather than invite people to participate in his SB framework. Lastly, I will offer several ways one can approach social development in favor of a more modest, and arguably freer, development of human communities.

SOCIAL BUSINESS FRAMEWORK

In order to strengthen and publicize its possibilities, Yunus has taken the time to develop other wider implications of his SB framework. Not only does he develop SB as a business entity, as different from NPOs and CSR, but Yunus goes on to imagine other aspects of SB that will compliment its organizational structure like social trusts, a social stock market, and Social Business Master's of Business Administration (MBA) programs.

Besides the first type of SB organizational structure that has so far been described, Yunus also created a second type of SB called social trusts. A social trust can be described as a profit-making company owned by poor people, either directly or through a trust that is dedicated to a predefined social cause. The benefits of this second type of SB is twofold, as the business is focused on addressing the social problems of the poor and the poor are direct beneficiaries of its profits.

Considering the future of social trusts, there will need to be a way to determine if its owners have achieved self-sufficiency, and thus no longer qualify to be beneficiaries of the SB. Perhaps Yunus will use the Progress out of Poverty Index (PPI) to make those decisions. PPI was developed by the Grameen Foundation to help organizations working in poverty intervention to identify the clients, customers, or employees who are most likely to be poor or vulnerable to poverty, integrating objective poverty data into their assessments and strategic decision-making. One could imagine owners of social trusts becoming self-sufficient and having to resign their position, hopefully for another position that will lead to more personal growth and profit. With his aversion to profit, it is unclear if Yunus would advocate such a decision. Yunus is adamant that he is not against making profit, only that it interferes with the resolution of social problems. Yunus' position then makes it difficult to understand if social trusts are more of a short-term solution or if the threshold of poverty will grow and thus justify the necessity of social trusts.

Part of the future of social business will include the creation of a social stock market. This market would only trade shares of SBs. Prices of shares in the market will reflect the consensus of social investors as to the longer-term value of the company. Consistent with the SB rhetoric, value within this market will be determined not by anticipated profits, but rather in terms of the benefits produced.

The idea of a social stock market certainly is consistent within the SB framework. Yet, it assumes a value for this social benefit when such a determination would require a rather sophisticated index to measure these benefits. Following his teleological position described previously, we can detect Yunus' bias concerning the nature of social benefits. However, social benefits can be ambiguous and sometimes contradictory of other potential social benefits.

Not to assume his position, but Yunus may reply that the value of social benefit is to be determined by up to the market. And if one is a keen investor, they will have done research concerning how the public understands the value of social benefits produced by a given sector of the market. This is valid, but there still seems to be an assumed standard of benefits, one that fits into Yunus' teleology.

With these mechanisms in place, Yunus believes that next will come the creation of Social Business MBA programs, which will support and preserve the structure and rhetoric of the SB framework. Yunus has already developed some educational infrastructure, like the Yunus Centre in Bangladesh and the Grameen Creative Lab in Germany, to support the development of his framework.

Yunus has carefully accounted for many key mechanisms to support and expand of his SB framework. The construction of this SB framework should be admired, as it is clear that Yunus expects to create a more dimensional, selfless individuals focused on strengthening the human community. While seductive, there are still many concerns over the SB framework and its implications that involve addressing and understanding issues like happiness, liberty, and freedom.

PROFIT VS. HAPPINESS

The strongest motivation for SB seems to come from Yunus' suspicion of all profit-maximizing business. Not that he is against profit, as he has explained many times, but that Yunus is quick to assume that large profits will accentuate human flaws like greed and selfishness.

This has long been a concern about Capitalism, but it is certainly not the only concern that Capitalism creates. Other concerns, according to historian Dr. Joyce Appleby, include "responding to shorter-term opportunities to the neglect of long-term effects, dispensing power without responsibility, promoting material values over spiritual ones, commoditizing human relations, monetizing social values, corrupting democracy, unsettling old communities, institutions, and arrangements, and rewarding aggressiveness and—yes—greed." So, while Yunus may have disdain for greed, there are certainly many other spillover effects of Capitalist markets.

To this end, Yunus gives three reasons for why SB cannot pursue profits: morally, SB cannot profit off of the suffering of those living within the social problems its trying to address; pragmatically, SB must not allow the stress of generating profits influence its mission of solving a social problem; and systematically, SB is meant to be a clearly defined alternative to business and charity, as a way to encourage new forms of thinking.

Of the three reasons, the pragmatic argument seems to be the most compelling, as the other two reasons are ideologically imposed, and thus lack necessity. Dr. William Easterly offers a different definition of profit seekers, as those who evaluate the chance of reaching many different goals and then choose the one that promises the highest expected benefit at the lowest cost. What Easterly suggests is a more pragmatic person, with a more morally ambiguous intention for seeking profit.

While it may be true that Yunus is attempting to account for selfishness, he also advocates for a model that gives a subtly negative connation to profit-seeking, which sends mixed messages to people wishing to increase their profits so as to get out of poverty. Yunus' social agenda clearly informs his understanding of profit, and to some extent, does offer a tangible solution to limiting human selfishness. However, when we imagine the future of SB and its approach to more complicated social problems, it may be more feasible and fair to admit the pleasures of profit and provide a framework for how to balance these pleasures when addressing a social problem.

While it may seem like an issue of semantics, there is a fundamental difference between the freedoms allowed to someone who wishes to encourage the earning of profit among all people and one who wishes to manipulate the desires of profit-seeking, self-interested, individuals.

SOCIAL CONCERN VS. MUTUAL BENEFITS

The desire to create social impact at every stage of the value-chain guides the creation of SB organizational strategies. Management plans and decisions must always take into account how to widen their social impact. This will require employees to embody the selfless worker, the enlightened consumer, and the compassionate humanitarian, all at once.

Yunus remains strong in his crusade to achieve a more selfless human community by pressing the SB agenda on his employees. This is a certainly sharp criticism, since employees would work at for a SB of their own free will. However, its sharpness cuts to the more central difficulty of incentives within the SB business structure.

Low-profit limited liability companies (L3C) are an alternative to the SB model. L3C is a for-profit company that purses a social purpose. Under law, no significant purpose of the company is the production of income or the appreciation of property. L3C is an example of a structure that balances incentives and social benefits. Yunus still distinguishes SB from L3C, saying, "In my judgment, making selfishness and selflessness work through the same vehicle will serve neither master well."

Yunus is steadfast in his suspicion of any financial benefits gained from a corporate entity addressing a social problem. It is fair to imagine that some people who will work for a SB will also be interested in maximizing their quality of life. Yet, Yunus asks for SB employees to deny the very spirit and opportunity that they offer to their customers. To go a step further, it is possible to imagine that poor people will most likely be SB employees and that even a small profit will make a large impact. In one light this may seem logical, but in another, it patronizes those living in poverty by its assumption of what people, like them, should earn. And, to some extent, SB could very well produce a more passive and selfless human being.

With this human construction, there is a fear of the loss of vitality necessary to foster innovation and nuance. What is most compelling about Capitalism is its way in which it causes people to change their minds about fundamental values and seek new forms of order and progress. Simply put, the focus of a development strategy should be on liberating human spirit instead of manipulating it, as SB seems to suggest.

Self-interest vs. Freedom

Capitalism is a system based on individual investments in the production of marketable goods. Many times in his explanation of SB, Yunus takes issue with the assumptions that, he believes, Capitalism makes about human nature. He often blames the market's inefficacy to solve social problems on its distorted view of human nature. He believes people engaged in for-profit business activities are portrayed as one-dimensional beings whose only mission is to maximize profit.

Yunus further defines his ideological position on human nature by admitting "my belief is that it [human nature] is fundamentally good. That is why religion good governance, social values, arts, culture, and charity have flourished throughout history, even in the face of tyranny and selfishness."

It is strange that Yunus takes this position considering the limits SB must maintain in order to ensure a company's *goodness*. The structure of SB seems to suggest that the opposite is true about human nature: its inherent depravity.

Whether we are fundamentally good or bad, or if we want to do good or bad things, regardless we must each be given the opportunity to participate in the exchange of the market equally. Yunus may very well agree with such a statement, but where we differ is in our paths to defining equality. Where Yunus would like humanity to stagnate its growth while the bottom billion catches up, some are interested in advocating for more balanced and dynamic growth of humanity.

Milton Freidman said, "Capitalism is a necessary condition of freedom, but not a sufficient reason." What is not needed is to hamper human potential, but to encourage it. Criticisms like environmental degradation and humanitarian relief could be posited as arguments in favor of hampering human potential. While fair, it seems immoral to assume a preconceived future, as developed in Yunus' teleology, wherein one can predict all of the mistakes humanity will make.

In all of his writing and lectures, Yunus does show a deep concern for the freedom of those struggling to survive on this planet. He creates SB to be a mechanism through which we can offer freedoms, both financial and social, to the impoverished. In the short-term, it does seem like SB has potential, but its long-term impact on human freedom warrants some investigation.

REFORMATION OF CONCERN

In an attempt to counterbalance the organizational rhetoric and strategy of SB, I would like to offer a reformulation of several social problems. Also, I will offer some specific examples organizations implementing modest social interventions.

Yunus often shows real concern for the most difficult struggles of people living in poverty: hunger, disease, illiteracy, and unemployment. Each of these terms lay a heavy burden at the feet of the individual. With terms such as these, it would take tremendous sacrifice to believe that they can address and overcome such difficulties. These struggles are burdensome, not only because of the particular horrors that lie within the terms, but also because of their ambiguity.

In an effort to avoid being overwhelmed by their descriptive magnitude, let us redefine these development ideas: hunger as proper nutrition, Disease as preventative healthcare, illiteracy as intellectualism, and unemployment as underemployment. Each of these ideas now creates a more realistic social problem. Programs to address these social problems can now be organized to foster sustainable solutions, while acknowledging the unpredictability of reality and, specifically, the future of humanity. What makes these reformulations realistic is their acknowledgement that social problems simply do not end, but merely transform with history.

Similar to these reformulations, Dr. Easterly points to the work of Lant Pritchett, Harvard's Kennedy School, Deon Filmer, and Jeffry Hammer, the World Bank, who have criticized the oversimplification of global public health interventions that seek to address health treatment rather than offering preventative healthcare. This is an example of program mismanagement informed by teleological assumptions; mainly that one has a duty to end sickness, today, which certainly seems disingenuous.

The work of economist Dr. Dean Karlan and his organization, *Innovations of Poverty Action* (IPA), describes another reformulation of the approach to global economic interventions. IPA "design(s) and evaluate(s) potential solutions to global poverty problems using randomized evaluations, the most rigorous evaluation method available." By advocating for better data collection and analysis methods, IPA offers an opportunity for more insight into the effectiveness of social impact. Instead of focusing on a fundamental change in human nature, IPA takes a more practical approach in its evaluation of government and individual social programs. This research may offer insight into human tendencies within a particular geographic and cultural context and, unlike SB; there is no predestined end or universal conclusion.

These reformulations of social problems are an attempt to offer more modest approaches toward global development. While SB does offer its own model, it may be more realistic to enact more mutually beneficial models that are concerned about the present state of humanity, rather than its future.

CONCLUSION

Yunus believes in a fuller, more dimensional concept of humanity, one that acknowledges its selfish desires and overcomes those desires with personal sacrifice. SB is an attempt to create a role for this selfless dimension of humanity in the free market. Concurrently, Yunus' aim is not to just explain the ills of a profit maximizing market system, but to create a framework wherein wealthy individuals can invest large sums, only being able to recoup their initial investment. Ultimately, SB is an attempt to encourage a more conscious and empathetic dimension of human nature within the free market.

The pitfalls of an ideological framework like SB is that it leaves little incentives for individuals to participate, while it indoctrinates them with a weak conception of human potential, lending to the encouragement of benevolence, entitlement, and expertise. Each of these qualities could be considered negative effects on human nature. Adam Smith offers that it is not "'benevolence' that causes people to serve one another, but 'their own interest', as competition on these terms will lead to the best allocation of resources."

Most frustrating, Yunus' teleology seems impenetrable, thus making criticism of SB hollow, as it has already determined its end. Dr. Easterly eloquently explains the difficulties with such teleological theories, "Unfortunately, like all other teleological theories, the claims of this approach to economic development are nontestable and nonfalsifiable. (You can test hypotheses about the past by not about the future)." This renders SB nearly impossible to critique, as it is presumptuous, let alone irrelevant, to make an argument for how humanity should be.

As we begin to see the worldview of which SB is a part, it is possible to think that thoughtful, modest social mechanisms are possible to provoke global development, and that ensuring equal freedoms among human beings is tantamount to any other social problem. And though we are moving faster toward this development, every day, the focus must not be on what we should be, but what we could be.

Client-Firm Relationship Dynamics: A Model for High Risk Clients

Susan L. Wright and Hema Rao

Susan L. Wright (susan.wright@oswego.edu) is an Assistant Professor at SUNY Oswego, School of Business, 310 Rich Hall, Oswego, NY 13126. Hema Rao (hema.rao@oswego.edu) is a Professor at SUNY Oswego, School of Business, 246 Rich Hall, Oswego, NY 13126. Correspondence concerning this paper should be directed to Susan Wright.

Abstract

As a result of a succession of 21st century corporate scandals, significant criticism has been leveled at the auditing profession with regard to auditor independence and financial statement quality. Although the Sarbanes Oxley Act of 2002 addresses problems stemming from the client-firm relationship, continued corporate failures demonstrate that more work is needed to strengthen the regulatory environment. This study defines audit failure and explores the causes behind it. The examination of audit failure is of critical importance as the European Union and the United States consider further options to reduce the occurrence of audit failures. This paper develops a model for interpreting the probabilities of an audit failure and proposes a plan, not yet considered in earlier studies, for regulators to consider in structuring auditing engagements for high-risk clients.

Keywords: Accounting complexity, agency costs, agency theory, audit engagement planning, audit fees, audit market regulation, audit quality, auditor tenure, earnings quality, ethics, mandatory rotation

Introduction

Agency costs arise from conflicts of interest between shareholders and managers of corporations. Agency theory is concerned with resolving these conflicts. This paper studies one aspect of agency costs by examining managerial influence over attestation services and its impact on auditor independence and audit quality. We propose an alternative that will reduce agency costs (especially for high risk clients, in high risk industries) and reduce the probability of audit failure.

Auditors provide a valuable service to the capital markets. They provide independent verification of the financial statements as prepared by managers and can report a failure by management to prepare the financial statements in accordance with GAAP, or to notify investors of a going-concern issue. With third-party attestation of the financial statements, investors have greater assurance as to the credibility of the financial statements and this assurance acts to reduce the cost of capital (Mansi et al., 2004). Auditors also provide an "insurance" function. Securities laws allow investors to seek recourse against auditors for failing to conduct a proper audit or to warn of a going-concern issue. Together, these facets of the auditing function provide value to the capital markets. (Mansi et al., 2004)

As a result of several recent audit failures, the auditing profession has a credibility problem. To examine these issues in greater detail, we address the following questions:

1. Why do audit failures occur and what factors contribute to them?

2. What does the literature say about this issue?
3. How do we proceed?

WHY DO AUDIT FAILURES OCCUR AND WHAT FACTORS CONTRIBUTE TO THEM?

In our opinion, an audit failure occurs when 1) an audit firm fails to report a material misstatement that causes the financial statements to be grossly misleading to those who depend on them, and/or 2) an audit firm fails to identify a going-concern issue. Audit failures may be caused by two factors: a lack of auditor independence, and/or a lack of auditor competence. Auditor independence relates to the ability of the auditor to carry out an audit in an objective manner and to provide certain assurances to external parties and other stakeholders including shareholders, employees, creditors, and customers. Lack of auditor competence refers to the technical inability of the auditor to adequately plan and carry out an audit for the same purpose.

The probability of an audit failure is relative to the strength of forces that influence the client-firm relationship. The first force in the relationship is related to the balance of power surrounding the contractual agreements between the client and the firm (Barrett, 2003). We propose three additional forces that influence the probability of an audit failure: (1) ethical values of the client, (2) use of complex financial arrangements/principles, and 3) the business risk of the client. We examine the four factors (power, ethics, complexity and business risk) below.

Power
The balance of power is an important force in the client-firm relationship. Power is determined by examining the nature of influence in the relationship. Barrett (2003) finds that unconscious bias influences these relationships. Further, if a particular client's fees constitute a substantial proportion of the firm's revenues, unconscious bias significantly

influences the auditor's judgment. In response to concerns over auditor independence and influence, the Sarbanes Oxley Act of 2002 required accounting firms to divest consulting operations from their auditing businesses; however, the taxation services remained. Even so, with or without the inclusion of taxation services, independence may be impaired as a result of the client-firm financial relationship and undue influence over auditor's independence may exist. Removing the consulting services may have reduced the magnitude of the dynamic, but the dynamic is still present and creates a conflict of interest between the client and the firm. This conflict of interest increases the probability of an audit failure when the balance of power resides with the client.

Other examples of power that can impact the risk of an audit failure include a dominant management style by the CEO or other top executives for the purpose of influencing accounting matters, and the development of snug client-firm relationships as a result of working together over long periods of time. The risk that the auditor becomes an advocate for the client and loses their objectivity and judgment is greater when power and influence resides with the client.

Client Ethical Values

Organizational intangibles, such as ethical standards, management style, integrity, reputation, and organizational culture contribute to the internal control environment, and are as important as traditional internal control measures[1]. Auditors should include an assessment of these variables when designing the audit engagement. Strong business ethics, cooperative management style and integrity lead to higher quality decision making for the purpose of creating value for all stakeholders. An organization has several reasons to operate in an ethical manner, including satisfied employees, higher productivity, stronger reputation, avoidance of fines and litigation, competitive strategic advantage, ability to attract talent and protecting shareholder wealth. Ethical decision-making may consider short-term impacts, but places a greater value on long-term consequences. Highly ethical businesses are unlikely to use their power in the audit engagement to commit fraud or engage in aggressive accounting treatment. Highly ethical businesses avoid developing close ties and relationships with auditors to maintain a culture of independence and integrity. Even in audit engagements where the client has substantial power over the firm, they are unlikely to use it to if they value and exhibit strong ethical behaviors. Highly ethical firms lower the risk of audit failure. (Kerns, 2003)

Complexity

Many organizations have complex financial and operational relationships. Complexity can create two types of problems. The first type relates to the ability to analyze the nature of the complexity and to apply the appropriate accounting principles. This analysis requires strong technical knowledge, critical thinking ability, and clear communication skills. Auditors and managers must have the expertise to accurately assess and evaluate transactions, valuations, and estimates for proper accounting treatment. Knowledge of advanced accounting issues such as fair value accounting, asset securitization, consolidating special purpose entities, foreign currency translation, accounting for derivatives and hedging transactions, leases, revenue recognition, pensions, equity compensation, and other advanced topics are necessary to effectively manage the engagement. Conservatism should be paramount to the auditor's application of various choices in applying GAAP. (Weaver, 2012)

The second problem involves the use of complexity to obscure questionable activities. This is especially important when the client wields power in the relationship. Even in situations where the client has strong ethical values, firm complexity increases the risk of audit failure. (Churyk and Stenka, 2014)

Business Risk

Business risk includes any operational and financial factors that may contribute to an organization's failure. The auditor must ensure that significant depth and breadth is exercised in the exploration of the business, its culture, management style, use of external rating agencies, and other factors when designing the scope of the audit engagement. Table 1 provides a list of the potential risk factors and types of data that are indicative of high business risk[2]:

Failure of the auditing firm to adequately design and plan the engagement to assess business risk significantly increases the probability of audit failure.

Summary & Context

An understanding of the effect of these four forces on the client-firm relationship is crucial for determining the likelihood of an audit failure and designing appropriate regulation. Power, ethics, complexity, and business risk, are also important variables to consider when designing an effective audit engagement.

The mortgage crisis of 2008 provides a context for understanding these forces. The banking sector is composed of several large clients who wield significant power in the client-firm relationship. Questionable ethical practices were used in attracting clientele and in structuring derivatives. They utilized complex accounting practices and innovative financial securities that can prove difficult to assess for ensuring proper accounting treatment under principles of fair value accounting. In addition, a failure to conduct due diligence in validating third-party credit ratings (Moody's and Standard & Poor's) caused inaccurate fair-value calculations for valuing assets. These four factors were highly indicative of the escalating risk inherent in determining the probability of an audit failure. This combination should have alerted regulators and auditors to the possibility of an impending crisis.

The crisis was industry wide. Not one auditing firm warned the market place of the escalating risk and impending collapse. Even after the collapse, the blame was directed at Wall Street, credit rating agencies, and the unethical business practices of the banking sector. Little was said about the role of the auditors and the role of the government agencies charged with overseeing the integrity of the markets. Regulators and auditors must recognize these intricate dynamics that combine to create escalating risk to the market. Their leadership is necessary to direct resources toward areas of systemic exposure when the probability of an audit failure is high. Auditing firms must also recognize the importance of their role as third party verification toward ensuring the integrity of the market place for shareholders and other stakeholders affected by audit failure.

WHAT DOES THE LITERATURE SAY ABOUT THIS ISSUE?

The Sarbanes Oxley Act of 2002 (SOX) provides safeguards to strengthen auditor independence and the regulatory environment. SOX Section 301 requires the SEC to relegate the responsibility for hiring, firing and compensating the auditor to an independent group (internal auditing group). SOX also prohibit firms from providing services such as book-keeping, information system design, human resource functions, legal services, appraisal or valuation services, and internal audit outsourcing for audit clients. Auditors can, however, provide certain tax services to audit clients (Barrett, 2003).

The existing model, even though re-shaped by the Sarbanes Oxley Act, did not prevent the banking crisis in 2008. The European Union and the United States are currently considering auditor rotation as a solution to the problem. It has been suggested that mandatory auditor rotation will enhance audit quality and improve independence (Chasan, 2014). Several studies, however, find that auditor rotation does not enhance audit quality (Cameran et al., 2015; Lennox 2013; Jackson et al., 2007; Johnson et al. 2002). In fact, some indicate that long-term auditor tenure improves audit quality (Myers et al., 2003). Other studies find that auditor rotation improves the quality of earnings (Hamilton et al., 2005) and that mandatory rotation at the firm level would improve independence and earnings quality at the same time (Mostafa, 2010). Further, Lennox (2013) argues that policy-makers should limit the ability of management to switch auditors rather than change the client-firm relationship. Although these studies are useful in assessing future initiatives, they fail to address the underlying problem (the conflict of interest) that undermines auditor independence.

A fundamental conflict becomes evident in the literature stream: firm level expertise is necessary to effectively perform an audit, but long-term tenure reduces independence and increases the probability of audit failure. So what are the options for managing this apparent conflict and what is the cost or benefit of strengthening independence? How should it be measured and interpreted to further our understanding of audit failures? How important is the idea of independence relative to the health of our global economy? These are complex questions that call for further research. We believe that the compensation arrangement is at the heart of the problem and further reforms must address auditor independence more directly.

How do we proceed?

At the core of the problem is the conflict of interest issue. How can auditors be independent, especially when the client exerts power, when the very client they are auditing pays them? Can a firm be paid and be independent? Sarbanes Oxley did not deal with this issue. Even If we conditionalize this question and conclude that yes, they can be independent (if there is a balance of power between the client and the firm, if both are highly ethical, if transactions and relationships are clear, and if business risks are minimal), we still lack a properly structured attestation mechanism to ensure independence in audit engagements.

Independence is central to audit quality. Until recently, this idea was unrecognized. In today's global economy, many corporations are larger than the economies of several countries combined. These businesses operate in complex global environments. In some cases, organizations are engaged in transactions that have no historical precedence and the accounting principles have not yet been developed to guide decision making. "Too big to fail" corporations exist in multiple sectors. Economic failure of these entities (or industries) can have wide-reaching economic consequences for global stakeholders. The 21st century economy requires a critical examination of the global business environment for the purposes of assessing the risks that are now the norm rather than the exception to the rule and where independence is central to the design of the attestation function.

In the wake of major tax law changes, executive compensation packages have changed significantly over the last 20 to 30 years. Executives are motivated with strong incentives for increasing stock price, and in some cases, rewarding short-term risk taking behavior rather than long-term value creation. In the case of BP's Gulf coast oil spill, excessive risk taking and improper managerial incentives, led to excessive cost cutting and mechanical failures that caused the oil spill, took lives, caused severe environmental damage, and destroyed billions of dollars in shareholder wealth. Although one might conclude that this wasn't the fault of the auditors, one might argue that they should have disclosed information related to the business risk of the client. Investors need stronger, more detailed disclosures that allow for informed investment decisions. Auditors must strengthen the audit design and provide a warning bell for protecting shareholders and other stakeholder interests for high-risk clients.

SHORT-TERM RECOMMENDATIONS

We recommend that the structure for providing attestation services be altered for high-risk clients in too big to fail industries. Our model for the client-firm relationship serves as a framework for policy makers to focus their attention on clients that are most susceptible to audit failure and that presents the greatest risk (see Figure 1). Large clients, with the potential to create systemic shocks in the global economy, should they fail, must undergo a more stringent audit. Experts in the industry, experienced auditors, and regulators would design these audits. Firms in high risk industries will pay for attestation services by contributing to a general fund used to pay for expenditures related to services, commensurate to the scope of the audit design. The pool of experts would be rotated on a frequent basis to further strengthen independence. The direct financial tie between the client and the firm, and the potential for developing cozy relationships would be virtually eliminated. There are several options for structuring these services: within the SEC, the FASB, or the stock markets in which these companies are listed. High-risk client profiles are depicted in the far left of the model shown in Figure 1.

There are several alternative methods to providing attestation services to those clients who are not at high risk of audit failure or may be of moderate risk. If the existing structure is maintained, regulatory bodies must strengthen the independence of private firms providing attestation services by requiring that no single client compose more than a stated proportion of its business for a prolonged period of time. Low risk client profiles are depicted in the far right of the model shown in Figure 1. Future research is needed to operationalize the four variables: power, ethics, complexity and business risk, for determining those clients most at risk of audit failure.

CONCLUSIONS

For the long-term, a new approach for providing attestation services is necessary. Tweaking the existing system by requiring auditor rotation, or as we suggest, restructuring the financial arrangement between high risk clients and the auditing firm, is a short-term solution that does not fully remedy the issues. Redesigning the process, the procedures, and the types of required disclosures, are central to the transformation. Reassessing accounting information disclosures, asset valuation and accruals is paramount to long-term reform. To be relevant in the future, the accounting profession must examine the purpose of their core services and consider how to best serve the needs of the global community.

External users require firm-specific information to accurately assess risk and to generate estimates for proper valuation. Transparency is the key to this innovation and striving for structures that are self-regulating (by clients, not regulators) is central to the restructuring process. The information regarding the critical elements for assessing the risk of audit failure for publicly traded organizations is readily available within the walls of the firm. What do we have to do to make it public? What cultural, structural, and systemic changes need to occur to instill within our systems the motivation to serve the interests of the public that we are privileged to protect?

REFERENCES

Barrett, Matthew J., Enron and Andersen - What Went Wrong and Why Similar Audit Failures Could Happen Again. 2003. Available at SSRN: http://ssrn.com/abstract=794831

Cameran, M., Francis, J., Marra, A. and Pettinicchio, A. 2015. Are There Adverse Consequences of Mandatory Auditor Rotation? Evidence from the Italian Experience. AUDITING: A Journal of Practice & Theory: February 2015, Vol. 34, No. 1, pp. 1-24.

http://dx.doi.org/10.2308/ajpt-50663

Chasan, Emily. 2014. European Parliament Approves Mandatory Auditor Rotation. Wall Street Journal, April 3, 2014

http://blogs.wsj.com/cfo/2014/04/03/european-parliament-approves-mandatory-auditor-rotation/tab/print/

Churyk, N. and Stenka, R. (2014). Accounting for complex investment transactions. Journal of Accounting Education

http://dx.doi.org/10.1016/j.jaccedu.2014.08.001

Hamilton, J. and Ruddock, C.. and Stokes, D. and Taylor, S. 2005. Audit Partner Rotation, Earnings Quality and Earnings Conservatism. Available at SSRN: http://ssrn.com/abstract=740846 or http://dx.doi.org/10.2139/ssrn.740846

Jackson, Andrew B. and Moldrich, Michael and Roebuck, Peter, Mandatory Audit Firm Rotation and Audit Quality. 2007. Managerial Auditing Journal, Vol. 23, No. 5, 2008. Available at SSRN: http://ssrn.com/abstract=1000076

http://dx.doi.org/10.2139/ssrn.1000076

Johnson, V., I. Khurana, and J. Reynolds. 2002, Audit firm tenure and the quality of financial reports. Contemporary Accounting Research 19 (4): 637-660.

http://dx.doi.org/10.1506/LLTH-JXQV-8CEW-8MXD

Kerns, Charles (2003). Creating and Sustaining an Ethical Workplace Culture. Graziadio Business Review, Vol. 6, Issue 3 http://gbr.pepperdine.edu/2010/08/Creating-and-Sustaining-an-Ethical-Workplace-Culture/

Lennox, Clive S. 2012. Auditor Tenure and Rotation. Available at SSRN: http://ssrn.com/abstract=2165127

MANSI, S. A., MAXWELL, W. F. and MILLER, D. P. (2004), Does Auditor Quality and Tenure Matter to Investors? Evidence from the Bond Market. Journal of Accounting Research, 42: 755–793. http://dx.doi.org/10.1111/j.1475-679X.2004.00156.x

Mostafa, Diana. 2010. The Impact of the Auditor Rotation on the Audit Quality: A Field Study from Egypt. Available at SSRN: http://ssrn.com/abstract=1676224

http://dx.doi.org/10.2139/ssrn.1676224

Myers, J., Myers, and T. Omer. 2003. Exploring the term of the auditor-client relationship and the quality of earnings: A case for mandatory auditor rotation? The Accounting Review 78(3): 779-799.

http://dx.doi.org/10.2308/accr.2003.78.3.779

Weaver, Lisa, (2012). Planning an Audit of Financial Statements. SA Technical ACCA http://www.accaglobal.com/content/dam/acca/global/PDF-students/2012s/sa_oct12-p7-planning.pdf

WEB APPENDIX

A web appendix for this paper is available at:

http://www.businessresearchconsortium.org/pro/brcpro2015p19.pdf

Notes

1. https://na.theiia.org/news/press-releases/Pages/Strong-Policies-Regarding-Ethics,-Integrity,-and-Management-Style-Identified-as-Key-Element-of-Preventing-Governance-Failur.aspx
2. http://accounting-simplified.com/audit/risk-assessment/audit-risk-business-risk.html

CPSIA information can be obtained
at www.ICGtesting.com
Printed in the USA
FFOW01n0704080416
23071FF